Sweet Spot

Finding Your Career
at Any Age

Bruce Roberts Dreisbach & Katybeth Lee

* * *

DEDICATION BY

Bruce Dreisbach

To Kim Bain and all my other protégés.

DEDICATION BY

Katybeth Lee

To each of you who have showed me through the example of your life how
to follow God's call to where your deep gladness meets
the world's deep hunger.

Table of Contents

SECTION ONE

Work: Search for Daily Meaning & Daily Bread 1

Chapter 1

Chasing the American Dream..3

Chapter 2

Facing Reality 10

Chapter 3

The School of Hard Knocks...21

Chapter 4

Launching a Career...31

Chapter 5

The Road to Hell..43

Chapter 6

Understanding the Why of Work 53

Chapter 7

Discover Your Best Self 61

Chapter 8

Mid-Career Course Corrections 67

Chapter 9

Springboards to a Better Career 87

SECTION TWO

Finding Work You Can Love 103

Chapter 10

Finding Your Unique Path 105

Chapter 11

The Bent of the Twig 115

Chapter 12

Temperament 127

Chapter 13

Tap into Your Talents 139

Chapter 14

Putting It All Together 147

SECTION THREE

Finding a Job You Can Love 155

Chapter 15

Landing the Job -- Part I 157

Chapter 16

Landing the Job -- Part II 173

Chapter 17

Bridging the Gap – Academy vs. Workplace 187

Chapter 18

Corporate Culture: Context is Everything 199

Chapter 19

Attitude Determines Altitude 213

Chapter 20

Strong Careers are Built on Relational Capital 227

Chapter 21

Building Balance into Your Life 241

APPENDIX **256**

READER CHECK LIST **257**

ENDNOTES **259**

BIBLIOGRAPHY **265**

For a Better Work Experience

There are a lot of books on the market that promise they can help you find a job. When you need a job, often the promise of a steady paycheck may seem like it's enough. We often think, "Who cares what the work is? I'm sure I can learn and adjust!" Yet the astonishing fact is that almost two out of three Americans who now have jobs want desperately to trade their present job for another! 61% of those with jobs feel their present job, company, industry, or career is not a good fit. They want out – just as soon as they can figure out how to find a better job.

This book is designed to help you learn how to find a job that fits your unique and best self. One that connects to your passions, that leans on your unique strengths, and that allows you to find personal success, and satisfaction in the workplace. In short, a job you can build into a fulfilling career, not just a means of bring home a paycheck. The contents of this volume will help you identify your unique self and how to find a job that fits you. It will then demonstrate how to grow that job into a career. These strategies and tactics will work for you no matter what age or stage of career you are in.

Sweet Spot. Just what is a sweet spot? This term is used in tennis to describe the area of a tennis racket which gives the most bounce to a ball coming off the strings. While you can hit and play the ball off much of the surface of the strings, and even off the frame in a pinch, experienced players learn any stroke will have more velocity, more power, and better accuracy if they hit from the "sweet spot." To get the most from your game, you must learn to find and play off the sweet spot of your racket.

This same principle can be applied to the world of work. Whether you are launching your career in the marketplace; if you've decided to change careers some way down the track; if you are side-tracked - involuntarily in need of a new job or career; or, if you are looking to re-career yourself after concluding your normal working life; you know the truth of the following statement. **Finding the right job is not easy.**

Understanding what makes you tick, what makes you uniquely you, and matching that to a job or career, which actually pays you to be you, is tough. Many of us wrestle for much of our life trying to find a square hole to fit our square peg. While finding your own sweet spot in career and vocation isn't easy, it can be done, and this book was written to help you find just that place.

Are you starting out in the world of work? This book is for you. When you are fresh out of school it is easy to struggle with the difficult task of landing your first position. Having a mid-career crisis? This book is for you! It will help you sort out where you are and get you back on your feet.

Perhaps it's not a career crisis -- more like a malaise. You have a job but it's beginning to bore you, cause real frustration, and misery. You're starting to wonder, "Am I headed in the right direction? Is this *all* there is?"

Or you may be headed towards retirement – and you honestly wonder; "Am I really done? Is this my legacy? Have I made a mark on the world?

This book was written to help you successfully launch your career, to overcome the speed bumps along the way, and to continue to grow, transform, and improve your work experience to the very end. No matter where you are in the course of your career, this volume will be useful for helping you identify what makes you uniquely you. The purpose of a job is not just to earn enough money to pay the bills, although that's quite helpful. The purpose of your job is to discover "The place where your deep gladness and the world's deep hunger meet" as Frederick Buechner so aptly put it. It's about being you…the best you!

Once you begin to identify those things that can help lead you to your unique competence, and the specific place in the world of work where you can make a contribution that both satisfies you and makes the world a better place, you need to enter into the process required to find the right job in the right career. This handbook will help you navigate the adventure.

Nurturing a healthy work experience and career requires skills that can be learned. This book will not only help you find a job you can love, it will teach you to cultivate your career. Maximizing the job opportunities which come your way is one of the key issues we will help you with in this volume. To be successful over the long haul, you have to learn to look for work after you get a job.

Finally, our goal is to teach you to keep your balance because a flourishing career is only one part of living a healthy, successful life. If you let your career spin out of control and destroy the equilibrium of the rest of your life, no amount of workplace success will make up for the sorrow and pain that you will reap in the future. Those who lose balance at work can destroy their careers, health, relationships, and our loved ones – just about everything we hold dear. We will give you the tools and the perspectives you need to build a satisfying career, which is also part of a balanced and rewarding life.

While some are born wealthy and never choose to work, and others have limitations which prevent them from employment outside the home, most Americans invest the largest portion of their waking hours in some kind of work. For many of us, work is the canvas upon which much of our lives are painted, where we seek to find ourselves, our unique competencies, our special talents and a means of giving back to the human community. We need work, not just to put food on the table and a roof overhead, but to find the whole person we were meant to be. Don't settle for less than the best you. Come along on the adventure as we find our 'sweet spot' in career and life.

Section One

Work: Search for Daily Meaning

& Daily Bread

Chapter 1

Chasing the American Dream

Janna Hebner was born and raised by a single mother in Gilpin Court, a public housing project in Richmond, VA. Gilpin Court is reported to be the largest and most infamous public housing project between Baltimore and Atlanta. Completed in 1943, it provides low-cost shelter to almost 750 households. Seething with unemployment, street crime, drug use, human trafficking, black-on-black violence, Gilpin Court demonstrates all the dysfunctions of government facilitated poverty. Many agree Gilpin is the most dangerous neighborhood in the Commonwealth of Virginia. This is the kind of neighborhood where dreams go to die.

Yet Janna's dreams have not perished, but have mysteriously flourished in this tough, gritty district in the east end of the old capital of the Confederacy. Janna's mother was just one of the many unwed teens in Gilpin Court who together have produced approximately 1,150 children under the age 18 in the projects. Like Janna, over 80% of the children born today in the city of Richmond are the offspring of unwed mothers. In Gilpin, 689 of the 750 households are headed by single females with an average annual household income of just $8,158. In the midst of this grinding poverty, racial injustice, and social deprivation, Janna has blossomed into a young woman with a mission.

Against all odds, Janna worked her way through the George Washington Carver Elementary School, Hill Middle School, and Thomas Jefferson High School, graduating with the Class of 2012. Through hard work, perseverance in the face of overwhelming obstacles, and help of significant mentors from the community, Janna became the first in her family to graduate from high school. She went on to win a full scholarship from Old Dominion University, where she hopes to become a doctor who can go back and serve the needs in her community.

Her story is a classic American tale of faith, hope, and love allowing someone from very difficult circumstances to overcome and pave a pathway to success. Janna's story can stand as a modern version of the American Dream. This belief and hope is that in America, anyone can rise above his or her circumstance to achieve their dream and aspirations.

All of us begin our working career with some kind of dream in mind. Like Janna Hebner, we often see ourselves as having arisen from modest origins, but aspiring to something greater and for the noble good, which will enrich us and benefit mankind. Much like the books of Horatio Alger, who penned over 100 juvenile novels during America's Gilded Age, we have high hopes, regardless of our birth or circumstances in life. Alger's books, such as *Ragged Dick*, featured impoverished boys from humble backgrounds who rise to lives of middle-class security and comfort through hard work, determination, courage, and honesty. His characters and stories illustrate the rags-to-riches narrative, which had a formative effect on America during the late 19th century.

Since that time, psychology of the American Dream has so permeated every aspect of our culture that it has almost become ubiquitous. It saturates our thinking to such an extent we do not realize what a powerful influence it has over our expectations and the choices we make in life. While the phrase "The American Dream" was originally coined by James T. Adams in 1931, it has morphed into a subtle, but pervasive expectation that America is a land of opportunity and prosperity for all. Our United States' Declaration of Independence proclaims that "all men are created equal" and that they are "endowed by their Creator with certain inalienable Rights," including "Life, Liberty, and the Pursuit of Happiness." Adams used the term to indicate his conviction that American society, unlike European or class-driven cultures, would allow anyone to aspire and rise to the level of their innate ability. In common usage, however, the American Dream has expanded into a generic expectation that everyone has the right to a life of personal peace and prosperity.

Billy Joel talked about this expectation that everyone in America has the right to shape their own destiny in his 1981 hit song *Allentown*. According to Joel, the American Dream makes a promise that if we work hard in school, if we behave, if we graduate, then "every child has a pretty good shot to get at least as far as their old man got."[1]

According to the American Dream, your socioeconomic class, your parents' education, and even the legitimacy of your birth should produce no limitations on your ability to achieve great things. Your origins don't matter and should not create a handicap which hinders the long-term accomplishments of a life.

We love to recount the story of Abraham Lincoln who was born in a log cabin in rural Kentucky, and tragically lost his mother to sickness at the age of nine. His father remarried and moved the family to Indiana, then Illinois, where Lincoln survived a hand-to-mouth existence on a hardscrabble rural farm, teaching himself to read and write then eventually becoming a lawyer. After many trials and tribulations, including numerous failed attempts to win elected office, Lincoln became the 16th President of the United States and perhaps one of the most important and influential presidents in United States history.

A Myth Exposed

Our take on the American Dream is vague but sure. If we do our best, get into the best college we possibly can, apply ourselves with a modicum of effort, and finally manage to graduate, then the world is our oyster. We should be able to choose any destination and have a very good chance of getting there or awfully close. CEO of a Fortune 500 company? No problem. Faculty member of a prestigious university? A bit of effort and that should be possible. Successful young actress on Broadway? Easy! Compassionate and effective inner-city school teacher? No sweat. Peace Corps volunteer traveling to exotic destinations around the world, while experiencing life and making the world a better place? Let's get started!

When I (Bruce) was at university, the underlying assumption was that the harder you worked, the further you would go. If you're willing to give it your all, then there could be no limits to your career prospects. During grad school, those in the MBA program would periodically be visited by hoards of hungry recruiters from big-name American corporations like Procter & Gamble, General Electric, Ford, and Deloitte. Many of the investment banks and financial services consulting firms from New York would also send their representatives. The rumor among my fellow grad students was that there was one perfect set of answers to land a great job with any of these recruiters and their companies. The conversation went something like this:

Recruiter: *What's the most significant accomplishment of your career to date?*

Student: *I worked a hundred and five hours one week.*

Recruiter: *When you think of your future career, how do you picture yourself in your working life?*

Student: *I see myself as O.J. Simpson, racing through the airport at top speed, hurtling luggage carts in order to make my next plane.*

Recruiter: *When you contemplate the next five years of your career, what goals or objectives would you like to accomplish?*

Student: *I'd like to see myself work a hundred and ten hours in a week."*

In our understanding of the American Dream, there was a direct connection between unbridled ambition, hard work, and enormous rewards. Perhaps our fixation on the American Dream is not so much about what we do vocationally, but more about what the rewards of our career can purchase for us. Our desire is to find a secure and interesting job which is able to produce a high income. This more-than-adequate income in turn will yield a lovely white Dutch colonial home, complete with black shutters, nestled into beautifully landscaped grounds in a neighborhood of similar homes and other "nice people." This version of the American Dream often includes a handsome or beautiful mate, two or three lovely children who are bright, healthy, and not too troublesome. These children are growing up in a clean, happy, crime-free neighborhood, attending excellent schools, making outstanding progress, and in every way are producing a future of personal peace and prosperity. This notion reminds me of Garrison Keillor's description of his hometown of Lake Wobegone, the mythical town in Minnesota where "all the women are strong, all the men are good looking, and all the children are above average."

The Myth Debunked

Unfortunately, much of the evidence available indicates that the American Dream is not a common experience for those seeking a satisfying job or career in the 21st century. The American Dream may be more of a myth than reality. Take the case of Melissa Meyer, who graduated magna cum laude from the George Washington University Business School in May of 2009.

Raised in Missoula, Montana, Meyer was an honor student in high school, valedictorian, class president, outstanding chemistry student, editor of the school newspaper, served as an intern in the U.S. Senate, and the only student from her class to attend college on the East Coast. For 23 years she toed the line, producing high levels of performance in all of those things which "the Dream" indicates will produce success. Perfect grades, a $200,000 college degree, a box overflowing with business cards and network connections, hundreds of resumes mailed out, dozens of job interviews and then…nothing. Her university career counselor indicated Melissa is "energetic," "enthusiastic," "flexible," "assertive," and "a good communicator." After six months of banging on doors, Melissa's post college experience indicates she is simply, inexplicably, "unemployed." With few other choices, Meyer has moved back home to Missoula, living with her parents, and is currently working part-time at Rockin' Rudy's, a local record shop where she also worked in high school.[2]

Often, we see people launch careers which appear to have every chance of resulting in the success and the fulfillment of the American Dream. Yet after five or ten years, what we thought was a career with great promise and much potential, has turned sour. Much like the case of Amy Lewis, a successful educational professional working in Washington, DC. After nine years of rapid promotion and accomplishment on her chosen career track, Lewis, a single mother with a young son, had an epiphany. As the youngest member of Howard University's executive team, she had a high-powered job with a six-figure salary. Yet Lewis realized her stress-laden position did not bring her joy and was ruining her life. All she could think about was doing something else and spending more time with her five-year-old. Even though all her mentors told her she was committing career suicide, Lewis quit her job, fired her nanny, got a part-time job, and put herself through acupuncture school. Today, she works as an acupuncturist in the shadow of the White House. She enjoys her patients, makes her own schedule, and doesn't miss a single one of her son's football games.[3]

Others, like friend Carmen, commit themselves wholeheartedly to a career that appears to be a great fit and is in line with their personal passions and interests. Even with a powerful desire to spend a lifetime in a career with a particular company, they wake up one morning and find themselves unemployed. Carmen graduated from high school, and during her college years worked as an intern in the graphic design department of a large regional newspaper. Before she graduated, the newspaper convinced her to quit school and go to work full time as a graphic designer. Carmen worked hard, investing in her own training and education. She came in early and worked late. Whatever the job required (no matter how unreasonable) Carmen was there. She was part of the hard core employees at the newspaper who called themselves "Lifers." Based on her outstanding performance, she climbed the ladder until, by her 20th anniversary at the paper, she was promoted to Advertising Services Director heading up a staff of 15 professionals. Two years later, the parent chain that owned her paper decided to outsource all graphic design. Carmen and her entire team were let go. Now she is 46 years old, a single mother with a 12-year old daughter, no college diploma, and she is beginning her career all over again. The prospects do not look good.

Years of experience and great success are no protection against an unexpected flameout in your career. Often we assume, peering in from the outside, that people who are very successful are concurrently happy and fulfilled. Looks can be deceiving. One of the most common experiences in the workplace today is to have a job, at which you succeed, but at the same time, which slowly but surely undermines your happiness and health. Over time, the stress and pressure of your job begins to erode the foundations of your life. It may be that your life is out of balance, but more often the expectations and pressures of your job are so enormous that they cause burnout.

Take the experience of Lorraine Murry of Atlanta, a fast-track executive in public relations. She made good money, landed important promotions, and was given increased responsibility in her firm. But she found her success had a dark side.

"As my responsibilities and pay increased," she says, "so did the mental anguish. My job was like a hundred-headed monster in a cheap movie, always breathing down my neck and stalking me, even in the middle of the night. When I chopped the head off of one publication deadline, five more took its place. "On Sunday morning, I began to dread Sunday evening—because it led to Monday morning. On Monday morning I dreaded digging through the mounds of work awaiting me."

Finally Murry found herself confronting a shocking question. "Was I making a living or was I making a dying? As I looked at my typical day with its frenzied commute, harried meetings, and endless deadlines, I realized suddenly what the answer was - my job had devoured my life."[4]

A Road to Hope

No matter at what point you are in your career, it is critical for you to understand the American Dream is just that – a dream. It's a myth. It's simply not true for most people. Finding the right career and job may prove to be an exceedingly difficult endeavor. If you are feeling you are "hitting the wall" in your search for a good career fit, join the club! There are lots of us in the exact same place. There is no easy road to finding your sweet spot in career and vocation. **But there is a road.** Finding a career that will utilize your unique strengths and interests is not easy, but it's entirely possible to accomplish. The purpose of this volume is to give you practical steps you can use to find your own unique sweet spot, where your unique passions meet the world's great need.

With the help of some fresh perspectives and several easy-to-use diagnostic tools, you can gain deeper insight into what makes you tick, and ultimately, what will bring you satisfaction in the workplace. If you're prepared to take some time to read and apply the balance of this volume, you will learn how to plan a strategy and develop tactics to enable you to create the career track you truly desire.

Chapter 2

Facing Reality

The Joyless Workplace

Steven Slater, a Jet Blue flight attendant based in New York City, made national headlines when he finally blew his stack and confronted his feelings about his job and his work situation. As all business travelers know, flying on commercial airlines has become increasingly difficult over the last ten years. A great deal of the friction has been created in the system by fewer flights, fewer aircraft, fewer seats, more passengers, more security, more rules, more fees, and more delays. This rising mountain of frustration gets dumped right into the laps of flight attendants, whose job it is to help people get through this increasingly annoying experience.

After 20 years in this high-friction position, Slater reached his limit one August afternoon on a flight to New York. After being abused by one too many passengers, Slater exploded with an angry, curse-laden tirade over the plane's intercom system. Plucking a pair of beers from the kitchen, he triggered the emergency escape chute and left his job with a flourish which made him a folk hero to many across America, especially those who have labored in difficult jobs under difficult circumstances for far too many years without any relief.

Slater tapped into an enormous vein of feeling which many working people in America share. If you're struggling in your search to find a good place in career and vocation, let me assure you -- you are not alone. The vast majority of people you work with, the vast majority of those in the workplace, struggle from time-to-time with similar feelings as those that sent Steven Slater down the inflatable slide.

At the time of this writing, the national unemployment rate hovers close to 8%. Another 8 to 10% are either underemployed or are so frustrated that they've given up looking. If you total those who are unemployed, those who are underemployed, and those who are mis-employed (are in jobs that really don't fit or don't meet their basic needs), close to 40 percent of Americans are presently involved in a full blown career crisis. Research among those with a job reveals this astonishing finding—84 percent who now hold a job say they'd like to change jobs in the coming year.

The overwhelming pandemic of poor job fit and miserable work experiences in American culture is both widespread and deeply rooted. A good case could be made for the assertion that one of the reasons we're going through such a serious recession in the job market is that people have never really learned to look for a job which fits their unique attributes and interests. Studies of recent college graduates indicate the majority simply want to make the most money possible, in the shortest period of time, so they can retire early, and then get to doing what they like to do.

It seems the majority of working Americans approach work as a nihilistic experience where we expect to be miserable and are rewarded with our expectations being thoroughly fulfilled. This reminds me of the rock band Loverboy's mega hit in the 1980s - *Working for the Weekend*. The chorus is of this popular rock ballad is a lament most workers in America sing more often than not. "Everybody's working for the weekend, everybody wants a little romance, everybody's gone off the deep end, everybody needs a second chance..." This song was enormously popular because so many people could relate to the feelings it describes. Work sucks. The best you can hope for is to get through it to 5 PM Friday afternoon - then you can start living your life again.

CEO Dennis W. Bakke reports that most American companies have "made the workplace a frustrating and joyless place where people do what they're told and have few ways to participate in decisions which fully use their talents. As a result, they naturally gravitate to pursuits in which they can exercise a measure of control outside of their work lives." Bakke claims that working conditions in large organizations today are no more exciting, rewarding, or fun than they were 250 years ago at the beginning of the Industrial Revolution. In the modern workplace an employee's full talents are rarely used and often go unnoticed. The result is people work hard so they can escape work. They literally are working for the weekend.

They work and scrape and save so they can spend a week at Disneyland, or they spend years planning and dreaming for retirement.[5]

There is a hidden contradiction in our desire to work, to work hard, to work hard for financial reward, and yet our willingness to suffer through the most miserable, degrading, pointless work experiences at the same time. It almost seems as if without thinking, many Americans have developed the ability to commit ourselves more fully and more diligently to investing in what is clearly abusive behavior. And the person we are abusing is ourselves.

Author Frederic Buechner summarizes the conundrum. "Jobs are what people do for a living, many of them for eight hours a day, five days a week, minus vacations, for most of their lives. It is tragic to think how few of them have their hearts in it. They work mainly for the purpose of making money enough to enjoy their moments of not working.

If not working is the chief pleasure they have, you wonder if they would do better just to devote themselves to that from the start. They would probably end up in bread lines or begging yet the chances are they would be happier than pulling down a good salary as an insurance agent, a dental technician, or a cab driver, and hating every minute of it.

'What does a man gain by all the toil at which he toils under the sun…?' If he's only in it for the money, the money is all he gains, and when he finally retires, he may well ask himself if it was worth giving most of his life for."[6]

When Steven Slater erupted in anger at the conclusion of that August Jet Blue flight, his emotions at his working situation were not unusual, just his way of expressing his anger was. Many of us feel anger about our working situation. We need to recognize however, that anger is a secondary emotion. It arises in response to a primary emotion such as frustration, fear, or powerlessness. If you are feeling frustrated in your work situation, if you're fearful you are not going to be able to improve your working situation, or if you feel caught between the need to bring home a paycheck and the actual requirements of your current job; these primary emotions may in fact result in anger. Anger does not have to be negative; in fact, it just may be our soul's way of speaking up and saying "Hey, I'm in pain here, and we really need to think about doing something different."

Facing Your Feelings

__Work.__   How do you feel when we say that word? How do you feel on Sunday evening when you contemplate going back on the job Monday morning? When you close your eyes, and center into the honest gut feelings, what rises to the surface? Are you excited about getting back with the team? Glad to provide leadership or a needed service to others? Does it make you feel warm and happy like a sunny summer day or the smell of freshly cut grass? Does it make you feel like rising to the challenge and becoming the best person that you can be? Does it stimulate you, give you a sense of growing intellectual curiosity and excitement about learning and doing new things?

Or, do you find yourself drawing back, feeling ambivalent and uncomfortable when you think about work? Does it leave you feeling bored, frustrated, and aggravated? Is there push-back in your soul—a real resistance to having to go in on Monday morning? Does it cause you to recoil in fear and aversion? When you're honest, do you realize you actually dislike the people you work with— in fact, you find them somewhat unsafe, distasteful, nasty, even scary? Do you often find yourself wishing and daydreaming you were in a different line of work? Or thinking you'd feel better if you were working for a different company? Or fantasizing about being wealthy and not having to work at all?

For many of us, it's hard to talk about the feelings we have when we're in a job situation that's a poor fit for our skills, our talents, and our personality. But humor can help. Where I live, a large daily newspaper has been running a highly effective commercial on local cable television touting its job-search resources. The ad opens with a shot of a caged green parrot sitting in an empty apartment living room. The parrot squawks, "I can't take this, I can't take this. Not another day, not another day." In the next scene, the parrot's owner returns home. As he comes in his apartment's front door you can see his weariness, his frustration, his exasperation, his despair. Both his appearance and his clothing literally

13

droop with depression as he says, "I can't take this, I can't take this. Not another day, not another day. I have to find a new job."

Facing the truth of our current vocational situation may not be easy. Often we're reluctant to be honest about how we feel about work. It takes up so many of our waking hours. It forms the shape and structure of most of our days. Often times it provides much of our relational or social context in life. In many ways it cuts precariously close to our self image and our self-esteem. And, of course, we need the money! But if our work life is not satisfying, honesty will prove to be the best policy. ***Being honest, at least with yourself, is the first step to an improved work experience.***

The source of our discomfort could be the specific place we work in, the requirements of our position, the nature of our chosen profession itself, or for many, the process of trying to figure out what to do for work and career. Sometimes we recognize we were pressured into this career by someone else, perhaps a parent or spouse. If it was up to us, we would not be doing this. And if we're really honest, we recognize we're embarrassed about having these feelings. We make the assumption that everyone around us is well-adjusted and happy with their vocational life.

A Universal Problem

You are not alone! Almost from the beginning of recorded history, we see humanity wrestling with work. Since the expulsion of Adam and Eve from the Garden of Eden, mankind has struggled with their conceptual view of work as well as their actual experience of it.

A brief review of modern literature on work makes it fairly clear that most Americans, like Adam and his son Cain, struggle with our relationship to work. Many of us can relate to the feelings Adam and his offspring must have endured - of being a restless wanderer on earth, seeking a means of earning a living, and finding a way to gain some satisfaction from our work. In the 1970s Studs Terkel wrote an enormously popular book simply titled *Working*. In this epic piece he interviews and transmits the oral histories of dozens of real-world working people. For even the most pedestrian types of workers—grocery clerk, bookbinder, gravedigger, waitress, pharmacist, flight attendant—Terkel found that work was the search for both "daily meaning as well as daily bread." One conclusion he reached: "Most of us, like the assembly line worker, have jobs that are too small for our spirit. Jobs are not big enough for people."[7]

The national statistics on job satisfaction in America yield a visceral sense that something's wrong at the heart of our experience of work. "According to a recent survey, job dissatisfaction is widespread among workers of all ages across all income brackets. The study found less than half of all workers are satisfied with their jobs. Worker satisfaction has continued to decline across all income brackets over the last decade." [8] While there have been substantial increases in productivity over the past decade, they haven't resulted in higher wages or happier workers.

Research conducted for the Conference Board among 5,000 households found that half of Americans are currently working in positions they feel are not a good fit for their skills or interests, and approximately six in ten workers plan to leave their current employer within the next two years. Another study states that eight in ten workers plan to look for a new job when the economy improves.[9]

According to pollster Daniel Yankelovich, only thirteen percent of workers find their work truly meaningful.[10] In another survey, only twenty percent of 350,000 employees in 7,000 corporations who were studied over a 16 year period were in jobs that made use of their talents.[11] Even at management levels, good job fit is hard to find. Fully half of the managers hired over a 3 year period had "not worked out," according to a recent survey of 55 companies.[12] Only one out of every three managers was well suited to his position, according to assessments made over a period of almost four decades by People Management, a leading national human resource firm.[13]

Why We Hate Work

Some degree of distress with work is widespread – almost everyone has experienced it at one time during their working career. There are concrete reasons why we feel this way. Most vocational pain and job discomfort come from two basic causes. *Intrinsic job dissatisfaction* has to do with the kind of work a person does, their feelings about the purpose of their work or employer, and their view of how well they fit that particular type of job. *Extrinsic job dissatisfaction* relates to an employee's view of the conditions of their workplace—specifically their work environment, their supervisor, their colleagues, and their pay.

Intrinsic job dissatisfaction is often related to poor job fit. There are many different ways to analyze and measure how workers fit jobs, but our ultimate goal is to put square pegs in square holes. If you take an extrovert and give them a desk job, they will spend much of their time down at the water cooler chatting with people -- simply because that's the way they're wired. If you take an introvert and give them a sales job, they will spend a large amount of time at their desk developing enormously complex and strategic sales plans. But they may never actually make sales calls. This also is related to the way they're wired.

The common practice in American business organizations is to assume we can take a square peg, put them in round hole of a job, and educate out the sides of the person until they "fit" the position. This kind of thinking results in roughly $50 billion a year American corporations spend on education and training – trying to "round out the corners." In actuality, this almost never works. Peter Drucker, the leading management consultant of the 20th century recognized this when he taught business leaders they should hire for the one main strength they needed in a position. This standard would also be applied in promoting people into new positions. According to Dr. Drucker, if the candidate does not have the one main strength needed in the position, it's highly unlikely any amount of education and development will remedy the situation.

Research by the Gallup Organization found that among 10 million workers about 7 million are currently working outside of the area which they do best. That's 70 percent! For those whose work does not let them focus on their strengths the costs are overwhelming. A recent poll of 1,000 people found not one person working outside their core strength was emotionally engaged on the job. By comparison, Gallup's ongoing research shows that people working in their area of strength were six times as likely to be engaged on the job and three times more likely to report having an excellent quality of life.[14]

Extrinsic job dissatisfaction more often has to do with the organization you work for and the people you work with, than your suitability for a particular type of job. You may have the temperament and skills to be a great lawyer, nurse, or accountant, but that does not mean you can be highly effective in just any business organization. Corporate culture is one aspect which significantly affects your level of comfort in a specific business. Working for the government, the military, or a state agency is considerably different than working for an entrepreneurial startup or a high-tech firm.

Not only the culture, but the people you are surrounded by will have a lot to do with your job satisfaction. Yes, it is true that being able to use your individual talents and skills to do something significant is important to employees, but this is not nearly as important as who your supervisor is. Research conducted by Harvard Business School and others have demonstrated for decades that the most important issue in job satisfaction is not pay, your work load, nor your working conditions. The most important factor in job satisfaction is your relationship with your direct supervisor. If you feel appreciated, respected, and valued by your supervisor you will be able to overcome many other negative workplace issues. On the other hand, if you consistently feel disrespected, run down, demeaned, or slighted by your supervisor; no increase in benefits, pay rate, or decrease in work load will improve your negative feelings about work.

The Cost of Dissatisfaction

Workplace dissatisfaction is easy to identify. As one anonymous employee remarked, "I hate knowing that nothing much is expected of me, and I hate even more that I seem to be willing to give them no more than what they expect."

Frustrated workers mention the layers of red tape, bad management, poor leadership, and dumb decisions. Scott Adams has made a fortune and given a great many laughs to countless people through his *Dilbert* cartoon series. Mocking the various kinds of incompetence commonly found in the workplace. Among his favorite targets are poor managerial decision-making, life in cubical land, idiotic coworkers, and—most scathingly— inept outside consultants. As a management consultant, my own stock of teaching materials is heavily illustrated with dozens of Dilbert cartoons, because he so nimbly captures the angst we feel in many of our work experiences.

When exposed to high enough levels of dysfunction, some workers reach a boiling point. They not only constantly complain about work, but also find themselves frequently frustrated and even filled with uncontrollable rage. Several workers describe feeling a ball of rage in the pit of the stomach on a daily basis, or feeling contempt for most of the people they see in the elevator or around the building. Academic researchers have been able to itemize the annual cost of this kind of stress on a national basis. The National Science Foundation claims 80 percent of employee emotional problems are stress-related, and 75 to 85 percent of all industrial accidents are caused by an inability to cope with stress on the job. Other costs from work-related stress include high levels of premature deaths, disability payments, medical bills, heart disease, alcoholism, and absenteeism. Ultimately, stress-related costs reach $100 billion every single year.[15]

When the Pot Boils Over

The symptoms of dysfunctional work experiences result in a serious economic cost to both employers and our national economy. Yet, even more troubling is the toll on individuals in the workplace. The vast majority of us regularly experience a multitude of negative feelings, concerns, and questions about our vocational life. Often we do nothing about it. Others, like Steven Slater, are so stirred up they actually respond by taking some type of action. In Slater's case, while his response was not pretty, it didn't hurt anyone.

In the best cases, these pent-up feelings translated into actions can produce the catharsis of quitting a bad job. Johnny Paycheck captured the joy of this in a hit song:

> *The foreman, he's a regular dog; the line boss, he's a fool;*
> *Got a brand-new flat-top haircut; Lord, he thinks he's cool;*
> *One of these days I'm going to blow my top, and that sucker, he's gonna regret it;*
> *I can't wait to see their faces when I get the nerve to say,*
> *"Take this job and shove it!"*[16]

This little ditty had such resonance with working Americans it was actually made into a full-blown movie. In the intervening years, many people have silently thought this themselves as they tear out of the plant parking lot on Friday night, "Yeah, you can take this job and shove it! I'm not workin' here no more!"

In the extreme cases this hostility on the job can lead to aggressive outbursts (described unfortunately as "going postal") which result in shootings or other forms of violence at one's place of work. Between 1986 and 1997, more than forty people were killed in at least twenty instances of workplace rage. Over the past several years, a number of these outbursts of workplace anger have made the national press. The mass shooting in November 2009 at Fort Hood by Army psychologist Nidal Hasan resulted in twelve dead, and thirty-one injured. Some observers concluded this incident was a typical example of a workplace avenger seeking retribution for episodes perceived as harassment or victimization.[17]

In February 2010 a college professor who had been denied tenure, a Harvard-educated neurobiologist, inventor, and mother of four, went on a shooting rampage in a University of Alabama faculty meeting, shooting six people and killing three fellow faculty members.[18]

These are not isolated incidents. According to an editorial in 2012 in *USA Today*, over 400 people each year are shot dead at work. Gun violence is becoming a frequent response among disgruntled workers, those who are struggling from workplace problems, those who have been terminated from a position, or even those who perceive some mistreatment in the workplace. [19]

The vast majority of us, however, do not react in such extremes. Instead, we endure, day after day, through difficult work experiences. Yet this is a serious issue! Think about it – with over 10 million interviewed; only three in ten of us have found our sweet spot in career and vocation. We struggle to confront, understand, and respond appropriately to the problem. *Is it really just my attitude that needs to change? Should I work on getting a different perspective on the people and situations that confront me at work every day? Do I just hold my nose and put up with it? Should I be researching alternative training and career paths so the balance of my working life will be more positive and fruitful? Do I need to find the same kind of work in a different organization? Should I consult a career coach? What is a reasonable plan for my vocational life? Am I headed in the right direction, or have I lost the path and become totally turned around in the woods?*

We ask ourselves these questions, and we should! Life is too short to spend most of it in a dead-end job or in a career that ends up sucking out the very soul of our being. If you, like the great majority of American working folks, find yourself struggling with some of these issues in your work life, read on. We have crafted this book to address these problems and to give you practical answers for your situation. If you read on then follow through, you too can discover the joy of working in your sweet spot.

Chapter 3

The School of Hard Knocks

At this point, you may be asking yourself, what qualifies the authors to give me advice on finding my sweet spot in career and vocation? An excellent question! In many ways, my co-author, Katybeth and I, come at this topic from opposite directions. I hope I represent the voice of experience, both as a worker trying to find a career on the way up and as an executive responsible for hiring individuals and building teams. In my 30+ years in the business world, I have been responsible for hiring a great many people. I've also had to fire some along the way, but that is a basic function of being a line manager. The key to success in any management position is the ability to get the right people on the team.

Katybeth, because of her age, stage, and experience, has a much better grasp on what it feels like to be a "20-something" who is transitioning from an educational experience into the workplace for the first time. In addition to having just recently survived her 20s, Katybeth's professional training is in career counseling (Masters, Ohio State) and in her position as Associate Director of Career Development at The University of Richmond, and now Associate Director at VCU, she has had many opportunities to help soon-to-be grads and alumni find their way to their sweet spot in career and vocation. But let me digress and fill in some detail.

Probably my most obvious credential is the experience I've had in working my way up from an entry level position in marketing research to one of the top executive positions in my field during my career. I started as a minimum wage grunt, doing "go-fer" jobs for a privately-owned marketing and advertising research vendor in Princeton, New Jersey. While working my way into project management, I built strong relationships with client organizations, and then moved over to the client-side of market research. After managing several corporate market research departments, I was promoted to brand management where I had the opportunity to supervise a number of sales and marketing functions. Additional stops along the way included experience in new business development and strategic planning. I finished my corporate career as the Director of Marketing Research at M&M/Mars, Inc.

After Mars, I founded a boutique management consulting company (Deer Haven Partners) which specializes in strategies for business growth, corporate culture transformation, and strategic planning. My role as an organizational consultant has allowed me the opportunity to help numerous clients recruit and build staff teams to grow their businesses. This process involved creating workforce development programs and procedures to help individuals transition their careers in new directions. Not only have I worked in this area on a strategic level, I've been involved in the nitty-gritty of hiring and teambuilding. Many evenings, I sat on my sofa with 150 resumes and cover letters with the goal of finding the best five or six candidates to interview for a new position.

Among my academic credentials, I have a Master's of Science in Organizational Leadership. Perhaps this most qualifies me to help diagnose organizational cultures and to lead change initiatives, but I don't think this has equipped me to address to your concerns about work and career.

Truthfully, I think my best qualifications for speaking to the issues contained in this volume come from the 'school of hard knocks.' In short, my own career -- my thirty years as someone working in the marketplace, has given me a wide variety of experiences and scores of insights contained herein. I come to this topic as someone who has struggled for years with the painful and difficult questions we'll examine throughout the course of this volume. The subject of work isn't merely an academic topic to me; I've had vast experience with it. The good, the bad, and the really ugly are the categories which cover most of the jobs I've endured.

There have been times in my career when I felt I was really working in my sweet spot—highly productive; using my gifts, talents, and experiences; working with a great team of people; and making a significant difference in the world. And yet, there have also been years where I felt I was wandering in the wilderness. I've tasted career success, and I've been fired. I've started a number of businesses, and have had several businesses fail. Most of the symptoms and experiences we'll examine in this book are things I've tasted and lived.

Learning from the Bottom Up

One of my first jobs after college was an entry-level position with a marketing and advertising research firm in Princeton, New Jersey. This was simultaneously one of the worst and one of the best work experiences of my entire career. My boss—let's call him Jack—was a terrible manager. He was very high-control. Jack loved to micromanage every piece of work done by everyone who worked for him. This was problematic, as his position as vice president required him to supervise a half dozen project directors and ten to twenty research studies at a time. Jack always had to get the credit, the praise, and the acclaim for every good piece of work done by every person who worked for him. Conversely, he was sure to pass on to others any blame and criticism for every mistake he made. Every report, every project, every analysis, had to have his thumbprint of authorship all over it. If it wasn't passed by Jack, it wasn't leaving the shop.

My two years working for Jack were the most miserable period in my three decades in the business world, but they were also the most valuable. In my first management position, and throughout the balance of my career, whenever I needed to make a decision about how to handle people or situations I would ask myself this question. "What would Jack do in this situation?" And then I would proceed to do the opposite. In almost every situation, I found myself developing into a highly effective manager, able to supervise people and organizations, build teams, and accomplish tasks solely by focusing on doing just the opposite of what Jack had done when he was managing me. I have to credit much of my success as a leader and executive to those two years of misery working for Jack.

Workplace Lessons

I've worked in some fabulous organizations. Some of the large businesses I've worked for have had superb corporate cultures, great values, top-quality people, and effective management decision-making, and they produced brilliant products and services for their customers and stakeholders. One of my employers, a Fortune 50 corporation, would make a textbook example of how excellent leadership and strong core values can produce an exceptional work environment, motivated and happy employees, a world-class product, and year after year of excellent growth and earnings.

On the other hand, I have seen a good deal of organizational dysfunction during my career. In my first corporate market research position, I worked for a Marketing Director whose stated goal in managing his department's culture was to leave everyone just a little bit insecure and unsure of their position. We all worked in a large warehouse that had been retrofitted into offices by installing a maze of cubicles (think Dilbert). My boss delighted in rearranging the cubicles. Almost every nine months he went to work: shaving a foot or two off of this person's office, adding a little more space to someone else's office, giving the Advertising Department more space or higher walls (a sure sign of favor), taking space off the Catalog Department (an indication of displeasure), or lowering the walls on some out-of-favor, high-ranking officer.

In another company my boss would invite associates into his office and depending on his mood and intention, would have you sit either in a rocking chair in front of his desk or on a sofa with a coffee table in a separate conversation area. Here was the secret -- if his intentions were positive and kindly, you would be asked to sit on the sofa, which created an atmosphere of being equals and being on a firm footing in your relationship with the boss. On the other hand, if he had something unpleasant up his sleeve, or you were in trouble, you would be invited to sit in the rocking chair. This particular chair was very nice-looking, and I think it had his college seal printed on the back of it. However, one of the back legs had been trimmed by about a half inch and replaced in the rocking chair rockers. Consequently, whenever you would sit in this chair, it would make you feel like were tilting backwards at an awkward angle and perhaps were in danger of falling out of the chair. The awkward physical symptoms caused by this chair made the occupant feel at a disadvantage in the relationship and the conversation, regardless of the content, and produced a psychological advantage for the boss sitting on the other side of the desk.

When I turned thirty, I went to work for a large multi-national manufacturing company that was listed on the New York Stock Exchange. I was so excited; this was the big time! Here was high-quality American business leadership at work, and I was part of the team.

Then I discovered many of the clever little strategies developed by management to keep plumping up the books for the market analysts who reviewed our company performance each quarter. For example, right after Christmas, every vice president had to come into work and spend days loading tractor-trailer trucks with product; the trucks were then driven around the countryside for two weeks. By the time the trucks returned and the product was put back into inventory at some point in January, the year-end close of our financial books had recorded these increased shipments as sales, even though none of the product had been sold. Not only was this deceptive, but the returned product meant that much more that had to be sold in the next fiscal year to keep up our string of consistently positive earnings reports.

Everyone Needs to Know Their Sweet Spot

After being hired into my first management position, I moved from the East Coast to Chicago. On my first day of the brand new job, my new boss mentioned in the course of our orientation, "Oh, by the way, I want you to fire Susanna." As I probed for more clarification, I found out Susanna was one of the staff members in the department I had just been hired to manage. Previously, she had worked directly for my new boss. About two years ago, he decided she wasn't doing a good job, so one Friday afternoon, he fired her. Susanna's response was to simply ignore this distressing experience. On Monday morning she was back at her desk doing her job. She came in every day and worked and every two weeks she received a paycheck. This had been going on for two years with no resolution when I arrived on the scene.

Before I did anything drastic, I investigated the situation and discovered Susanna was actually a very good worker. But she was a square peg in a round hole -- she was in a job that simply did not fit her strengths and talents. After a few interviews, and several diagnostic tests to obtain a focus of her abilities and interests, she was transferred to a new position in a different department. At last report she had continued to do excellent work for this company for twenty-five more years and then accepted full retirement.

This experience, and many others like it, gave me my first insights into the value of an assortment of diagnostic tools which we will explore in Section Two. Over the course of my career, I learned a great deal about what sort of vocational opportunities to seek out and which to avoid. Over the years, I have been saved thanks to these diagnostic tools, and they have offered me a better understanding of what actually makes me tick too. At the same time I've been able to help others learn to use these tools to guide and direct their own careers. Helping others discover their sweet spot over the years has been a particularly rewarding experience and one stimulus which led to the writing of this book.

Katybeth's Experience

As you might guess from reading some of my dad's stories, my parents placed a high value on the role of work. Growing up, I had a myriad of opportunities to learn about what work might do for me, and what it might not!

When I was twelve, my mom arranged my first externally paying gig with a neighbor down the street. She had two small boys and was a potter, trying to earn some extra income by making ceramics in her basement. Her toddlers were a bit of a hindrance, so my job was to play with them upstairs while she worked in her studio downstairs. Often they would go down for a nap while I was there, and my immediate impulse was to tidy up their playroom. I loved how neat everything was…until they woke up again! My official title was "Mother's Helper;" my compensation was a whopping 25 cents/hour and one pound of clay a month to be used under the guidance of the mother-potter. Let's just say I was not included in the negotiations, and was less than pleased. I was hoping for more money and less clay! Ironically, I have since taken up pottery and now pay for the privilege of using a studio and buy my own clay at $10/bag.

The first summer I was old enough to work legally, I arranged for two jobs. The first was an assistant at a summer theater program. Among other things, I was in charge of the props. I enjoyed the process of identifying the necessary materials and locating each to enable the play to be performed with excellence. The rest of my time was spent herding rowdy children.

When I wasn't in the summer theater program, I was at my other job—scooping ice cream. I grew up in a lakeside resort town in New Hampshire, where most establishments were open from May through October to cater to the tourists. Our town had 5,000 year-round residents, and about 25,000 in the summer. I worked every Fourth of July from age 14 until after college. *The Bubble*, my ice cream employer, was owned by a local couple and staffed by their children's friends. Our supervisor acted more like our mom than a boss, and the team was energetic, creative, and mostly fun.

While I was at college, I worked as a Resident Assistant and scooped more ice cream, this time for Baskin Robbins. When I graduated, I decided to travel around the world, volunteering for different mission organizations and non-profits. It was the first time in a long, long time that I hadn't had a job—and it was really hard. I realized I gained a lot of satisfaction from knowing I had work to do and doing it well. I liked the sense of purpose I gained from work, even unglamorous work like scooping ice cream. Not having a set of responsibilities was surprisingly difficult for me. It's good to remind myself of this after a long week in the marketplace.

In graduate school, I had the brilliant idea to be a live-in house mother for a sorority at a large state university known for being a bit of a party school. I had two rooms off the first floor of the house, and about 20 undergraduate sorority sisters lived on the second and third floors. There was a full-time cook and a housekeeper whom I supervised, and a whole lot of shenanigans after the sun went down. The cook would lock the kitchen when she left in the evening—one morning I came down to find the door had been kicked off its hinges. No one would fess up to it, or rat out a belligerently drunken boyfriend, so the entire sorority paid for repairs together. There were suicide attempts, cat fights, and full beer cans thrown through our windows in the middle of the night. Though it provided free room and board in addition to a $10,000 stipend, it was not worth the trouble, and I moved as soon as my contract was over.

When I graduated from my Master's program, I had a few job offers for Career Counselor positions—making the decision between them was quite difficult. Though I think any could have been good, I chose the one where I thought I would have more access to professional development and mentoring, since it was my first position as a professional. I had no idea what an impactful choice that would be. Though I'm a product of entirely public education and deeply believe in its importance, the private institution at which I work has an abundance of resources which have enabled me to grow professionally over the last five years.

The Career Development Center staff with whom I work are immensely talented. My supervisors have had years of experience in the field, and are always looking for ways to improve the way we serve students, alumni, faculty, staff, and employers. They are creative and compassionate. They are inspiring advisors and effective team leaders. I have participated in workshops and conferences with the National Career Development Association, the Mid-Atlantic Career Counselor Association, and the National Association of Student Personnel Administrators. I am trained to administer the Myers-Briggs Type Indicator, the Strong Interest Inventory, and Strengths Finder 2.0. I serve as an academic advisor for undeclared students, as well as a career advisor for first year students through retired alumni. I have given presentations at national conferences, published articles, and individually advised nearly 1,000 clients.

Learning For a Lifetime Journey

As I reflect on the odyssey and adventure of my career (Bruce), I see a number of high points, a smaller number of very low periods, and a variety of experiences that fall somewhere in between. My dad, a taciturn industrial engineer, used to tell me, "Son, if you find a job where you like 25 percent of what you do, and hate 25 percent of what you do, and the other 50 percent is just okay—hang onto it! It's a good job." Spoken like a child of the Depression, my father's only career advice didn't seem helpful to me, especially in light of his own experience.

At heart Dad was a tinkerer. He loved to fool around with mechanical processes and find better ways to do things. He was gifted at finding manufacturing solutions which improved efficiencies, lowered costs, and sped up production. My grandfather told stories about him as a boy. "I could never give him a chore to do on the farm, where your father wouldn't study the task and invent a better way to do it before he set to work." Dad earned a Bachelor of Science in Electrical Engineering and went to work for a growing manufacturing firm. They discovered his giftedness with improving processes, and sent him to night school to get a Master's degree in Industrial Engineering. His career seemed to be developing along the lines of his natural talents and interests. Then success spoiled his career.

After a few years, and with every significant accomplishment at industrial engineering, Dad got a promotion. With every promotion, he had fewer systems to tinker with and more people to manage. An introvert, he was always uncomfortable around people. The more people they gave him, the more miserable his work made him. I watched him spend the last thirty years of his career getting big promotions, making more money, but still hating his work. The last twenty years he just loathed getting up and going to the plant to deal with all the people problems. Outwardly, he was seen as a successful executive. The truth is, his job eventually sucked out his soul, destroyed his joy, and left him a shell of the man he had been.

Why does it seem so difficult for most of us to find career paths which lead us to a positive work environment, one that uses our gifts and talents, which provides an adequate living, and allows us to make a contribution to the world we live in? My dad's meager advice and the example of his own career simply made me fear the workplace. No one in college offered me much advice about finding a job, let alone finding one that fit my competencies and interests. As a college graduate, I was left to stumble around on my own in the dark looking for a job and a career. Until I met the woman I eventually married, my secret ambition was to go live as a mountain man in the Snake River Wilderness in Idaho.

While many in the world may see career as a hopeless muddle, my own experience, and that of many people a lot smarter than I am, tells me you and I were not made to spend the bulk of our working lives in fear and misery No matter where you are in your journey into career, you can redeem your experience. We were each designed with unique skills and interests and were created to experience work as a blessing.

While you may be mid-career or even late career and think you don't need to look at the foundations of how you got where you are, I would urge you to reconsider. Recent research among American workers by *Parade Magazine* found nearly 60 percent of workers would choose a new career if they could start over again.[20] The strong majority of your co-workers feel the need for a total career makeover. Maybe you should give these issues your attention before it's too late.

Many careers develop an unintended hook or slice (to use a golf metaphor) because of the way they were launched. Our motives, our goals, and our ability to transition from academic training to a real-world working environment all influence choices we make which have a long term impact on our careers. Most of us simply fall short in terms of learning to understand our own unique strengths, interests, and passions. This lack of insight into our core values leads to poor choices of a vocational nature. If you are in mid-career and you're hitting the wall, the seeds of your current career crisis may have been planted twenty years ago.

Section Two gets to the heart of making midcourse corrections in your career. We will investigate your own unique design and understand critical factors which affect your ability to improve your satisfaction during the course of your career. This section will also present a variety of diagnostic tools you can use on your own to get a better sense of what does it mean to be in your sweet spot which fits your unique self.

Section Three lays out the process of growing, and sustaining a career that will be a blessing in your life. Our goal should be to find ways to discover our unique self, find a path to make a significant contribution to the world and to reap the satisfaction of leaving the world a better place than when we came into it. These last chapters will enable you to hang on to a good job once you find it and to build a strong career that is rewarding to you and to many other people in your life.

Chapter 4

Launching a Career

Launching any new enterprise can be a perilous endeavor. As Bilbo Baggins, the famous hobbit of *Lord of the Rings*, once remarked, "Just stepping outside your front door can be a risky business." When we contemplate launching a career which will potentially span four decades, consuming the majority of our time, attention, and energy, we recognize the stakes are high.

I'm reminded of the launch of the space shuttle *Challenger* on January 28, 1986. The *Challenger* was a state-of-the-art spacecraft which contained the best aeronautic technology developed over the previous three decades. It also contained seven of the most highly trained professional astronauts in the NASA program. The *Challenger* broke apart 73 seconds into its flight on that fateful morning, killing all seven crewmembers. The disintegration of the entire vehicle began after an O-ring seal in the right solid booster rocket failed at lift-off. This small, $2 part apparently lacked sufficient flexibility at the unusually low temperatures experienced the morning of the launch over the coast of Central Florida. As a result of the breakdown of this one small detail, a cascade of technical failures surged through the spacecraft, resulting in its structural failure and crash.[21]

The American educational system traditionally leaned towards a liberal arts philosophy -- the student was exposed to the classics and a variety of other areas of academic study before graduation. This broad background of knowledge then presumed to create an adequate foundation for learning almost any type of professional, leadership, or management skill. Today, however, the pendulum has swung in favor of technical education, where the student is actually expected to be trained to function in a particular kind of position upon graduation. Approximately 85% of college students in America today are enrolled in university training which is technical in orientation rather than following the liberal arts pattern.

The fatal underbelly of this hyper-focus on graduating from university with a specific job skill is the fact that so few people entering university have any clear idea of their unique strengths, their interests, and their passions, all of which are foundational for success in a career. This conundrum is much like the old computer slogan: **GIGO** or **Garbage In = Garbage Out**. If you haven't developed a clear set of parameters to guide your selection of university training, the output isn't going to be very helpful in terms of finding a job or career which you ultimately find satisfying and rewarding.

Recently I read an article entitled, *The 10 Worst Jobs in Science*. These distinguished jobs included that of **armpit detective**, a position at Florida International University to "study human odors, mainly from the underarm, to try to isolate the compounds that give us our unique aroma." Also listed was the **feces piper**, a hospital position which involves transplanting fecal matter from a healthy patient through a tube into a sick person, in hopes the good bacteria can wipe out the infected bacteria. Then there's the **oceanic snot divers**, scientists from Italy's Polytechnic University who dive in the Adriatic Sea to collect samples of "gelatinous masses of dead plankton and decaying cell material that look like large loogies and smell of seafood and decomposing eggs."[22]

When starting out to university at the tender young age of 18, does anyone have any idea they could end up as an armpit detective or an oceanic snot diver? How exactly do we move from a vague, unformed, adolescent phase which typifies the American high school graduate, into the highly complex process of sorting out the many different kinds of jobs and careers and finally to identifying a career direction suitable for a specific individual?

Frederick Buechner points out a major problem with identifying your individual call is that "There are all different kinds of voices calling you to all different kinds of work, and the problem is to find out which is the correct voice..."

Buechner goes on to say, "a good rule for finding out is this. The kind of work you are best called to, is the kind of work (a) that you most need to do and (b) that the world most needs to have done. If you really get a kick out of your work, you've presumably met requirement (a), but if your work is writing TV deodorant commercials, the chances are you've missed requirement (b). On the other hand, if your work is being a doctor in a leper colony, you have probably met requirement (b), but if most of the time you're bored and depressed by it, the chances are you have not only bypassed (a) but probably aren't helping your patients much either."[23]

One Main Thing

Finding your sweet spot in career and vocation involves a great many issues and requires study, analysis, and multi-faceted decision making on your part. Yet, at the heart of this process, there is only one critical piece you have to figure out to find career success. Peter Drucker describes this critical element thusly: "To know one's strengths, to know how to improve them and to know what one cannot do – this is the key to continuous improvement." Identifying your main strengths, this is the one thing you must do to build a successful and satisfying work life. Your weaknesses don't really matter. It is helpful to learn what one cannot do. But ultimately, weakness lead nowhere. All the things people do to throw obstacles in your career path, these won't ultimately knock you off track, so long as you find and build on the one main thing: your unique strengths as a person.

After decades of helping thousands of people find their sweet spot in career and vocation, it's obvious to me this issue must be addressed. Knowing your unique strengths contributes the most to those who are successful in finding a job or career they can love. You may not have heard about this in school. I doubt your parents sat you down and had a little chat about career planning like they did about the birds and the bees. Even if you utilized your university's career counseling service, you may have not caught this when it came up. I can assure you, there is almost no likelihood your current employer is going to let you in on this secret. **Yet, it is the one thing you have to discern in order to find a job you can enjoy and a career leading out of that.**

There are many different ways to screw up your job search and your career development process. Trust me, it's easy do it wrong. As we start though, let's focus on the one positive thing you can do to invest in a secure foundation.

When you clear away all the underbrush, this whole process is relatively simple. We're trying to figure out what kind of square peg you are, so we can identify what kind of a square hole of a job to put you in.

Far too often, I see people who are launching a career or trying to redefine a career, spending the bulk of their time on tactical issues: how to network, how to use job search sites on the Internet, writing an effective resume, doing research on a company, doing practice interviews, and learning to communicate effectively. These are helpful issues, and we will cover some of them, or point you to other resources which expand on issues. But they are simply tactical issues--they tell you the *how* of trying to land a job.

The one strategic issue is to *understand the core of who you are as a person*, what makes you unique, what strengths you bring to the world of work, and what attributes need to be part of your vocation for you to be the best you can be and make your largest contribution to the world at large.

How many of us actually begin our work life by making a careful assessment of our talents, unique gifts, temperament, educational skill sets, and the potential career paths we might investigate, let alone where they might lead us? A lack of self-knowledge, a failure to research, and a lack of knowledge of our interests and passions could very well land us a 30-year assignment as a sneeze modeler (the person who researches where spit lands on another's face when someone coughs or sneezes, in order to find the areas of the body most susceptible to the flu virus entering.) A major reason I think many Americans struggle with vocation is that we tend to be ignorant about our own unique gifts, talents, and temperament and the types of work that might best utilize our distinctive skills.

When I lead corporations through a strategic planning exercise, we begin with the guiding principles of the organization. It is essential to get a crystal-clear focus on the mission of the organization. Why do you exist? What measurable results do you want to accomplish? How will you know if you're succeeding as an organization? What are the core values you refuse to compromise or change? As I tell my clients, these are the hardest things to identify and to articulate in the strategic planning process -- but they are absolutely essential to creating an effective strategic plan.

This is much like the process a tailor uses when he makes a custom suit of clothes for a client. The first step is always to take measurements of the client's physical body. The customer's unique body dimensions is the basis for the suit of clothing to be created that will be a perfect fit. While I (Bruce) am 6 foot 2 inches, weigh 250 pounds, and as my mother used to say, have always been a "husky boy." Katybeth is 5 feet 9 inches and wears a size 6 dress. Clearly, we are never going to be able to swap wardrobe items. I expect our respective custom suits will be dramatically different. This is as it should be.

Understanding your own mission and core values is essential to launching, growing, and sustaining a successful career. Your core values are the measurements of what it means for you to be a square peg and what you need to look for to find your matching square hole in a job or career. By core values, I mean your own unique gifts, talents, and temperament.

Some parents project their own hopes and dreams on their children, often with good intentions, but unfortunate consequences. One student told me (Katybeth) her father had attended Yale and expected her to go to Yale, just as he had. She was wait-listed at Yale, but admitted to Dartmouth, Princeton, and a number of other fine institutions. He refused to contribute financially for her to attend any of the universities to which she was accepted because it wasn't the one he had attended.

Another student's parents told him he could be either a doctor or a businessman. He took a heavy load of science courses his first year, and in doing so, realized that he didn't particularly like science, nor was he as good at it as he would need to be to compete for medical school. Sophomore year when registration time arrived, he declared a business major, though he had yet to take a business class to know whether it was a good fit for him. He presumed it was his only other option if he wanted his parents' support.

Often students today have been pressured by the high expectations of their parents since before kindergarten. These unfortunate young adults have been shaped by demands for high grades in school, exceptional performance in athletics, and participation in lots of social, civic, and community experiences—all as a prerequisite for getting into the best college thus receiving parental approval. When they reach their last years of college, it begins to dawn on them: they've spent so much time pleasing their parents and the other people around them that they have no idea what makes them happy. They've never had time or opportunities to consider: *What gets me excited? What are my interests and passions? What skills and talents do I excel in?*

Avoid Two Dangerous Myths

As we begin to identify your core values and unique strengths, I must caution you about two prevailing myths which are part of the fabric of the American Dream, and which often derail individuals who are seeking to find their vocational sweet spot.

The first is what I call the **Myth of the Renaissance Man**. It's built around the belief that successful individuals, over time, can and should develop the capacity to do everything well.

Leonardo da Vinci is probably the original model for this. Universally recognized as an exceptional genius, da Vinci excelled in a variety of disciplines—painting, sculpture, music, engineering, and the physical sciences. While he leaves to his credit a number of significant accomplishments, including the paintings *Mona Lisa* and *The Last Supper*, perhaps his greatest legacy is his many voluminous sketchbooks in which he drafted his ideas and thinking about a wide variety of subjects. Unfortunately, the great diversity of his interests prevented him from pursuing and completing most of the ideas he was engrossed in.

In my work in the business world, I occasionally come across individuals engaged in headlong pursuit of this dream of universal competence. They labor under the impression that they ought to be the best in every discipline required in business or organizational life. They not only strive constantly to improve their areas of individual strength, but seek to succeed in areas in which they lack significant skills and aptitudes.

The frequent result of pursuing this myth is a person who's struggling with guilt because he's not able to improve his performance in certain areas, who's crippled by perfectionism, or who lives in denial, pretending to have capacities he simply doesn't possess. Those who work with this type of individual are fully aware of his shortcomings. But they're unable to help him because he has bought into the myth. Typically he rises to a position of influence in management where he then proceeds to clog up the process. In his attempt to keep a finger in every pie and to influence every area under his control, he creates delay, confusion, and a staff of frustrated, unhappy people. Not only are his subordinates unable to contribute their unique skill sets, they suffer from the bungling incompetence of their senior officer.

Dr. Peter Drucker, , articulates the solution to the Myth of the Renaissance Man in his groundbreaking volume *The Effective Executive.* First published in 1966, it continues to be a crucial handbook for those who manage others. Drucker advocates staffing from strength: "Whoever tries to place a man or staff an organization to avoid weakness will end up at best with mediocrity. The idea that there are "well-rounded" people, people who have only strengths and no weaknesses, is a prescription for mediocrity if not for incompetence. Strong people always have strong weaknesses too. And no one is strong in many areas."[24]

During my corporate career, whenever I had the opportunity to mentor or develop staff, I would instruct them about the Myth of the Renaissance Man. Not only is it false, it will point you in exactly the opposite direction you need to go to become successful. In truth, you have the capacity to do one or two of the needed tasks better than anyone else in the organization or in your chosen field. Your goal in developing your career should be to eventually identify the one or two percent that are the pinnacle of your capacities. You develop a successful career by building on your strengths—learning the unique value you contribute to a team, to an organization, to an industry. Always remember to build on your strengths—manage everything else away.

A good friend who's an executive coach told me of an exercise he uses with clients. He gives them a 3x5 card and asks the client to write on the front the three things they like best about their job. On the back of the card they are to write the three things they like least about it. When the card is complete, Jeff and the client review the items. Then he encourages the executive to find ways to do more of the things on the front of the card (usually stemming from the person's strengths) and to find ways to delegate away the items on the back of the card. Jeff observed that tasks you don't do well are typically the items which end up on the back of the card. These have a tendency to be from your areas of weakness. His advice on delegating is to look around for somebody who absolutely loves to do that particular task and delegate it to them.

A Second Myth

A second myth has been identified by some as the **Myth of Becoming**. It's the notion that we can all be anything we want to be.

Arthur Miller, Jr., the founder of People Management writes, "This idea, deeply ingrained in the American psyche, is that one can become and do whatever one wants. This is without doubt one of the greatest lies ever promoted.... 'Whatever the mind can conceive, the will can achieve' is how the myth is often framed. This widespread belief in unlimited options for personal destiny has to be among the chief deceptions and destroyers of our age."[25]

The Myth of Becoming is based on the notion that people are like putty and can be shaped into a variety of forms to fill their own wishes, to fulfill the needs of their employers, or to become exactly that which society values. The truth is each individual human being is remarkably unique. We each have a distinctive pattern of capacity and competence which defines our options. No matter how much we long to be someone else, nor how much education and training we receive, humans really aren't capable of sustaining a long-term productive existence outside of the pattern God has designed at the core of their being.

The myth's appeal, however, is almost irresistible: "You can become *anything* you want!" In our culture, this almost feels like a God-given right. If you're willing to apply yourself, work hard, and get education and training, you should be able to do and be anything you desire. Yet, even the simple evidence of human physique tells us this myth can't be true.

Different people have different body types and physical attributes. One person is a short, rather light, agile horse-rider, gifted at motivating animals. Another may be six-foot, four inches, weighing 285 pounds—all bone and muscle—with hands like hams. Can both be great athletes? Maybe, but only if they pick the right sport. The small fellow would make a great jockey riding in flatland races or the steeplechase. The large guy with big hands may make an incredible rugby player, which involves a lot of physical contact, running, scrumming, and tossing the ball.

Yet what would happen if our five-foot, one inch, 105-pound friend insisted that he too could be a great rugby player? My guess is that he would become crushed under a couple of beefy giants in short order. The problem isn't his ability to become a fine athlete; it's that his expectations lead him to pursue a sport where he simply wasn't designed to be successful. Likewise, if our six-foot, four inch giant decides he needs to succeed as a jockey, he most likely will be turn his mounts into mush under his excessive weight and certainly won't be winning any races. Both these body types have a great potential for athletic success, but only if they're willing to compete in sports appropriate for the way they have been created.

You are Unique

Understanding that each person has been designed uniquely is the bedrock and foundation of every successful career. Certainly, as a human being, we all have a number of things in common with other people. Generally, we have two ears, two eyes, one nose, one mouth, and various other appendages and physical attributes we share with the bulk of humanity. We also have a number of psychological and emotional characteristics we hold in common. And yet, in our essential self, in the combination of attributes, interests, temperament and other vital aspects of ourselves as a person, we each are unique! **You were made to do one or two things better than anyone else on earth.** It's critical for you to figure out what your unique focus and purpose is so that you can become all you were meant to be, and so you can have an influence which leaves lasting benefits to the world at large.

Some people have perfect pitch. From an early age, they can sing with near perfection. Others are tone deaf and cannot carry a tune in a large bucket. These are not judgments of ultimate value. These are observations from nature. All the research says that the taller a man, the more likely he is to be promoted into positions of leadership. But try as I might, I have not yet figured out how to grow another three inches taller. Rather than fight my unique design, it is imperative that I learn to understand what makes me uniquely me. And celebrate it!

Now when we argue that each person is unique, we do so recognizing that in many ways this contradicts the tenants of the American Dream and much of what your educational experience has tried to teach you. We are perfectly happy arguing uniqueness from simple observation. When was the last time you walked into a room of people and found yourself staring at someone who looks exactly like you? Even "identical twins" have characteristics which distinguish their appearance so that those who know them well enough can easily tell them apart.

While the world's population is approaching 7 billion, every single individual is unique. Your fingerprints are unique. Your eyes are unique. Your DNA is unique. Even the rhythm of your heartbeat is unique and varies with every individual such that it can be patterned and identified by those with the appropriate tools and training. That means you're unique! There's no one else like you on the planet. You've been designed for a special purpose. At the same time, it's critical to understand there are certain things you cannot do at all, and a great many things you cannot at all. Still, there are also things you can do better than anyone else.

Find Your Voice

In the process of trying to discover our unique design and our special place in the world of work, we are often pressured and influenced by others. Instead of seeking our uniqueness our tendency is to compromise. It's easy to compare yourself to someone else and think, "I should be more like them."

Tina McBride grew up loving music in the small town of Sharon, Kansas. Even in high school, her fondest memory was the thrill she got standing at a microphone belting out country tunes as a part of her family's band. After graduation, she moved to Wichita and worked as a professional musician. On the advice of her musical mentors, Tina switched to singing Pop 40 tunes on the club circuit. It was music people wanted to hear, but it wasn't the music that fed McBride's soul. Singing became more like drudge work, she suffered from fatigue and exhaustion, and she even began to lose her voice from strain. By age twenty-two, McBride felt forty and was ready to give up.

On a weekend back home, her dad asked her to sit in and play with the family band. "I was barely a few bars into a Patty Loveless number when I felt something. A feeling of connection with the audience. And something larger, something bigger than the music. Like when I was a kid. That old thrill. That feeling of doing what I was made to do."

McBride realized she was made for country music. She turned her back on the club scene, moved to Nashville, and committed herself to finding a music career that fit her. She got her first break in the business selling t-shirts at a Garth Brooks concert. Over the next fifteen years she gradually worked her way up as a country music performer. Martina went on to break into the top tier of country music, selling over sixteen million albums, and wining most of country music's top awards multiple times.[26]

Your goal in finding your sweet spot in career and vocation should be to find your authentic voice. Much like a budding writer, each person who seeks to find an appropriate role in the marketplace, needs to find their own authentic voice. Don't compare yourself with others and don't compete to try to be like someone else. Mary Pipher, the author of the best selling nonfiction book, *Reviving Ophelia*, describes the essence of finding your voice as a writer:

> "By diving into the experience of writing, you will learn what you truly think and who you really are. Your self-exploration is a way to pay attention to the world, within yourself and outside of yourself...Try different tones and styles and take note of what sounds most natural for you. Eventually, you will be able to winnow out those that sound false...People from all circumstances, all ages, all personality types and all cultures can be powerful writers. With self understanding, over time, writers learn to work with your

strengths, and to use their flaws as accent notes to enrich their work."[27]

Begin the Journey

Finding work you can love is a process more than an outcome. I'm afraid we sometimes approach career planning the same way we might a vending machine. I draw near, spread my feet at eighteen inches in the power stance, and square off to the selection window. I insert the money, decide which candy bar I want, press the right combination of buttons, and...*drum roll*...out comes my career!

Actually, the process is more like a journey. There's as much joy from the process as there is from arriving at the hoped for destination. Consider the process an adventure you have the privilege of embarking on. It might be helpful to see your search for work you can love as being a lot more like a quest like Frodo's in *Lord of the Rings*. Beginning is the first step.

We understand this process of identifying what makes you unique is challenging for most people to work through. It's true! We recognize the great blessings and great difficulties of living in America where there are so many different ways of earning a living and building a career. On the other hand, having too many choices is probably not as painful as having too few choices. There's no easy answer. As Os Guinness has written, "We are all on a search for significance. We desire to make a difference. We long to leave a legacy."[28]

Chapter 5

The Road to Hell

They say the road to hell is paved with good intentions. Likewise, the road which leads you into the journey of career and vocation is often paved with good intentions. And yet, somehow, so often, it leads you to a place of doubts, disappointment, suffering, and even torment. While your intentions may have been positive, your methodology or choices, led you to a living hell of a job or career. Perhaps you think, "That's not going to happen to me!" In fact, almost six in ten American workers look back on their work life and conclude, if they could do it all over again, they would select a different career.[29]

Let's look at some of the common mistakes people make in either launching or building their career which leads them into unfortunate predicaments and see if we can't help you avoid these pitfalls on your journey to vocation.

The Empty Promise of Money

Many young adults think the primary purpose of a job or career is to make money. Preferably lots of money. Not so fast! If you lift your eyes from the starting line of career and gaze a decade or two down the track, you might be surprised at what you see. Building a career solely on the love of money can be a huge mistake which too often leads to tragedy.

After the global economic crisis began in mid-2008, there followed a tragic string of suicides of formerly wealthy and well-connected individuals. The acting chief financial officer of Freddie Mac hanged himself. The chief executive of Sheldon Good, a leading U.S. real estate auction firm, shot himself in the head behind the wheel of his red Jaguar. A French money manager who invested the wealth of many of Europe's royal and leading families, and who had lost $1.4 billion of his clients' money in Bernard Madoff's Ponzi scheme, slit his wrists and died in his Madison

Avenue office. A Danish senior executive with HSBC Bank hanged himself in the wardrobe of his $750-per-night suite in Knightsbridge, London. When a Bear Stearns executive learned that he wouldn't be hired by JPMorgan Chase, who had bought his collapsed firm, he took a drug overdose and leapt from the 29th floor of his office building.[30]

Often our *motives* for selecting a career are the reason we end up in trouble somewhere down the line. Many people chose a vocation merely from pragmatic expediency. Where are the good jobs? What fields are hiring, and how much money can I make? Recent research among college students found the number-one life objective among freshman students (cited by 78 percent) is "being well-off financially." This goal came out higher than any other, including "raising a family" (75 percent), or "helping others in difficulty" (69 percent). Concern about money permeated "just about everything," according to John Pryor, author of the study of 220,000 full-time freshmen at 297 four-year colleges.[31]

Even after graduation, many young adults say their primary impetus for selecting a job is that it will make them rich or famous. According to a Pew Research Center poll, 81% of 18- to 25-year-olds say getting rich is one of their generation's most important goals and 51% said the same about being famous. Often Millennial graduates, absorbing many of the Boomer values of their parents, choose work or a career which has high potential for producing material rewards or a luxurious materialistic lifestyle.

Parker Jeffs was in his early twenties when he got his Master's degree in Accounting from American University in Washington, D.C. He chose that degree not because he had any real interest in the field, but because he figured if he worked hard enough, he thought he could make partner in a big firm and earn a $1 million per year. Even without making partner, Jeffs felt a good accounting job would have high potential to produce a four-bedroom colonial house in a nice suburb, membership in the country club, good private schooling for the kids, and exotic vacations for his family. This choice, and the 80+-hour workweeks that came with it, gave Jeffs a bleeding ulcer by age thirty, a divorce by age forty, and estrangement and broken relationships with his kids. Ultimately, it was the path of self-destruction for a talented young man with great potential.

This approach to career planning is really not focused on the work, but on financial security. In the end the fixation on money may prove to be an illusion. American society bombards us with advertising and other impressions which misinform us about the true nature of happiness. In a thumbnail, advertising tries to convince you that to feel good you need to buy something you do not need. Comedian George Carlin crisply captures the absurdity of this philosophy when he says, "Trying to be happy by accumulating possessions is like trying to satisfy hunger by taping sandwiches all over your body."[32]

Failure to Launch

Failure to Launch, a movie starring Matthew McConaughey and Sarah Jessica Parker, tells the story of a not so young man (age 39) who has managed to avoid becoming an adult in terms of his relationships with the opposite sex. This can also be seen in the journey to find an adult job and career. Some people have no plan, so they simply drift. They live for today and hope tomorrow things will sort themselves into a better situation.

At times, it may feel like the best thing to do is toss a dart at the board of chances and do "whatever." Join the circus. Become a monk. Teach English in Botswana. This laissez faire approach was taken by a family friend who graduated from college about five years ago. First she went to New Zealand and worked as a farm laborer. Then she landed in Antarctica (minus 80 degrees) and waitressed in the dining room of a research station. Next she spent a summer on a dude ranch in Montana doing carpentry and construction. Following a stint as a tourist in Argentina, she moved to Park City, Utah, where she worked as a firefighter in the summer and snowboarding instructor in winter.

The major difficulty with this approach is that eventually, the consequences catch up with you. Day to day, the choices may seem harmless enough. After a decade or two, a spouse, two kids, a mortgage, two car payments, and a lot of credit card debt, your laid back lifestyle may come to haunt you.

Skipping Your Homework

Why is it so hard for us to get a grip on this whole area of vocation? For one thing, American life today is so full of background noise--the Internet, smart phones, e-mails, instant messaging, texts, apps, Facebook, tweets, television, and iPods—they are blaring into our subconscious all day long. Frankly, it's hard to think. All this chatter and lack of margins in our schedules tend to squeeze out adequate opportunities for reflection and thinking. It takes time to develop a clear understanding of our interests and passions. It takes patient reflection to gain a clear understanding of our unique strengths, skills, and talents.

Finding a job you can love doesn't just happen. Finding a job that allows you to become all you were made to be is not just luck. Getting into a career that doesn't cause you serious regret decades later is not simply a fortuitous event. Why do you think "mid-life crises" are so common among middle-aged workers? It's because haphazard career planning is often worse than no career planning at all. We all make choices as we seek to find meaningful and productive work. The choices we make—and often the motivation behind them—form the hidden foundations of the career consequences we reap years or even decades later.

Wake Up! Pay Attention! This is your life! Your failure to plan or to do adequate homework is most likely to result in negative consequences for decades, which is a very long time.

External Pressure

A significant number of people end up in poor fit jobs, or the wrong fields due to external pressures. A friend who majored in wildlife biology, his true passion, eventually obtained an M.B.A. and entered the field of finance due to pressure from his father, a successful investment banker. A bright and talented young 25-year-old I know, with a heart for social policy issues and their effect on the working poor, ended up in nursing because of family pressure to get a "practical" job. A talented Ivy League college grad with a yearning to teach history is working in the law field due to pressure to help his dad carry on the family business.

There are many variants of this story, all the result of what psychologists call an "external locus of control." It means a worldview dictated by forces outside us, telling us where to go and what to do, and leaving us little choice about it. These folks feel that they are merely a leaf floating on the stream of life, blown about by wind and currents with little or no control over their destiny. This fatalistic perspective constrains our choices in life and may prevent us from becoming the person we were created to be.

Parental pressure is probably the most frequent source of external influence that misdirects people in their career search. It is very common for recent college graduates to be unsure of their next step. Roughly 60% of college graduates move back in with their parents for some period of time after finishing university. They do this not only for financial support, but also for emotional support. Setting out from the highly structured environment of education, which these twenty-somethings have spent most of their life working through and transitioning to a completely chaotic and unmanaged marketplace with millions of choices is a difficult step to take.

In some cases, parents can make a bad situation worse by injecting additional pressure to what is already a stressful situation. Many twenty-somethings find their parents harassing them weekly with specific job opportunities and other suggestions about what next steps should be taken. Phil, a 25-year-old New Orleans native, was working at an entry-level help desk job less than a year after finishing his economics degree. "I was fed up with my mother calling me every week and telling me stories about how she read an article about some kid my age making five to six times my salary. She would say stuff like, 'There was an excellent article in *Newsweek* about Jeremy Snot-Nose who's 24 years old making $90K/year programming a computerized toilet flusher.'"[33]

Internal Pressure

Sometimes the pressure we feel about career choices comes not from external sources such as our parents, but rather from within ourselves. This may be an even more difficult kind of stress to cope with. The anxiety and pressure for many college graduates has been building for years. First, it's the pressure in your sophomore year to declare a major. Many students think their major will directly correlate to their career. In some cases, particularly in more technical fields, this may be true—for instance, to be an accountant, not only must you major in accounting, but you must also accumulate 150 credit hours to be eligible to sit for the CPA exam.

For those students who have elected to study a liberal arts curriculum, they need to sort out a connection all on their own. This can be overwhelming to a 19 year old who may not have done her homework yet, or has no idea how she might want to apply a Religion degree to a career. Many students have lived life thus far on scheduled, pre-planned, and highly predictable time tables. The idea that the journey toward a satisfying career may unfold slowly over time, without a magic schedule to dictate exact turns at specific times to achieve success simply petrifies these students. Some will elect a technical field of study, such as business or engineering, simply because it comes with a clearer timetable.

More problems can arise when these students don't actually like the coursework in their major, and merely stick with it for the comfort of having a preset path. Let's think about that—if you don't like the classes now, what are the odds that you'll like the careers they are preparing you for? Not very good.

Many things can happen as you head toward the real working world. One friend of mine, Rachel, ended up graduating from a prestigious school with a major in Math. I asked if she liked Math or was good at it. "Well, no," was her reply. "When my parents got divorced, they specified in their agreement that each would pay for half my college, and I had to graduate on time – or no more financial support. At that point in time, I just had more Math credits than anything else, so it seemed the easiest way to finish in four years." I asked, "What do you like to do?" "Well, I'm pretty creative. I like art, and I'm a great wordsmith." Here's a young woman whose resume is at war with her career interests.

Finally, for the last 18 months of your undergraduate life, everyone you meet asks you the dreaded question: "So, what are your plans when you graduate?" All of the emphasis is on what you're going to do, where you are going to go, and who you are going to be.

"Samantha, a 25-year-old living in Minneapolis, had always considered teaching as a possible career because of her love for children. 'But in college, the low pay and low prestige of teaching made me think I should find another path -- something that would sound impressive at my high school reunion. In college, I was so worried about having a job and impressing people, even though I had no clue what that job would be.'"[34]

Liz, a 29-year-old in New York, found most of her pressure was self-induced. After college, she planned to go backpacking in Europe. During her senior year she panicked because she didn't want to leave the country without a job lined up, so she took the first one she found. Settling for a job simply to ease the internal anxiety about what you're going to do is not a good strategy. Liz describes what she learned when she returned from Europe to begin the "really awful job," she had accepted earlier. "'Looking back, it was extremely stupid to take a job just to have a job, but there's a lot of anxiety during the last couple months of school.' Liz spent her work days counting the hours until she could leave, and losing confidence in her abilities because her boss viewed her as very young and treated her that way. From the start of her eight-month stint in this awful job, she was constantly looking for another job."[35]

Fear of failure is another source of internal pressure and anxiety which can produce negative effects on your journey to find your sweet spot. I think most of us struggle to some degree with fear of failure. I, too, have suffered from this malady at times. In hindsight, as I look back over a long career, I see far more people suffering regret at choices they never made. Taking risk, and even the occasional failure, seem to be characteristics associated with those who find joy and personal growth along the journey of their career.

My suggestion is not to worry too much about the fear of failure. My counsel to my daughters when they were launching their post college careers was simple. You can try three or four different kinds of careers in your first ten years out of college, without it having any negative impact on your long-term career prospects. Many employers look favorably on people who do a 'Gap Year,' serving in an orphanage in the foothills of the Berber Mountains in Morocco, do home reconstruction to damaged family homes in the aftermath of Hurricane Katrina, or find some other role in community service as an intern, even if it's an unpaid internship. These sorts of experiences tend to broaden a person and make them a better employee no matter what kind of career they ultimately select.

Remember, you're embarking on a journey! Try to teach yourself to think of it as an adventure. Like all adventures, parts of your quest to find your sweet spot in career and vocation will prove tedious. It may even be a bit boring, at times even painful, and sometime experiences simply to be endured as you look forward to better days ahead. Not every position you hold will be fun. And from time to time, even when you're in a job that uses your skills and strengths, while a good fit for your interests and passions, the position will not always be pleasurable.

It's important for you to realize **your job isn't who you are.** Many people try to create a direct connection between their job and their self-esteem. This is a serious mistake. Even if you are in a job that is right on your sweet spot, you will grow to the point of maturity where you realize that you are more than your successful job or career. Many of us will experience numerous positions where the primary thing we learn is another kind of work or work setting we don't really enjoy. There's often a lot of trial and error, and learning before we find that 1% to 2% we can do better than anyone in the world.

Trade-offs

It's important to acknowledge at this point, there are jobs and careers which are a better fit for you. Still there are others that will fit your friend well, but ultimately, no job is perfect. Just as there is no perfect spouse, do not expect to find a job that will be everything you ever could hope it would be. Knowing this, you need to think about what trade-offs you are willing to make to get as close as you can to that 'impeccably tailored suit of clothes.' Let me present you with several models to help you digest this.

Who/What/Where

When students are graduating from college, they are frequently asked, "What are you going to do when you graduate?" Isn't it interesting that people focus on the *what*, but rarely do people ask "Where are you going to settle" or "Who do you want to be around?" If you are poised to make a transition, chances are that you are actually weighing each of these factors. If you really want to go into publishing, you probably know most of the best publishing houses are in New York. The *what* determines the *where* which leaves the *who* in last place. This may mean you will not have many friends in New York City in the beginning, and will have to work hard to develop relationships.

Consider another example: you are recently engaged. Your fiancée is in another city. By deciding to relocate for this relationship, you are prioritizing the *who* which determines the *where* leaving the *what* in last place. This may mean you choose to take a job that may not be your ideal *what*, but it allows you to invest in your future marriage. The *who, what,* and *where* cannot all be your first priority. Weigh your values and situation in life to determine what works best for you at this point in time.

Economic, Social, and Moral Incentives

This is another decision tree to help you consider the trade-offs required in job selection. Various people are motivated by different things. The bestseller *Freakonomics* describes three types of incentives: economic, social, and moral. Economic incentives might include the amount of pay, discounts, fines, and other monetary rewards or penalties. People motivated by social incentives are likely to work toward a certain type of interaction with people, whether they are clients, customers, or colleagues. A moral incentive is shaped by how a person perceives right and wrong. Each of these can impact what sort of career is a good fit for you. Helping careers might be a good fit for someone motivated by social incentives-- such a person might be motivated both by the people they are able to help as well as their colleagues who are similarly oriented. A person who is motivated by economic incentives may find sales to be a good fit. The more she sells, the more she is economically rewarded, perhaps becoming eligible for bonuses or other incentives. A third person who operates on a moral incentive may find a cause-based organization appealing, whether it be a religious organization which advances his moral beliefs, or something like the Sierra Club which fights for another type of cause and belief system.[36]

Achievement/Affiliation/Power

David McClelland's acquired-needs theory provides a third framework for considering some of the trade-offs that exist in finding your sweet spot in career. He proposes that people's needs are related to their life experiences, which impact motivation and effectiveness in the workplace. People with a high need for achievement want to excel at what they do— they have a need for regular feedback to assess their progress and prefer to work with other achievers or alone. People who seek affiliation desire harmonious relationships with others and want to be accepted by others. They like work with a lot of interpersonal interaction. People who seek power may desire two different types: personal or institutional. Personal power wants to direct others; institutional power (or social power) wants to organize the efforts of others to further the goals of the organization.[37]

Ask yourself-- how do you know that you're doing a good job? What gives you a sense of satisfaction? How do you measure your impact? If it's the yearly performance evaluation where you received top marks with a comment that your work goes above and beyond, you may have a need for achievement. If you have a need for affiliation, you may think of the relationships you have at work, and how you feel about your connection with your co-workers or customers. If a promotion, new title, or increased staff come to mind, you may be motivated by personal or institutional power.

As you think about all these components that contribute to what and how you choose your work, remember -- there is no perfect job. Challenge yourself to think through each of these potential sets of options. Which is most important to you? Which is most motivating? What makes you feel most needed? It's okay if some of your priorities change over the course of your working life. The key is to develop the ability to reflect on your internal drivers and know how they fit in with the world of work.

In conclusion, while there is just one key to finding a successful career (identifying your unique strength), there are many ways to sabotage your future career. Understanding the intrinsic role of work in the human experience—how it changes us and lets us change our environment—is essential to navigating through the obstacles to a satisfying conclusion.

Chapter 6

Understanding the Why of Work

Almost from the beginning of recorded history, we see humanity wrestling with work. Since the Biblical account of the expulsion of Adam and Eve from the Garden of Eden, mankind has struggled with our conceptual understanding of work as well as our actual experience of it.

Some people view work as a punishment. A sentence of hard labor, like a prison chain gang breaking rocks under the hot Alabama sun or as a curse pronounced against us for crimes against humanity or for simply being human. Is it merely a consequence of living in a broken world?

I think Studs Terkel gets closer to the truth when he concludes in his book entitled *Working,* **"Work is the search for both daily meaning as well as daily bread."**[38] Work is part of the process of discovering our own unique self. I prefer to see work as a blessing. It is where we begin to discover our own unique strengths as we experience the privilege of impacting others, giving back, and leaving a legacy.[39]

The Two Purposes of Work

Work is about far more than earning a living, it's a journey of discovery! Work has purpose. Work is a unique opportunity given to us to discover our unique self and to make a contribution to the world in which we live.

Work is an important environment in which we are able to grow and become the true person we were meant to be. This is the environment which helps us mature into the unique person, the original self. There is one thing you are better at than any other person in the world. Work is the environment where you are to discover what you're uniquely made for. It will also help you to find the unique setting or specific set of circumstances which will allow you to become your best self.

In the final analysis, work is really not about the money or the things the money can buy. **Work is where we discover our unique competencies. Our passions. Our unique relationship to other people**. Some of us have been designed to be the Chief Executive Officer of huge corporations. Some of us have special creative skills which allow us to be artisans or craftsmen, working solo and creating art that may last many lifetimes. Some of us can lead teams or teach others how to meet pressing physical, personal, or societal needs. You may have unique skills in problem solving or in creating a new entrepreneurial business. Work allows us to discover what challenges us and inspires us.

It could be rock climbing or working with severely handicapped children. It could be discovering a cure for macrobiotic fevers. Perhaps, it's the challenge of engineering bridge repairs or the satisfaction of crafting a perfect, handmade chocolate confection. It could be teaching inner-city children to succeed in math. Or the joy of patiently cleaning a school full of classrooms after everyone has gone home for the day. It could be helping the illiterate through the wall of reading and writing which has held them back for a lifetime. It could be getting the cash drawer to balance every night. Perhaps painting the sunset or encouraging a child to imagine things in their own way.

The second purpose for work is the opportunity to contribute, to give back to others, to make the world a better place. Work is where we discover the purpose and meaning of life. It's where you discover all you were made to be as a human being. Not always directly from your job, but this endeavor is where you can learn much of what you have to give to the world – to make a difference in the world. This is where you can determine how you might leave a legacy that lives on beyond your time on earth which makes a contribution to better the human race.

Making Work Meaningful

Albert Schweitzer was born into a family which had been renowned for several generations for excellence in religion, music, and education. Yet Schweitzer struggled for years to find work he was not only good at, but meaningful to him--work which addressed his interests and passions, work which gave him a sense of calling and purpose, work which enabled him to give back in a significant way to others in the world. A highly successful student, Schweitzer obtained a PhD in 1899. He held a number of posts as a college professor and obtained notoriety for his contributions to theology. Meanwhile, he continued an outstanding music career which was nurtured in his childhood. His work as a concert pianist provided funding for many of his academic pursuits. In 1905 he decided to go to Africa as a medical missionary so he enrolled in medical school. After graduation in 1913, he moved to French Equatorial Africa where he fulfilled a plan to build a hospital. Most of his friends and colleagues told him he was committing career suicide by leaving the celebrity and financial success of his concurrent careers in academics and music, which kept him among the wealthy and elite of Europe. When Schweitzer was awarded the Nobel Prize in 1952, it was not because of his accomplishments in academia, nor in ministry, nor in the field of music. It was because of his lifelong commitment to building a hospital in a very poor area of West Africa and pouring his life into the people in the community.

Finding meaning in work is often where our own vocational experience breaks down. Barbara Ehrenreich set aside her PhD and career as a successful journalist to spend a year exploring the world of the minimum-wage worker in America. She started out working as a waitress in a family restaurant in Key West. She moved to scrubbing dishes in a retirement home in Portland, Maine, while augmenting her income working as a Merry Maids housekeeper several shifts a week. Finally, she hops a bus and ends up doing retail work at a Wal-Mart in Minnesota.

In her bestselling book, *Nickel and Dimed*, she describes trying to survive the exhausting mental and physical work required to earn the minimum wage in America. Not only does this work often provide too little income for food and shelter, it is frequently full of indignity and injustice for the worker. Ehrenreich is treated to the humiliation of always having to use the back door, having to take a drug test to make $6/hour, and having to work extra shifts in order to make enough to pay for a roach infested one-room place to sleep at night. Working as a maid she was prohibited from even taking a drink of water in any of the homes she was cleaning. Even at a large multi-national corporate giant like Wal-Mart, most of the front-line workers make so little money they cannot afford any of the health benefits offered employees.

What makes meaningful work? Malcolm Gladwell describes the American-Jewish immigrants in New York City who founded the garment industry stitch by stitch, apron by apron, as having meaningful work. "When Borgenicht came home at night, he may have been tired and poor, but he was alive. He was his own boss. He was responsible for his own decisions and direction. His work was complex; it engaged his mind and imagination. And in his work, there was a relationship between effort and reward; the longer he and Regina stayed up at night sewing aprons, the more money they made the next day on the streets selling aprons." Gladwell defines three things -- autonomy, complexity, and a connection between effort and reward - as the three qualities work must have if it is to be satisfying and meaningful.[40]

Author Daniel Pink's recently published book paints a similar picture of what makes work meaningful. In *Drive*, Pink draws on decades of research and concludes people are most motivated in work environments characterized by purpose, autonomy, and mastery. Purpose represents our yearning as humans to be connected to something significant, something larger than ourselves. Autonomy speaks to the freedom for an individual or workgroup to determine the best means to achieve goals rather than following rote "how to" prescriptions. Mastery reflects every person's inner drive to be excellent and explains why people enjoy becoming experts in avocations which do not provide external rewards."[41]

What Is a Good Job?

There are a wide variety of views as to the purpose of work and what constitutes a "good job." Most of us assume if someone holds a position generally held in high regard in our society, such as a doctor, lawyer, or airplane pilot, that person has attained a career position of significance and success. Others think if the financial rewards which accompany a job are high enough, it must indicate the person in the position will feel a high degree of vocational satisfaction. As Malcolm Gladwell points out, what ultimately makes us happy about our vocational life often has nothing to do with how much money we make, or how esteemed our profession is in the public eye. Gladwell concludes the only work that really makes us happy is work that fulfills us. He presents a hypothetical question of whether you would choose to be an architect for $75,000/year, or choose to work in a toll booth every day for the rest of your life for $100,000/year. His assumption is that we would take the architect's job even though it paid less, simply because it was more interesting.

I think Gladwell's only partly right. On a fishing trip in Alaska one year, I met two men who were both having a midlife crisis. One fellow was a 40-year-old physician (an ear, nose, and throat specialist) living in the Northeast, who made a lot of money and only worked four days a week. While his career offered him wonderful opportunities to do things only money can buy (like fly fishing in Alaska), he was pretty bored examining people's ears all day long. The other fellow was 50 and owned a large glove manufacturing business based in Chicago. He was a successful CEO of what had originally been a family business. Under his leadership this business had grown and expanded its size and significance. This gentleman was responsible for the employment of several thousand people and the well-being of their families. He had an ideal opportunity to lead and influence others for good, and he, too, made a lot of money. In spite of what appeared to be outstanding career circumstances, both men were very dissatisfied with their positions and were casting around wondering if there wasn't something better they should be spending their lives doing. Their jobs may have provided plenty of money but they were coming up short on both satisfaction and significance.

Ultimately, individuals who find satisfaction with their vocational situation in life are not driven by money, nor are they driven by societal esteem. I think of people who I have met who have experienced enormous satisfaction and fulfillment in their jobs. Marcy Fry, a social worker in an urban setting with an extremely demanding caseload, might make the same salary as an airline flight attendant, yet she finds herself fulfilled by the opportunity to meet the needs of her clients. High school science teacher Jake Blandton, laboring in a small, unheralded Christian school in rural Maine, finds the thrill of passing on his excitement about ecology, and all things outdoors to his students. This keeps him engaged and excited. While his job means he has to work a second job during the summer and drive a school bus everyday to make ends meet for his family, this doesn't keep him from feeling joy. His satisfaction stems from the influence he imparts to budding young adults.

Coach Don Norford has labored in obscurity for decades, serving as the leader of a high school football program. Few have heard of his work at Long Beach Polytechnic High School, but Coach Norford has produced more players for the National Football League than any other high school in America. Norford has declined numerous NFL and college coaching opportunities, along with luxuries and esteem that accompany that job. Although Coach Don is well known for coaching football, he is also the head coach of the track & field program. These boys and girls teams have been ranked No. 1 in the nation for many consecutive years. A dearly loved and highly respected leader in the community of Long Beach, California, Norford has found the internal rewards of his job far more significant than money or fame.

Is Money the Answer?

It's easy for us to think money's the answer. *If I just had a big bag of cash, all my problems would be over, and I would live a great life.* The longing for easy riches is something most adults have entertained from time to time. Even my pastor has confessed a lifelong addiction to faithfully filling out the Publishers Clearing House Sweepstakes entry forms in hopes of winning $10 million. There are a multitude of get-rich-quick schemes which play upon this frail human craving to become instantly wealthy beyond belief.

How about day-trading stocks? The advent of online electronic stock trading convinced many a work-weary soul he or she could quit a crummy job and earn riches while sitting pajama-clad before the computer, clicking through stock transactions. But much like other forms of gambling, almost all day-traders eventually burn through all their savings, the family loans, and the credit on their plastic cards before collapsing in despair and bankruptcy. Easy riches rarely come their way.

The cheapest perceived route to easy riches is buying a lottery ticket. Millions do, and some occasionally win. However, if you read the follow-up stories about those who win vast sums through the lottery, in 9 out of 10 cases, the winners' lives end up much worse off than before they won the jackpot.

If you had $10 million in the bank and never had to work another day in your life, would that make you happy? Would you be satisfied? We often think if we were financially independent, we could relax and enjoy life— no worries! It's not true. Money won't make us happy. This idea is a great falsehood spread by a philosophical worldview which tries to convince us money is the answer to all of life's problems.

Bret Boone, a professional baseball player, had a very successful 14-year major league career. Between 1990 and 2006, Boone played second base for a number of the best teams in the MLB. He retired March 1, 2006, surrounded by a loving wife and children, his extended family, financially secure for life with over $50 million in earnings from his professional career. Waking up after baseball he found himself successful, wealthy, and retired at the age of 40. Boone soon was mired in a deep depression. Instead of enjoying his unique place in life, he found himself playing several rounds of golf a day, descending into alcoholism, and wondering what to do with the rest of his life.

"It's weird. You retire, and everyone says, 'Oh, it must be awesome to be young and retired and you're set for life and this and that.' It's usually a young guy saying it. And I always tell them (wagging his index finger), it's not all is cracked up to be. All my friends are still playing baseball and all my buddies are now 65-year-old men who are retired because they're the only ones who can play golf on Tuesday mornings. What do you do next? How do you go on? Where do you start?"[42]

Or take my friend Tina DiMato. Tina is in her early 50s and financially independent. She owns a gorgeous waterfront mansion on a lake in Michigan and a beautiful winter home in Naples, Florida, where she spends the cold weather months. She can afford the best in any thing. She is able to travel, has her health, and her children and grandchildren. Yet Tina finds herself dissatisfied. She doesn't need to work, yet finds her life lacking structure. She often tells me, "I just don't find boundaries that help me use my time and my energies in ways that seem productive." In her heart she wonders, *so what is my purpose in being? What makes my life worth living?*

Pity the person who's born to riches and never needs to work. Often this handicap can destroy a person's character and distort their experience of life from an early age. But this is a handicap that can be conquered. Eunice Kennedy Shriver was born the fifth child of Joseph and Rose Kennedy. Born to wealth and privilege, and the sister of a president and three U.S. senators, she was lauded after her death in 2009 for a towering achievement of her own. Motivated by her love for her sister Rosemary, who was developmentally disabled, Eunice Kennedy Shriver devoted much of her life to raising money and awareness to help people with mental disabilities. Her signature accomplishment was the founding of the Special Olympics, which has become a worldwide program serving almost three million children each year in 180 countries.

While raising her own family of five children, Shriver sought to eliminate the stigma associated with mental disabilities. In 1962 she turned a portion of her estate in Maryland into a summer camp for mentally disabled children. In 1968, just weeks after her brother Robert was assassinated, she held the first Special Olympics in Chicago. Looking back on the impact of her life in 2006, Shriver declared, "If you don't have an idea that materializes and changes a person's life, then what have you got?[43]

You may be one of the fortunate few born with a trust fund to take care of all your living expenses for a lifetime. Even if you have plenty of money and never need to work to take care of your financial needs, you cannot lead a satisfying and fulfilling life without finding meaningful work in which to engage. Simply managing and multiplying your funds will not satisfy most of us. We need to be needed. It does not have to be a paying job; it could be a volunteer position.

No matter the outlet, we can use work to discover the two key components of a fulfilling and satisfying life. Work gives the opportunity to discover our best self. It is where we discover what makes us unique and special as a person. It is also the place which gives us the opportunity to contribute, to give back to others, to make the world a better place.

Chapter 7

Discover Your Best Self

So how do you discover your best self? When I think of people with a highly developed sense of their unique self, I think of Coach Tony Dungy. Coach Dungy has been successful in his chosen occupation as a professional football coach. "He debuted as a head coach with Tampa Bay in '96. After six seasons, he became the winningest head coach in the franchise's history. Then in 2002, he moved to the Indianapolis Colts, leading them to the playoffs seven years in a row before winning the Super Bowl Championship."[44]

However, I believe Dungy's success is about far more than the external accomplishments of his teams. Coach Dungy has figured out his own unique strengths and how they connect with one of the world's great needs. His core purpose through work is not just about football and winning. He is out to build better people.

Dungy has a heart to help players achieve their potential. "I want them to leave here as better people and better men than when they came...so if they come and play for me, win a lot of games, make a ton of money, but they don't leave as better people, I haven't done my total job. Winning is what we get paid for, but I think my job is more than that."[45]

Competence

One of the primary ways you know you're in the process of discovering your best self, is if you begin to develop competence. **Competence serves as a litmus test indicating you are well on the way to finding your sweet spot.** If you want to have influence on the people around you in the marketplace, then you need to find your own place of competence. By its very nature, competence requires working in an area of natural talent and ability. There is a strategic reason this book looks at exactly how to find your sweet spot before discussing how to find a great job and build a successful career. It's critical for you to discover the specific kinds of work you are designed to excel at as a basic prerequisite to becoming competent. You'll never develop competence trying to be a square peg in a round hole.

There is a direct correlation between being competent at tasks required in your work life and having a high sense of self-esteem. When you go to work and are able to excel at those activities and relationships which make up your job, you begin to see yourself in a positive light.

Authors Peel and Larimore point out that the foundational requirement for influence in the marketplace is competence -- the pursuit of excellence in one's daily work. "By excellence and competence, we don't mean to imply you have to be better than everyone else. It does mean, however, that you are serious about doing good work -- about doing your best." [46]

Competence in the marketplace includes teamwork. In the workplace you are often part of an organization or a team. Or, perhaps you are an individual providing services to a group of customers. No matter your workplace context, your peers will evaluate you in terms of being a person who cares about your work and caring about your customers. Some people are exemplary members of the team. They're positive, encouraging, happy to be at work, and excited to serve customers. They're willing to help associates with their jobs, and they're supportive to those who work under them. They know their jobs well, and they work hard at trying to perform at a high standard.

Now for the tough question--are you the weak link on your workplace team? Are you willing to help others with their tasks, or do you use the excuse, "That's not my responsibility?" Do you constantly complain about your coworkers or about what management asks you to do? Are you a grumbler, slow to participate, negative, critical, or simply not very good at your job? This lack of competence will completely undermine your ability to grow both personally and professionally in the workplace.

Compassion vs. Competition

Many think it should be our goal to out-compete our fellow workers in the marketplace. Actually, this approach may do more to harm than good in building your career. There is a second attribute which determines who has the most positive impact in the workplace. If you're going to win the right to be a friend, to influence others, and succeed in the marketplace, you'll need to be perceived as a person who is compassionate. This doesn't mean you need to be soft or weak, but it does require a willingness to be considerate of others. Nothing reveals more about your character than how you treat people, particularly those people who are peers or subordinates.

Captain Holly Graf was on an upward tear through the ranks of the Navy. Ever since her graduation from Annapolis, her peers and superiors sensed she was on a fast track to flag rank. Hidden underneath her polished exterior, however, was an angry, bitter core that would destroy her career and rock the Navy to its foundation. In 2003 when the 9,000-ton destroyer, U.S.S. Winston Churchill, shuddered to a dramatic stop outside the mouth of a Sicilian harbor, everyone on board assumed the ship was aground. In the U.S. Navy grounding a ship means an instant end to a captain's career. What followed next was even more startling. "Sailors on the Churchill's stern…broke gleefully into the song, 'Ding dong, the witch is dead!' One officer reported, 'They were jumping for joy and singing on the fantail.'"

As it turned out, one of the ship's propellers had broken, and the ship wasn't aground after all. The jubilant reaction of the sailors, however, was a powerful demonstration of how damaged the relationship was between captain and crew. Even though Graf went on to become the first woman to ever command a Navy cruiser, several years later she was relieved of command for "cruelty and maltreatment of her crew."[47] Even the highest forms of competence cannot outweigh a lack of compassion, let alone a cruel and abusive manner toward others. Compassion will impact your career potential as much as competence.

Some people approach the dynamics of the workplace in a strictly competitive framework. The people who always have to win. Even if it isn't their idea, they try and claim credit for it so others above them will think it was their idea. It's not that you can't be competent and competitive, some very competent people are quite competitive. But an excellent worker, or manager learns to balance the demands of accomplishing tasks while building relationships. You cannot afford to damage either element balance means success. Successful workers eventually discover you can accomplish almost anything, as long as you don't worry about who gets the credit.

The unfortunate truth in organizational life, is that those who emphasize competition too much end up burning rather than building bridges. They eventually alienate other people in the organization. Often times those who are too competitive find out this strategy may offer short-term advantages but a long-term demise.

As team members in any organizational setting, we need each other for success. Each member should desire to continue to grow in one's own area of excellence, while supporting and encouraging other associates as they make their contributions to our overall achievement. **When it comes time to considering people for promotion, management will examine whether or not you're able to make friends and create allies.**

What's Your Legacy?

In addition to being a medium that allows us discover our best self; being engaged in the workplace also gives us the opportunity to contribute. Sometimes our success in a particular job in the marketplace spins off other opportunities to leave a legacy to those who follow us. Andrew Carnegie began life in America as a poor Scottish immigrant working on the plant floor of a textile mill as a bobbin boy. Uneducated, Carnegie taught himself to read and write and was an avid life-long learner. He worked his way up through several organizations and eventually founded Pittsburgh's Carnegie Steel Company, which eventually became US Steel.

With the fortune he made from his business career, Andrew Carnegie turned to philanthropy, with a particular focus on education and helping others like himself who were trying to work their way up from the bottom. Among other things, he built Carnegie Hall in New York City, Carnegie Melon University, and established a multitude of libraries, schools and universities across both America and Europe. By the end of his life, Carnegie was more famous for philanthropy than for his success in the steel business.

You don't have to be a steel magnate to make a difference in people's lives. Anne Mahlum is a single woman living in downtown Philadelphia.

Her sport is marathon running. On her predawn runs through the city she kept passing a group of homeless men. Friendly greetings were always exchanged. One day Anne realized she could include these guys in her sport. "Running is so simple," Mahlum said. "You really only need a pair of shoes. You don't need a lot of equipment. You need heart and dedication." She thought running might make these homeless men feel as good as it made her feel. So she started a running club for the homeless and began asking businesses for help.

"I sent out an e-mail to a bunch of people, and I just said, 'I'm starting Philadelphia's first homeless running club. I need your shoes. I need your clothes.' And the support that I received back is just so astonishing." The group started with nine men; now it's not uncommon to see a much larger group hitting the streets at five o'clock in the morning. Their homelessness is invisible to others who see them running. "They look and say, 'Oh, look at the runners.' There's a positive association, because there's no separation."[48]

Sometimes we have the opportunity to make a difference in a person's life, and we hardly even realize the impact we are having. Often opportunities embedded in our workplace are small, quiet, and subtle. The effort it takes to respond in a caring, compassionate manner is so small. We often have no idea of the long-term impact we are creating.

Author and pastor Chuck Swindoll shares a story about the sort of impact we can have in a person's life when he tells the story of Miss Thompson, an elementary school teacher with a problem student named Teddy Stallard. All through elementary school Teddy struggled. He was disinterested, wore musty, wrinkled clothes, never combed his hair, and often was distant and unfocused. He was one who was easy for kids and teachers alike to overlook or scorn. The teachers knew why Teddy struggled—his mother was ill, then died when he was in the third grade. He lived alone with his father who had trouble coping.

Teddy's fifth-grade teacher, Miss Thompson, struggled to value Teddy. She was finally convicted by words of Jesus: "To the extent you did it to the one of these brothers of mine, even the least of them, you did it to me." Teddy Stallard certainly qualified as one of the least. Once God finally broke her heart with compassion for this sad little boy, "Miss Thompson had become a different person. She helped all the children, but especially the slow ones, and especially Teddy Stallard. By the end of the school year, Teddy showed dramatic improvement."[49]

Years later, Miss Thompson received a letter from Teddy announcing that he had graduated second in his high school class. Four years later, another note brought news of graduating first in his college class. Four years afterward came this note:

Dear Miss Thompson:

As of today, I am Theodore Stallard, M.D. How about that? I wanted you to be the first to know. I am getting married next month, the 27th to be exact. I want you to come and sit where my mother would sit if she were alive. You are the only family I have now; Dad died last year.

Love,

Teddy Stallard

"Miss Thompson went to that wedding and sat where Teddy's mother would have sat. She deserved to sit there; she had done something for Teddy that he could never forget."[50]

That's just it, you don't have to be rich and powerful to leave a legacy. You really just have to live life with your eyes open. Many of us brush up against people with needs. We see situations where we can, with a little effort and cost to ourselves, make a dramatic difference in life for other people. Often we change the world one person at a time.

Sometimes we leave a legacy through actual substance of our work and sometimes indirectly by influencing people we come in contact with in work or our community. As someone wisely pointed out, no one lies on their deathbed and saying, "I wish I'd spent more time at office." We have to get beyond seeing work as simply work and a means of earning a living. We have to recognize that work is our 'promised land.'

Chapter 8

Mid-Career Course Corrections

My grandfather was born in 1895 and raised in Germantown, Pennsylvania, a neighborhood of north Philadelphia. After high school, he went to work as a "slater," installing slate roofs on houses in the Germantown district. Early in this job he injured himself when he fell off a 2½ story roof. He decided it was time to change careers. His next position was working for the Budd Company, where he began as a sheet metal worker earning $5 per week in their Philadelphia plant. The pay was not great, but he was able to work with his feet on the ground. The Budd Company was a leading manufacturer of stainless steel passenger cars used by railroads all over the country. My grandfather spent the rest of his career at Budd. He worked his way up using his 'street smarts' and sweat equity attaining the position of General Manager of the plant by the end of World War II. As a child, I remember seeing black-and-white photographs of him escorting Presidents Truman and Eisenhower through the plant on personal tours. By the time he retired in 1965, he was a self-made multimillionaire.

According to the American Dream, my grandfather's story could and should be the standard for all Americans. When you contemplate your career, there is a standard imaginary screenplay about how your life is supposed to work out. You begin by getting training. Then you select a career and start to work for a good company. You work hard and you work for the same firm for 35 years stepping up the ladder of promotion until you reach the pinnacle of your ability. After reaping the rewards of a successful career, you get a nice party, the gold watch, then you head into retirement where you enjoy three rounds of golf each day. I hope you're laughing by now, because this, my friends, is pure fiction. If it wasn't so painful, it would be comedy. This "typical career" as portrayed in the urban myth of the American Dream no longer exists.

It may have existed at one time for some people like my grandfather. Back in the 1950s and 1960s when the American economy was at the peak of its post-World War II expansion, this was career path for some. But since the 1970s, the American economy has been seriously hammered by two conflicting forces. The first is the ever-expanding role of technology which has increased the productivity of our manufacturing/service sectors. The second force has been the globalization of the world's economy.

For every increase in computer technology, communication technology, and robotics, we see both increases in business productivity and human beings being made redundant. Since 1980, the increases in productivity from technology has effectively doubled the world's labor supply.

In conjunction, while technology improvements have made our businesses more productive, the transition into a global economy means work processes which used to be done locally, have moved offshore. When President Nixon opened relationships with China in 1972, he also opened Asian labor markets. Global access to this new pool of inexpensive labor also had the effect of doubling the world's labor supply. The result of these macro economic shifts has meant the outsourcing of millions of good American jobs, including jobs which require a college education, to countries with labor willing to work for less money to do the same job.

The consequences have been devastating to the American workforce over the past 30 years. Millions of jobs have been taken away from humans and given to robots, computers, and other electronic chip devices. Millions of other jobs have been shipped to Mexico, the Asian Rim, and India.

Plan for Transitions

The global economy we live in today, by its very nature, produces a lot of change in employment opportunities. There is a constant churn of jobs being eliminated by technology or being shipped overseas to lower-cost labor markets. Older manufacturing industries which used to provide millions of high-quality, blue- and white-collar positions, (like the auto supply chain in the Rust Belt states) shrunk, contracted, and finally died. New industries are born -- many of the job classifications that are now the fastest growing literally did not exist 20 years ago. The remarkable fact is the average lifespan of a Fortune 500 company in America is only 45 years. This is the tumultuous economic sea into which you are launching the small boat of your job search and career.

Your career, my career, and every career will experience transitions. In this chapter we want to help you be proactive. If you capture the opportunities which are presented through transition periods and use them to enrich and improve your experience in the workplace, you will have a more satisfying and fulfilling career than if you cling to the myths of the American Dream.

The most recent research I've seen indicates the average working American will have at least three distinctly different careers over the course of their working life. What's more, the typical person in the workplace will probably work for eight to twelve different employers over the course of a career and may change jobs every two years even if they stay with the same employer. **You need to be prepared for change**.

There are seven stages of transition common to most careers. These transitions include entry-level adjustments; early career changes; being laid off; being fired; realizing you are bored, burned out, or just in need of a change; to reaching the mid-career plateau which makes us wonder if we need to move from success to significance. Finally, we will suggest you should proactively be thinking about a new career for your retirement years. Planning and successfully navigating each of these periods of rough seas requires the same set of skills.

Entry Level Issues

The first transition is to land an entry-level job. We consider this a transition, because for most young adults, you are being torn out of the womb of a supportive and structured world of schooling and tossed into the maelstrom of a highly competitive, global economy. As many of you have discovered, a good education is not always a pivotal help to finding your first job. Most employers want people with two years' experience (and good educational credentials) to fill their entry-level positions. Yet even with a bachelor's degree, if no one will hire you, how would you ever get the experience to land an entry-level job? It's a conundrum, but the answer is simple. You probably need to start out lower than you expect.

A wise person once taught me that a problem is simply **a gap between your expectations and your experience**. To close the gap, you can either change your experience or change your expectations. Changing reality (your experience) is often tough to do. Modifying your expectations may be a better strategy to closing the gap. When I was in the corporate world, we often hired recent MBA graduates to fill entry-level positions in our marketing department. These students came from the top ten business schools in the country. Nine out of ten of these fresh graduates arrived fully expecting to make Vice President in a couple of years, then move on to COO or CEO within their first five years in the firm. In general, we found their expectations to be completely unrealistic. While the graduate training might have given them some of the basic tools needed in management, they were gravely inexperienced, lacked judgment, let alone familiarity with the key issues in running our multi-billion dollar business. These unrealistic hopes often led to disappointment, disillusionment, and sometimes derailed their potential for long-term success.

What are realistic expectations at the beginning of your career? In good economic times and bad, the answer is always the same -- **begin at the bottom**. While it's true some recent grads land enviable first-time positions, this is actually only the case for a small percentage of each year's class. And the quality of your first job bears little relationship to your long-term potential for achievement in your chosen career. For most of us, we need to adjust our expectations and get our head around the fact that our entry-level position might be much lower than you had envisioned for yourself while you were earning that fancy diploma.

When Jay Leno went looking for his first position, he wanted to work for a local auto dealership. As a teenager, he was a bit of a "motorhead" and loved cars. After being rejected several times by his dealership of choice, Leno decided to simply show up one morning and begin work. He washed cars, swept the lot, moved inventory, and gladly did any menial tasks no one else on the dealer's staff was willing to do. He was not paid for this work, nor did he ask to be paid. He came every day and labored diligently, demonstrating his enthusiasm, his willingness to work hard and his committed interest in automobile retailing. In less than two weeks, the management was so impressed with his dedication they offered him a full time position.

Leslie Stevenson, Director of the University of Richmond's Career Development Center suggests, "even if you know this isn't your dream career, even if the job is woefully beneath you, the job matters. Show enthusiasm; master the job." Other professionals recommend that you take whatever job you have, and like Jay Leno, make yourself a star in the position. As you increase your visibility and your value, you will increase your chances of getting a promotion or a strong recommendation. Ask your management for more hours and more responsibility. Let your supervisor know what your goals are. Be strategic and concise in promoting yourself in the organization. Identify the job you'd like to hold and work on developing the attributes and skills needed for that position. Use your customers and other professional contacts to increase your network to look for your next job.[51]

Some people labor under the impression that work ought to provide the same sort of fun, social life, stimulation, and satisfaction college life often provides. This is an expectation you need to discard immediately! I suppose if you were willing to pay your employer $25,000-$50,000/year like you paid your college, they might consider entertaining you, but in the working world you're hoping to be the one paid. This is why it's called *work!*

Your goal in your entry-level position ought to be to work as hard as you can at learning about both the business and profession you've been hired to work in and to learn about what makes you tick. The better a job you do at learning the basics during your entry-level phase, the more quickly you will rise to better positions. If you're a good entry-level student, you will learn, if simply by observation, the kinds of things you like at work and the kinds of things you do well. You will also learn the things you dislike or that you are not as effective in handling. If you become a good student of both the firm and the industry you're in, you'll be able to figure out specific areas which have more of what you like and less of what you dislike. You're now in a place to begin to build a plan to develop your career.

How long should you expect to be in the entry-level phase? Typically, this part of your career lasts three to six years. During this period, you might hold several positions and learn the basic skillsets of a particular job and industry during that time. If you are promoted from within the same firm, it's probably all right to change jobs every 12 to 18 months. Your resume should demonstrate you've held the position long enough to master the basics of position and to prove your potential for higher level service. If you are changing jobs by moving to a different company, you should probably aim at two-year stints in each position/employer. There exists a tension between aggressively seeking better positions/promotion and ending up with a resume that makes you look like you're a job hopper with a short attention span.

Early Career Transitions

As you move through your entry-level position(s), you should begin to make significant choices about where you want to direct your career. Hopefully, somewhere between Year 5 and Year 10 or 12, you will find a focus which points you in a direction leading to your sweet spot. This is not always the case, as some people have more difficult entry-level positions and struggle to identify a clear direction. Others begin with very clear direction and after 5 to 10 years of diligent work and achievement discover, after they've managed to climb the career ladder, they really don't like the building it's leaning on.

My daughter Megan started her professional career working in a college as a secretary/receptionist. About six months later she was promoted into a position as an Admissions Counselor. After 18 months in Admissions, Megan took a new position with a college in Boston. One reason she changed jobs, was the realization that her small first employer had few opportunities for advancement. The second motivator for change was the gradual realization that living in Washington, DC, was not all she had hoped it would be. In short, it was time to try something new.

Her new position allowed her to use her experience with adult continuing education students, but also gave her much broader areas of responsibility including: recruitment, enrollment, financial aid, academic advising, and supporting the students through graduation. Some of these new responsibilities she enjoyed, and others she found less satisfying. After several years in her third position, she was intrigued by the thought that she might enjoy working with traditional students (age 18-22) instead of the older continuing education adults.

When her alma mater posted a position for a Regional Admissions Representative, Megan leapt at the opportunity, which is responsible for recruiting traditional students from the six New England states to attend her college in central Pennsylvania.

A year and a half into this, her fourth position, she feels comfortable and increasingly competent in her job. She tells me it's the best job she's ever had! After six years in the marketplace, Megan has learned she enjoys working in an academic setting and working with young adults. She is particularly interested in focusing her career towards Admissions, Alumni Affairs, and perhaps International Study programs. She now feels confident enough in her career direction that she has begun working part-time on a relevant Master's degree.

The early career phase typically includes your first ten years at work. This includes your entry-level positions and developmental positions, which begin to move you into a more focused career path. Some careers have very specific training tracks that need to be followed to develop a successful long-term career in that profession. Medicine, law, and various nursing specialties would be examples of those. Other kinds of careers offer more latitude. Those interested in writing, editing, journalism, have a lot of freedom and flexibility to try different ways of earning a living with the written word. If you decide to work in management, you'll have opportunities to work in a variety of different kinds of departments as you seek to find an area that suits your skills and interests as well as being a good match to your organization's needs.

My first entry level job was as a researcher at the Kennedy School of Government at Harvard University. While the work itself was fairly tedious and boring, it was fascinating to rub shoulders with some of the brightest minds in Boston. After two years, I realized that this kind of research wasn't very practical--almost all of my excellent work was going to end up entombed on a dusty shelf between two covers and never read or used by anyone.

After getting married, I felt a lot of pressure to earn a living, so I accepted a position teaching middle school and high school students in a small private school. Everyone agreed I was an excellent teacher, but I hated the job, and I wasn't too thrilled about having to work 90 hours a week. The pay was wretchedly low and the benefits nil. So, after a year, I packed up my bride, moved to the West Coast and enrolled in graduate school, a common reaction to entry-level job frustration.

Later, I was offered an entry level position as a business researcher in a medium-size advertising and marketing research firm based in Princeton, New Jersey. Now here was work which was much more practical. My position entailed doing research which was actually going to be used to make multi-million-dollar decisions. The downside, of course, was that I had to start at the bottom again for minimum wage. Over the next year, I did all the dirtiest, thankless tasks that need to be done. My Harvard research experience counted for nothing. I ran the copier, took out the trash, delivered reports to clients, went out to pick up lunch for important meetings, lugged boxes of surveys to the storage facility then back, and hand coded thousands of surveys. The plus side was I learned the marketing research business from the ground floor up. Within a year, I was promoted to Project Director and eventually was awarded the opportunity to move into Client Service.

The first six years of entry-level positions in my career development path had their ups and downs. But by Year 6, after my promotion to Client Service, I realized marketing research was a good fit for me and I wanted to make a career out of it. My next position involved running a small marketing research department for a publisher in Chicago. This position gave me exposure to new business development and marketing, for which I had real aptitude and high interest. Eventually, I was asked to switch over to the Marketing side of the business and serve as the Brand Manager for some of the new businesses I had encouraged the company to develop. For the next half-dozen years I moved back and forth between staff positions in research and line management in the marketing department. At the end of my early career years, it was pretty clear that my sweet spot involved the intersection of marketing research, marketing management, and new business development.

The Stalled Career

Frequently, this early phase of your career doesn't have such a happy ending. Many people find themselves five to ten years down a particular career path and discover their job is not a particularly good fit for their interests and passion. Peter Wilson spent ten years working his way up to an excellent position as an account manager in a public relations firm in the Boston area. He realized he had reached an age when money was not the primary driver of his life. His wife and growing family were increasing in importance, and they were a lot more fun than many aspects of his PR job. He grew to dread the days filled with business meetings held for no identifiable purpose. He enjoyed interacting with the adults at work and occasionally was rewarded by having one of his ideas accepted by the client. But overall he found the bad far outweighed the good.

Wilson turned to his brother Ray for counsel. As they talked, Peter mentioned he'd always been attracted to teaching, but didn't think it was a feasible goal for a man with a wife ,a two-year-old, and plans for more children. With his brother's help he came up with a transition strategy and within three months was enrolled in a Master of Arts in Teaching program, which he completed in a year. He started student teaching English the next January at a middle school in Topsfield, Massachusetts, and was hired into a full-time position the following September. While his current salary is much lower than in the public relations job, every day is filled with the challenge of keeping 12- and 13-year-old kids engaged and connecting with ideas. Wilson finds himself rewarded by the opportunities he has each day to help students develop their critical thinking skills, and explore the richness of the English language.[52]

The Mommy Track

Another variant of this early stage transition is a working woman who takes time out to have and raise children. When they decide to return to the workplace, many women feel that they have been left behind or that they have become unattractive to potential employers. If they compare themselves to their peers, those who remain single or childless or put their children in day care then went right back to work, they often see themselves as falling short. Certainly a professional with 20 years' experience is going to be in a different position than one who only has 10 years, plus 10 years off raising a family.

The solution to this is a hybrid strategy -- something between an entry-level and early career transition approach. One of the best tactics is to re-think your branding (which we describe in the next chapter) and include your role as a manager in the family, and any volunteer or community service you have been involved in during your break to raise children. Writing a "functional resume" lets you describe skills and activities you have developed even if it was not in a marketplace setting.

It might also be helpful to take some courses to sharpen your skillset in areas you feel you may have fallen behind during your time out of the workforce. Finally, like our advice to the person seeking an entry-level job, you may have to get comfortable with the fact that you'll have to restart your career at a lower position than you left it. The key is to get back into the workforce and demonstrate your good attitude, your maturity, your excellent work ethic, a willingness to learn, and to work hard at whatever job you can find. Good work will find its reward.

Laid Off

If you go to work one day and discover you've been laid off, don't despair. This is a common experience, and you can recover from it. In many cases, your future will be much brighter without your old job. The most recent research indicates there are over 14.8 million people who have been laid off since the beginning of the Great Recession in December 2007. Significant layoffs, however, are not a new phenomena.

To some extent, many layoffs are the result of this macro trend towards globalization. When my father was working in aircraft avionics in the 1970s and 1980s, manufacturers' began to ship jobs and then entire manufacturing plants to Mexico to take advantage of the cheaper labor supply. When I worked in the toy business in the 1980s, almost all of America's toy manufacturing was shipped overseas to the Pacific Rim for the same reasons. After the boom of business productivity due to technology advances during the 1990s, companies began to ship many jobs overseas. India in particular, reaped great benefits from this movement to outsource labor to lower costs environments, while using technology to keep communication and service levels high. Millions of jobs in customer service, computer programming, software and technology support, accounting, and consulting services have been shipped offshore.

In other cases, large numbers of people have lost their jobs due to corporate misbehavior . These workforce meltdowns are not the result of economic displacement and globalization, but the result of unrestrained greed, ethical lapses and moral failure on the part of management. Enron is a classic illustration. On December 2, 2002, Enron declared bankruptcy after admitting they had been misstating earnings to the tune of $586 million since 1997. Within weeks, the company went belly up and all 21,000 employees lost their jobs. Most of these people also lost their life savings and 401k accounts which were loaded up with Enron stock.

A shrinking economy, even on a local or regional basis, can result in many businesses being forced to layoff workers. Fort Myers, Florida, was booming during the middle of this past decade both from Gulf Coast tourism and the expected retirement of Baby Boomers. Construction soared and home values nearly doubled from 2004 to 2005 as speculators bid up prices. When the bubble burst, the general economy fell hard as the real estate and construction collapse impacted other kinds of businesses.

Mike Cannington lost his job as the marketing director of a chain of motorcycle dealerships. Even with 16 years in marketing, and his experience as the president of the local Chamber of Commerce, Cannington, like 30% of Florida's unemployed, has been out of a job for over six months. David Bogart, who was laid off from his sales job at Jandy Pool Products, has been forced to sell his house, has exhausted his $20,000 in savings, and ran out of jobless benefits in July. Boyd Champion lost his construction job three years ago. Married with two children, they now rent a small spare house with unpainted walls and struggle to put food on the table on a daily basis.[53]

The macro trends affecting some industries result in a long-term shrinkage of consumer demand and a reduction in business. Honestly, if you're in an industry that is heading toward a decline, it would make sense to be proactive and plan your move to a new industry before you get a pink slip.

Occasionally, people are laid off not because of economic necessity, but simply because of some whim of management. About 10 years into my career, I was recruited from Chicago to run a new market research department for a Fortune 500 Company on the East Coast. My department was part of a division of about 35 high-value employees who had been carefully recruited to create a powerful engine for new business development and new business acquisition. About six months after this new business SWAT team was assembled, my wife and I went away for a long weekend in Boston. When I arrived back on the job at 8 AM Monday, I discovered my entire division had been laid off. Everyone--from my boss, the Vice President of New Business Development, to the lowest secretary-- came to work to discover their jobs had been eliminated.

After the dust settled from this unexpected turn of events, the circumstances of my first layoff actually produced a positive outcome. After several weeks, I was offered the position of Group Brand Manager, a significant promotion, which included a raise and responsibility for a $45 million product line.

If you find yourself laid off, don't take it personally. It's not about you. Unfortunately, many of us equate our self-worth to what some employer is willing to pay us. It is important during the course of your career to learn to separate your value as a human being from your pay grade. **You are not your paycheck, whether it is small or large.** At points in your career, you will get paid far more than you are worth. Other times you will have the chance to give far more in value than your cash compensation covers. There may be benefits other than cash compensation to that job. Recognize there is much in our work life we have no control over. Unexpected layoffs happen. None of us is immune to the impact of macro economic forces which sometimes consume thousands of jobs including our own.

While large numbers of jobs have been lost, other macro economic forces are busy creating new industries and jobs which simply didn't exist five years ago. Research by the Chronicle of Higher Education concludes the number of jobs requiring a college degree will outnumber the number of workers available in a few years. There could be three million fewer college graduates than the market demands by 2018 say the Chronicle's report. Research shows most people who go through unemployment, actually get better jobs in the course of the experience. Adults who found work after being laid off during the current recession say their new job is "better than the former job" (44%), about "the same as the former job" (30%), or for some, "worse than their previous position" (24%).[54] In the sections of this volume which follow, we will give you strategies, tactics, and effective tools to reposition yourself to find a better job after a layoff.

Fired

Okay, in all honesty, being fired is more personal than being laid off. But again, the best advice is to not take it personally. Being fired is a wonderful learning opportunity. It gives you the chance to re-evaluate your career and determine your most important values and priorities. It will also give you a chance to sharpen your focus on both your high-value skill set and those interests you're passionate about. If you take advantage of this golden opportunity, you will come out of being fired in much better shape than you were before the event.

The first time I was fired, I knew it wasn't my fault. After three years of outstanding success, the president who hired me was promoted to another unit and replaced by a man who was his polar opposite. Over the next several years, almost a dozen of the stars recruited and mentored by the previous boss, left the firm. I was the second to go. I knew a parting was inevitable--in fact, I had cleaned out my desk eight months before and was actively looking for a new job, when I got the call to meet my boss and the VP of Human Resources for a conference. When my supervisor indicated he was not pleased with my performance, I was able to calmly suggest that if they would offer me a year's severance pay and benefits, I would make the problem go away. Perhaps, technically, I wasn't so much fired, as I jumped before I was pushed.

The second time I was fired, it caught me by surprise. Well, not in the big picture sense, but more in the actual day and time it happened. I was recruited to launch a corporate change initiative in a medium-sized firm and turn it into a "marketing driven company." The CEO, and founder, was anxious to multiply the size of his business, and I was hired to find new strategies that would help them to grow. During my original two-day interview for this position, I saw with crystal clarity exactly how it would turn out. In this prophetic vision I saw myself being fired. While the CEO described himself as a "collaborative leader," his management style most closely resembled that of King Henry VIII. When anyone disagreed with him, it was, "Off with his head!"

Over the course of the next year, I developed 16 different strategies to help grow the business. Not one was accepted and implemented by "King Henry." Nonetheless, when the axe finally fell, and my head rolled into the basket--I was a little shocked. With 24 hours of reflection, however, I was actually greatly relieved. And over the long term, this hasty departure turned into a blessing.

If you get fired, it's best not to be defensive. It generally indicates a breakdown in your relationship with your employer. It is what it is. Research shows that two out of three management hires "don't work out," according to management. Management rarely accepts any blame for poor hiring decisions, but more often than not, these dysfunctional situations arise from putting a square peg in a round hole. Don't beat yourself up! In most cases you're much better off to part ways, forgive, and finally to forget. Holding a grudge or nursing a bitter attitude only hurts you. If you are given specific criticism during your exit interview, it is wise to take heed and see if there is any truth to those charges. You might also be at fault for trying to make your square peg fit in a round hole. **Learn what you can, and move on**

Sometimes, being fired is the encouragement you need to change careers. My friend Allison Dandridge went to work as a special education teacher in an elementary school right out of college. Special needs children have always been her passion and her area of competency. After a few years however, the school district asked her to transition into a regular classroom. For about 15 years, Allison managed to cope, although there was an increasing disconnect between her skills and what was required of her as a classroom teacher. Eventually her coping skills failed her; her classes became chaotic, and then went out of control. Finally, after three years of interventions, her principal dismissed her. In truth, Allison was really not able to handle the classroom or the teaching chores anymore. She was in way over her head, and had been drowning for a number of years.

After Allison was finally let go, she re-discovered her passion for special needs children. Encouraged by her adult daughter to reenter that field, she eventually found an excellent position which was a great fit for her skills and interests. The small class of three to five students was well within her classroom management capabilities. The need to constantly adjust and individualize teaching and learning styles to the children's needs was a good fit for her own rather creative/chaotic approach to education. In hindsight, Allison wishes she had not persisted in clinging to her traditional classroom position for the number of years she did. It caused her a lot of pain and suffering and prevented her from moving on to a better situation.

Allison's situation is a good example of why it's important to regularly reflect on whether or not it's time to consider Plan B. All of us should cultivate the habit of looking for constructive feedback on our work performance. We need to find safe people who will help us evaluate our skill and success at the core tasks of our position. Left on your own, it is easy to deceive yourself into trying to squeeze your square peg into a round hole. You need honest friends who will tell you when you're not succeeding, and to give help you be proactive on shifting to Plan B.

Burned Out, Worn Out, or in Need of a Change

At some point during the course of your career, you may hear that small quiet inner voice whispering to you, "You are not in the right job." Ariane de Bonvoisin was working as a managing director for Time Warner in New York and controlled a $500 million digital media venture capital fund when she began to hear that quiet message from her soul. She heard that 'inner microphone' go on every morning for two years before she was finally ready to listen. Eventually she resigned her position, traveled to Italy and India, spent time with her parents and learned to windsurf. She now works full-time as an author and speaker.[55]

During the course of your career, you can develop high levels of competence in a particular profession, and achieve significant success in that field, yet still get to the point where you're hitting the wall. For some of us, after working 80 to 100 hours per week in a high stress, high pressure job, we begin to recognize the toll this lifestyle is having on our health, our relationships, our sanity, and the rest of what's left of our lives.

I have always been someone who has responded well to challenge. I love big, tough, impossible jobs. One of my bosses used to say that I'm the kind of guy who loves to jump out of airplanes…without a parachute. In my first career, I reached a pinnacle of success in my early 30s, holding one of the top positions in my field. My normal workdays consumed 10 to 12 hours but often ran to 18. I left home in the dark and came home in the dark for the majority of the year. My frequent travel schedule ratcheted me back and forth through 15 time zones. Sure, I had lots of frequent flyer miles, but who would ever want to use them?

I was married to a lovely woman and had two beautiful children. We were fortunate to live on a bucolic farm in upper Bucks County, Pennsylvania. One day I had a sudden insight. I realized I never got to see my wife, my kids, or my farm in the daylight! It was if we lived in alternative universes which seldom connected. Like slowly waking from a bad dream, I looked at my friends who were ten years further down the career path I was on and saw that most of them had lost their marriages, their hair, their health, and even their relationships with their kids. All they had to show for their self-sacrificing lifestyle was money. Deeply disturbed by these new insights, I took a week' vacation and went to Sanibel Island off the west coast of Florida where I spent a lot of time walking, thinking, sleeping, and praying. Somehow, during that week, my sanity returned. My wife and I began to plan and prepare to launch my next career.

Not every turning point is a crisis like mine was. One of my friends got her law degree from the University of Miami and went on to practice labor and employment law. After 15 years of considerable success, she found that practicing law had just become stale. It was no longer challenging, nor very interesting -- although still quite lucrative. She prepared herself and transitioned into a second career in human relations management. Again, she was very successful at this new career and worked her way steadily up the ranks. She has held top HR positions for several of the best corporations in America. A decade into her new career, she found herself with those same old feelings of frustration with how she invested the bulk of her time every day. When she analyzed her current situation she realized it just wasn't fun anymore. Thoughtful reflection help her understand it wasn't merely a question of changing companies, but that it was time to think about a third career. One personal avocation has been teaching, and if not for the demands of her present position, she would seek more opportunities to teach. After significant consideration, she has decided it is now time to sharpen her training and seek to shift into a full-time teaching opportunity, probably at the collegiate level.

Shifting From Success to Significance

In his book *Half Time*, television entrepreneur Bob Buford popularized the concept that many mid-career professionals reach a point where they're interested in changing careers in order to find more meaning and fulfillment in the second half of their lives. Buford began his vocational life with a single ABC affiliate in Tyler, Texas, and grew it into a network of cable systems across the country. By the time he reached the age of 50, Buford found himself wondering if business success was all he would contribute to the world during his lifetime. Buford identified this desire as wanting to "shift from success to significance."

In my experience, when people in the workplace reach mid-career and begin to feel stale, bored, or burned out it, may be that their inner self is longing to find a way to give back to others, or make a contribution to society at large. Towards the end of one's career, we began to think about what we've accomplished and whether not we will leave a lasting legacy when we leave the workforce or even this lifetime. These feelings are symptoms of a new opportunity. You do not have to spend the rest of your career in a rut going through the motions of business as usual over and over again, if you find it is no longer rewarding. You have the potential to experience a whole new kind of career before your working life is over.

A great example of shifting from success to significance can be seen in the life of Richard Stearns. After earning a bachelor's degree from Cornell and an MBA from the Wharton School at the University of Pennsylvania, he worked his way up through the marketing functions of several blue-chip corporations. Then for over 10 years he served as the president and CEO of Lenox Inc. He enjoyed a seven-figure salary and all the benefits. He and his family lived in a beautiful mansion on the Main Line in the western suburbs of Philadelphia.

While Stearns was enjoying the success, influence, and benefits of his career in corporate marketing, he was wondering if this was the best way that he could make a difference in the world. In 1998 he left Lenox to become the president of World Vision, one of the largest non-profits in the United States. Under his leadership, World Vision, a Christian agency which provides relief and development aid to poverty-stricken countries, regions, cities, and individuals all over the world, has greatly expanded. Annual donations have tripled from $358 million to over $1 billion. Overhead expenses have been reduced by almost one third. By using his executive talents to leverage the impact of this nonprofit agency, Stearns has been able to be a powerful advocate for those affected by poverty and injustice.

Retirement and your "Encore Career"

Normally, American workers from the developed Western nations have come to think of retirement as the point in time when you stop working, kick back, relax, and enjoy your golden years. We have images of moving to retirement communities on some coast or desert where we play golf, go boating, and generally enjoy endless days of leisure. Others long to move to the mountains to ski, or bike, or hike or to simply do all those things they neglected to do for the past 40 years because they were too busy working.

The transition to retirement is not always easy. A friend of mine was a senior pilot with United Airlines and finished his career as the captain of the largest commercial airliners being flown in the world, usually flying United Airline's routes back and forth to Asia. Larry's job was very demanding, challenging, and financially rewarding. When he hit the mandatory retirement age for pilots of 60, it was not pretty. The best picture to describe Larry's entrance into retirement - it was like watching a guy running flat out on a treadmill when someone walks by and pulls the power plug. He went from 60 miles per hour to zero overnight. It was a tremendous shock. It took Larry close to two years to even begin to figure out what to do with his time, resources, and good health.

Most retirees should plan for and consider a new career in retirement. There are several reasons to do so. Staying active and involved is the key to long-term health in the senior era. Many people who retire from active professions and go right into a life of full-time leisure, find their health and vitality drained by this change. For many individuals, the shock of retirement undermines both their health and interest in living -- they die quite quickly -- often only several years after they quit working.

The other factor to consider - you may end up living for 30 or more years after you retire. When Social Security was instituted in 1935, the average life expectancy after age 65 was only three years. With advances in medical science and healthcare, Americans are living much longer. Today the average life expectancy is 78.4. Conceivably, two out of three retirees could live past 90. This means that you are going to have decades of health and vitality, that you need to apply in some constructive direction (like in your encore career). Given the switch to individually-financed pensions, you probably will also need some additional financing to underwrite this much longer period of retirement.

You should plan for your encore career, in the same way that you plan for your initial career. For it be successful it really needs to be driven by your unique strengths and abilities coupled with your particular interests and passions. These are the same elements which drive anyone's success in career at any time of life. Sure, you could probably get a job at Wal-Mart as a greeter, or land a spot down at the local Piggy Wiggly bagging groceries. These types of jobs do produce some supplemental income - but they probably don't yield much satisfaction.

Since the 1990s a movement has been growing to help match older workers with encore jobs in public service or in other ways to benefit society. Many nonprofit organizations now exist, from Boston, Massachusetts, to Portland, Oregon, which aim to help older workers find new work. Pat Daly is a good example. Following college Pat wanted to "save the world" by working with children. Instead, she went into investment banking becoming a director of Credit Suisse and working all around the world. When she retired from banking at the age of 57, Daly became the New York regional director of an organization which promotes science and technology education among children. While the job pays much less than her previous gig, Daly reports the satisfaction is infinitely superior.

Gary Maxworthy, wanted to join the Peace Corps in the 1960s, but instead went on to become the president of a food brokerage company. In retirement his desire to give back led him to join the VISTA program as a food bank employee. Six years, later he founded the Farm to Family program, which last year delivered more than 100,000 pounds of fresh produce to California food banks. Baby Boomers, like Maxworthy and Daly, often desire to return to earlier ideals of making a difference in socially meaningful ways. The willingness to seek out and build an encore career in retirement allows these people to stay active, to enjoy the camaraderie of working, to give back to others in need, and to earn a little money to help with retirement expenses.[56]

Surviving Career Transitions

In this chapter we have described the seven major job transitions you might experience during your career. Each move has a number of aspects which are unique to that portion of your work life. Most importantly, the driving motivation which launches a period of transition is different with each era. Seeking your first job puts you in the entry-level transition. Finding your current career path isn't leading you in the right direction gives cause for change, regardless of when it takes place during your work life. Involuntary transitions, like being fired or laid off, result from external forces you have no control over. Deciding to voluntarily change careers - from burnout, halftime, or retirement -is usually driven by your own internal motivation to improve your workplace experience.

No matter which specific transition you are experiencing, the solutions for each of these situations are remarkably similar. In the next chapter we will describe a series of strategies and tactics which will allow you to reboot your career and move it in a more positive direction no matter which transition era you're going through.

Chapter 9

Springboards to a Better Career

When you hit a speed bump in your career, you need to see it as a springboard to a better career. The seven transition stages we discussed in the previous chapter should not be viewed as setbacks, but rather as opportunities for new growth and development. The process is much like pruning a grapevine or a fruit tree. Removing old dead wood allows for, and even stimulates, the production of new, more fruitful growth. For most people, those with the right attitudes and the right tools, hitting a transition point can actually accelerate and improve the trajectory of their career.

The most important element of turning career transition points into opportunities for a better future is your attitude. Particularly, your attitude towards change. Often, we are inclined to think of change as a negative – almost by definition. When unexpected change comes, particularly if it feels forced upon us in some way, we can get upset and assume the only likely result will be negative outcomes. Hey, lighten up! You obviously haven't been paying attention to your life and career if you think any variation from the status quo will be unhelpful. Your life isn't that good -- yet!

Ariane de Bonvoisin, whom we met in the last chapter, had her view of change completely altered by her experience of dropping out of corporate success to find her own unique sweet spot in vocation. She says "The No. 1 lesson I learned was to change your view of change." De Bonvoisin urges readers to believe change is a good thing, that it's part of life and happens to everyone.[57]

Ariane also says, "Fear is the No. 1 'change demon' or dominant emotion that shows up during times of change. The best antidote to fear is faith -- faith in yourself, faith that things will work out, faith in God." Here's the "Change Guarantee" De Bonvoisin offers to friends and colleagues: "From any change, something good will come, something positive will happen for you. It might not happen in the way you think, or on the timeline you think, but it will happen. Have faith."[58]

Back To the Basics

The first step every person in a career transition needs to take is to go back to the basics. When Vince Lombardi took over as the head coach of the Green Bay Packers in 1959, he assembled his team for their first practice session. This was a team which had lost all but two of 12 games in the previous season, the worst record ever accomplished by a team of Packers. As the legend goes, he stood in the middle of this group of professional football players, held up a football and said, "This is a football." From there, Lombardi began to explain to his players the game and how he wanted them to play it. He went on from that fresh new beginning; a beginning focused on the basics, to mold this team into a powerhouse which would win five league championships over the next nine years.

Going back to basics, requires you to refocus on and identify what really makes you tick. I realize by now, we probably sound like a broken record to you, having thoroughly discussed this in Chapter Four, but identifying your unique skills and strengths and your personal interests and passion are absolutely critical to finding and growing in your sweet spot. "This is a football!" It's the basics; it's critical. Just as you cannot play the game of football without understanding what to do with the ball, you cannot build a career without understanding what makes you tick. Section Two of this book is dedicated to giving you practical tools to help you to do that. And yet, I'm amazed by how many people I meet in career transition who still don't understand who they are and what drives their engine.

When I (Bruce) saw how my father's career turned out, I began to develop a summary list of the ten factors which absolutely had to be part of any job I considered. The rough outlines of my *Job Fit Factor* list developed before I had been in the marketplace for ten years. I have refined it over the 35 years of my career. It is considerably sharper now than it was ten years out of the starting gate. Whenever anyone calls me and asks me to consider a job, or if I should wake up one morning and decide to change careers, I immediately whip out my *Job Fit Factor* list and see how this new position stacks up against these ten critical issues. I know for certain, unless any prospective position contains eight or nine out of my ten factors, there's no way I would succeed at the job over the long term. This list has saved me a lot of pain and heartache, as well as needless job changes. There is a copy of my personal Job Fit Factor list in the Appendix.

I feel bad my father didn't have a list like this to guide his career. If he had figured out what he was good at and what he really enjoyed doing, his career might have been dramatically different. He could have reached the point, ten years into his career, where he turned down a promotion. Each promotion he accepted gave him more responsibility and money but multiplied the people encounters he had every day. When he got to the place there were more people management issues in his job than tinkering with manufacturing systems, he should've approached his supervisors and asked for a demotion! You can ask for what you want! If you know yourself well, you will ask for those things that are on target with your sweet spot. You will decline the opportunity to improve your stature and income by accepting promotions which end up making you miserable.

Eli Schein is a successful computer programmer working for a large corporation in Philadelphia. Eight years into his career, Eli was offered the opportunity to move into management. As most of us would be, he was flattered by the affirmation of his competence and his potential for leadership. After he accepted the new position, he began to discover the hidden costs of management. Yes, his salary had increased, but the time he spent on the job began to creep up from 40 hours a week to 48 hours a week and then 54 hours a week. Schein discovered, as an introvert, he really missed solving problems on his own (as a programmer). He disliked all the people problems he had to solve and found the work exhausting. Finally, he discovered dealing with management issues for 60 hours a week was consuming his entire life.

While he is an extremely competent computer programmer, Eli's real love is singing opera. Eventually, he realized the time commitment required to be in management was going to eliminate his ongoing role as a member of the cast of the Opera Company of Philadelphia. So Schein did what few of us would have the courage to do. He went to his boss and asked to be demoted back to his old position as a computer programmer. Over the last 20 years, he has achieved a remarkable balance of health and happiness in his life with good equilibrium between his day job and his evening career at the Opera.

A Second Chance

Many of us reach a point in our careers where we need a do over. In golf we call it a *Mulligan*. Our first shot turns out to be off course, and we need another chance to begin again. Transitions help us to get this second chance in our vocational experience. If you find yourself in a career transition, recognize the opportunity it gives you to recalibrate your understanding of what energizes you, and what gives you satisfaction. Life is too short, and the workweek is too long to spend your life in a job which makes you unhappy. Or one you're bad at. Even if you've made a poor choice with your initial selection of job and career direction, you are free to make other choices. Don't ever feel it's too late. **You can always have a "do over."** Everyone is entitled to, and often needs a second (or third or fourth or fifth) chance.

When Michael Vick, the popular former quarterback of the Atlanta Falcons, was convicted of interstate dog fighting, he was sentenced to two years in the Leavenworth Federal penitentiary. Most pundits assumed his football career was over. After his release from prison, Vick was mentored by Coach Tony Dungy and several others who were willing to give him a second chance. Coach Andy Reid of the Philadelphia Eagles went way out on a limb when he hired Vick as his backup quarterback in 2009. In 2010 when Donovan McNabb was traded from the Eagles, Vick took over as the starting quarterback midway through the season. His high level of performance led the Eagles into the playoffs, and Vick was twice awarded NFL Player of the Month. Those courageous few who were willing to give Michael Vick a second chance, found their faith rewarded.

Measure Your Sweet Spot

Before you begin the process of your career do over, it is vital to honestly and accurately assess your unique skills and strengths. I am always amazed at the number of people who slide quickly past this step in their eager rush to get a new job. "Just get me a job!!!" This really matters. You may have skated past this step earlier in your career – and that's why you are in a career transition today.

Many of us are victims of our own idealized view of who we are and what we can do. Often this is not an accurate reflection, rather it is who we wish to be, than who we actually are. This problem of being lousy at self-evaluation bedevils many of us in a variety of areas. For example, the vast majority of us believe we are above average drivers. Ha, ha, fancy that! In psychology, this kind of belief is called a *positive illusion*. Other examples: only 2% of high school seniors believe their leadership skills are below average; 94% of college professors report doing above average work. Positive illusions cause enormous problems in our ability to change or improve simply because an accurate assessment of where we are is critical before we can move in new directions.

Susan Cain was an honors graduate of Princeton and Harvard Law School. After seven years in corporate law, she found herself chatting about career tracks with several of her law school classmates. One mentioned a classmate who recently argued a case before the Supreme Court. Susan realized she was not envious, not because of a self-less character, but because she really did not aspire to argue a case before the top court in the land. In fact she didn't aspire to any of the conventional achievements of lawyering. In her secret inner heart, what she really wanted was to become a writer and a psychologist. This sudden glimpse of self-knowledge became a turning point which dramatically transformed her career for the better. Eventually she left law, and through a series of incremental steps, became a New York Times bestselling author.[59]

Self-Assessment is a Process

In order to get at what really makes you uniquely you, you need to work through a process of steps. Perhaps this is like following a recipe when you set out to make a new dish. Using each ingredient, in the proper sequence, in the correct amounts.

Think about how you chose which college to attend, if you went to college. Did you read about those you were considering online? Did you research which schools had courses of study which appealed to you? Did you talk to people who had experience with the school, asking them what the classes and the social scene were like? Did you visit them, meeting students, faculty, and staff? Getting a "vibe" and assessing whether it seemed like a good fit for you? It takes time, careful research, and ideally first person experience to select a school that's a good fit for you. Finding a career to match with your skills, interests, and values is no different.

When I (Katybeth) was a high school junior, my dad sat me down and asked me what was important to me in a potential college. I said I wanted one with excellent academic programs, a successful pre-medical track option, an inviting Christian student group, and warmer weather than New Hampshire. He helped me make a spreadsheet with these factors and handed me the thick *Princeton Review* book so I could find out where each of the schools on my list stood in each area. Based on this, we selected a handful to visit over spring break. Two of the schools, which are highly regarded nationally, were so snobby in their information session, I didn't even bother to go on their tours. I knew that wasn't the environment for me. As soon as we arrived at William & Mary, I knew it felt right. My parents wanted me to explain why, but it was hard to put into words - I just got that "vibe" that this was the right place for me. If you really want to identify your sweet spot, you need to be willing to take the time to research, evaluate, and experience the options before you.

Many of the college students with whom I work complain that they should receive credit for their job search. They are surprised it takes as much time as it does, and they feel like it's not a worthy investment of this limited resource (time) without some sort of compensation. Unfortunately, what they don't realize is that the more time and thoughtfulness they devote to the process of exploration before launching their careers, the less likely they are to find themselves in a career that is a poor fit. Since you have the opportunity to realign at this point, consider this same principle— the amount of work you're willing to put in up front will directly correlate with the satisfaction you experience in the long run.

University professor Douglas Hicks talks about how many of the best students who come through his leadership classes end up taking entry-level positions with consulting firms. In conversations with the students, Hicks discovered the primary motivation was not any particular interest in consulting as a career or having unique skill sets that would be appropriate to consulting. The consulting firms were the first on campus every fall to recruit graduating seniors. They would extend offers to a top group of students and throw in a bonus of $500 cash plus a laptop computer. The driving motivation behind students accepting these offers was the anxiety that every senior feels when they are inevitably asked by parents, professors, and classmates: "What are you going to do next year?" Most of the students confessed they had simply "settled" in accepting this job because it was the first one offered and it took away the tension of having to figure out what they really should be doing with their career and life.[60]

Most of us do not know much about the world of work outside those careers in our families and those with whom we interact in our daily lives—teachers, police, doctors, and so on. A wealth of jobs and industries are available you may never have heard of. Take the time to explore them. Read about them in professional publications, magazines, or online. Talk to people who have been engaged in these fields, whether they are friends who work in the industry or people who hold jobs you think are interesting. Go test the waters—ask if you can shadow a professional for a day, volunteer your time and skills, take an internship. Just as in the search for a college, the more information you gather to compare to your needs and wants, the better a match you'll be able to make.

Career Assessment Counseling

If you are going through a career transition, it may be extremely useful to employ the services of a career assessment counselor. The assessment tools provided in Section Two can be applied with the simple diecions included in his book. Others may require you to purchase another book with more detailed instructions about taking a test, diagnosing the results, and applying the results to your individual situation. If you work through the material in Section Two and find yourself wanting to know more about what makes you uniquely you; you might consider going to a career assessment counselor.

A number of organizations offer career assessment skills over the Internet, but if they require you to take a self-administered test in under 15 minutes and then propose to tell you your best job fit, we would suggest you beware. Often you get what you pay for. If you pay for superficial help, that's what you get: superficial results.

Often state agencies will provide career counseling assistance. These programs provide various kind of assessment testing, and a range of levels of assessment counseling and coaching. Frequently state counselors can help steer you into particular kinds of jobs based on your strengths and interests.

If you're currently enrolled in a college or university, these institutions commonly provide career counseling services to students. They regularly offer services to alumni as well. It might actually be worth your while to enroll in a course in a local college, so that you can take advantage of their career services office. The college career center can help you measure your abilities and interests in several areas including your skills, your interests, your values, and the people environment in which you function the best. These counseling centers often teach seminars for those who are either seeking their first job or are seeking to change careers. They might help you improve your resume and give you coaching for your job search. In many universities, these folks can open up a wide network of alumni to facilitate your search for positions in particular organizations or industries.

There are also excellent private career assessment organizations in most major metropolitan cities. These might be for-profit organizations, or non-profits, but they offer similar kinds of services. These agencies typically provide a Career Assessment Package which includes assessment tests like the Myers-Briggs Type Inventory, the Strong Campbell Interest Assessment, the Clifton Strengths Finder and the Skills Scan. The package will also include a Skills Assessment process helping you identify areas where you have excelled and produced results in your previous work history. The counselor will then work with you to interpret and apply your individual strengths and to develop a Career Action Plan to help you land your next job. A package of perhaps five sessions might run $125. Other services, like polishing your resume, helping you build your network, coaching for interviews, and similar services can also be provided by these agencies.

Get Additional Training

If you find yourself in an involuntary career transition, you may discover your tooling for your chosen career has gotten a little rusty or out of date. Use the extra time being out of work to update your skill set through some training. It's a good investment for your future. This also shows the kind of initiative employers are looking for in new hires. Many people have discovered their jobs have disappeared permanently because the type of work they've been doing is in the process of becoming extinct. They need to retrain to equip themselves for a new career -- one that has positive long-term prospects. And if you find yourself voluntarily changing careers you will almost certainly need to invest in more education so you can land a job in a your new field.

Lori Rose graduated from college with a BA in English. She really had no idea what she wanted to do with this degree when she matriculated, but she eventually landed a job as an administrator for a family-owned construction company. While her position as the office manager, bookkeeper, and secretary for the firm didn't actually use her academic training, it was a good fit for her skills and temperament. Lori really enjoys working with detail, and as an introvert she does not mind working alone. When the Great Recession hit in 2007, home building in her area of the country quickly evaporated.

Recognizing both her company and her job were seriously at risk of disappearing altogether, Rose evaluated her strengths, her temperament, her interests and those things she had been successful at during her eight-year career. She went back to college and got a Master's degree in Library Science. It took her 18 months to finish the degree, but now she has a faculty level position as a research librarian in large university. In many ways, she has returned to her first love, the English language.

Ed Wozniak was a mid-career machine repairman for Chrysler Motors when he went through his second layoff in five years. Given the economic climate in Detroit in late 2007, Wozniak, who lives in Royal Oak, Michigan, decided it was time to get out the automotive business and find a new career. At age 36, Wozniak realized he probably had few long-term job prospects unless he changed fields altogether. During the previous layoff from Chrysler he had taken some college courses in anatomy and biology. Everything he read indicated nursing was always on top of the list of high demand positions. So after the second layoff, he enrolled in a one-year nursing program at Oakland University and graduated with honors this past December. He now has a position at Royal Oak Beaumont Hospital as an intensive care nurse. While his new occupation doesn't pay as much as his auto job, he reports it is certainly a lot more interesting and rewarding to be on the front lines helping patients, than to be constantly in fear of the next layoff.[61]

During the past decade, universities have become more responsive to the needs of working professionals. Some offer college-level credit for work and life experience to help people close the gap towards attaining an undergraduate degree. Others offer intensive evening courses which can lead to a Bachelors' degree in as little as 14 months or a Master's degree in just over a year. It is now possible to complete a university education, all the way through a PhD, while studying online.

Trade schools have also opened their doors wide to receive and equip those who need to upgrade workplace skills or to change jobs altogether. Anita Ray spent almost a decade styling hair. Hard economic times motivated her to put down her hair dryer and pick up a scalpel. She is now studying to become a surgical technician at the Tennessee Technology Center in Murfreesboro, Tennessee. Her classmate, S'ari Gian, 45, has a Master's degree in music and previously owned a Performing Arts Academy and gave private music lessons. A shrinking economy undermined her business and now she has enrolled in trade school where she is learning to become a licensed practical nurse.[62]

It may be hard to believe, but there are areas of our economy desperately short of workers. Precision parts maker Hamill Manufacturing, located just east of Pittsburgh, Pennsylvania, has more orders than it can fill. Yet only half the machines are running in the factory because of a shortage of skilled workers. "I would hire ten machinists right now if I could," says John Dalrymple, president of the company which makes parts for military helicopters and nuclear submarines.

A study of small to midsize manufacturers, those with up to 2,000 workers, cited a shortage of qualified employees as their No. 1 concern. These are positions that pay very well, about $60,000 a year, have good benefits and job security. Experts in the field fear the skills shortage in manufacturing will eventually cut into our country's economic revival. The US Labor Department recently released a study which found "Too few young people consider manufacturing careers and are often unaware of the skills needed in an advanced environment." Officials indicate that while less-skilled work will continue to move overseas where the pay is lower, both manufacturers and government officials are committed to keeping a skilled workforce and the high precision manufacturing sector based here in the United States."[63]

Join a Support Group

One of the best things you can do to help yourself through a career transition is to join a support group. Frankly, any career transition can be difficult and painful. If you're unemployed, it may take three months to three years to find a new position or career. Without the support of friends who are going through similar kinds of experiences, it is very hard to sustain yourself, let alone to be enthusiastic and aggressive in the job search. You say, "But I don't have any friends," or "All my friends are still working."

That's how we all feel when we go through a job search, particularly if it begins with an involuntary separation from our previous position. We feel alone, isolated, inadequate, scared, angry, fearful, and lonely. Even if you have voluntarily decided to leave your old position and set out on the great adventure to find new work in a new career, the excitement will wear off pretty quickly. In short order, you will want to have a support group.

A support group will provide emotional sustenance to help you deal with the roller coaster of emotions which come during the transition. It will also give you an opportunity to network and connect with others as you share stories and goals. Members eagerly pass along job tips and contacts, banking on the fact you're often only one connection away from your next job. Just knowing you're not the only person going through this experience can restore a measure of balance and humor to your outlook on life. Being part of a group helps you realize you are not alone, that there are others sharing this experience with you, and they are willing to help each other out; this is powerful therapy for the negative feelings which come with career transitions.

Career transition support groups have always existed, typically sponsored by church groups or local career centers. If you can't find one, it should be easy enough to start one. Wherever you live today, there are plenty of unemployed people you could ask to join you for a weekly meeting. The methodology is pretty simple: You meet at a convenient time, perhaps over coffee. You ask a few questions to break the ice and build community ("What's your favorite holiday dish?"). Take time to allow each attendee share, one at a time. Folks need to share about their feelings, their current status, progress made, doors both opened and closed. This allows people to vent their frustration and receive positive feedback. People will naturally offer encouragement, affirmation, and support to others as they share. Most people want to help others – being able to contribute ideas, leads, and advice allows them to do so. You will find yourself sharing those lessons you have learned to help cope with the impacts of unemployment. The group should intentionally focus on job search and career issues, where members can offer one another concrete help. Wherever possible, you might follow up to encourage progress with specific action steps someone previously shared.

The Job Club, a group of unemployed folks in San Francisco, has been meeting for over two decades. They gather for informal community, sharing, and mutual support. Unlike the cutthroat atmosphere of a job fair, a support group will help you develop friends who really care about your employment prospects. They can offer perspective, contacts, encouragement, and when required, accountability -- to make sure you continue to work hard at the process which will lead to your next job. Support groups can provide a confidential place where you can share your honest feelings. You can ask for advice and get feedback on how you're conducting your search. Your focus turns from your own circumstances to how you might be able to help others. And in the final analysis, you find people and friends who are willing to help new friends -- including you.[64]

Redevelop Your Brand

In my role as a management consultant, I am often called upon to help clients sharpen their brand image. I explain that if they do not know what makes their brand unique, consumers will not take the time to figure it out for them. Positioning your brand requires three steps:

1) Build upon the felt need the consumer has and wants met.

2) Build upon unique strengths you have to satisfy that need.

3) Finally, effective positioning requires understanding the consumer's perception of your place in their competitive set. How do you stack up against other brands in their group of potential choices?

If you've been in the workforce for any length of time, you may simply think of yourself as an engineer, a software programmer, a machine operator, a secretary, or a nursing tech. Back in the day, people came up with a title for the work they wanted to do; and when they were looking for a new job, they simply looked for a job wearing that same title. Things are not so simple today.

In today's rapidly changing economy, most employers are looking for skill sets rather than job titles. For example, if you have skill sets as a graphic designer there are potentially hundreds of different jobs which can apply those skills to diverse kinds of products or services. Perhaps, the newspaper advertising business where you've previously applied your graphic design skills, is on the way to extinction. At the same time, there is a rapidly growing demand for good graphic designers in Web advertising. You may have to take several courses to increase your competence in applying graphic design in web applications, but if you understand your core skills, it's fairly easy to find new applications of those talents.

When you begin to think about yourself as a brand, you'll recognize the importance of identifying the features and benefits you offer to an employer. As Martha Goldsmith, an image consultant who helps older clients develop their personal brands, explains, "Self-branding isn't really about you at all, at least not in the way you think. What we should focus on is what does my target (employer) need and what value can I provide my target? Goldsmith claims this self-understanding becomes our "Unique Selling Proposition. USPs, as they're known, are vital to developing our own brand because they demand we pinpoint what sets us apart, and play up our achievements."[65]

Often workers who are mid-career or older fear that unless they have a very sophisticated social media presence, they will be left behind in today's job market. It is true that many younger job seekers use social media like Twitter, Facebook, and LinkedIn to search for new jobs. And research from Career Builder.com indicates that 50% of hiring managers vet and recruit applicants through social media. But it is critical to differentiate the role of technology from the role of branding.

Technology never drives your brand. Positioning -- understanding what makes you unique, what high value skills and assets you bring to potential employers and the benefits you could deliver to an employer -- drives your brand. After you have clearly identified your brand's positioning, technology can accelerate your brand. "Once you have figured out what your USP is, what value you can bring to the table, you need to tell stories -- narratives that connect the pieces of a job history and convey who we are and what we want. When you go to build an Internet presence on a social media site, this is the story that you want to tell."[66] If you can authentically describe your skills, your history, your direction, your goals, through social media, then it will accelerate your job search in a very positive way.

Start Your Own Business

Sometimes the best way to reap the value you have developed during the course of your career is to start a new business. You might consider starting your own business if the industry you are coming from has been shrinking and laying off people. You should also consider it if you have advanced well beyond your academic credentials, and changing jobs would require you to take an enormous step down in both responsibility and pay. My friend Carmen, who managed the Advertising Services Department for a regional newspaper, found when she was laid off that her actual skills and accomplishments were far greater than her academic credentials. Not only is she an excellent graphic designer, she has years of project management skill, an outstanding portfolio of advertising projects, and seven years of management experience. When she was laid off she had 22 years of experience, increasing responsibility, outstanding results and she managed a professional staff of 15. But without a college degree, she simply could not land a comparable position as a manager of graphic design services.

As Carmen was working on her Brand identity in preparing her pitch for potential employers, she realized when she totaled up her strengths, her interests, and her assets, that she was a virtual one person advertising agency. Selling the brand "Carmen Carey Advertising" to potential clients was hardly any different than selling the brand "Carmen Carey" to prospective employers. Carey's career demonstrates her outstanding ability to conceptualize and implement effective advertising across multiple media outlets. Project management skills are top shelf. Her management experience enables her to recruit and use both inside and outside vendors to complete large-scale advertising projects.

The better Carmen understood how she *contributed value* to a potential employer, the easier it was for her to understand how she could contribute the same value as an advertising agency. She took on one client and then a second, while simultaneously continuing to look for a job. Hands-on experience convinced her she would make a lot more money per hour working as a vendor than as an employee. Plus owning her own company gave her a lot of control over her time schedule, which, as a single mother, is invaluable to her. Eventually she concluded her best future was in building and operating her own ad agency.

Viola Chisholm was 55 when she was laid off from her position with a community service agency. She had great difficulty, as many workers in their 50s do, in finding a similar position. Her daughter encouraged her to use her sewing skills instead of her administrative talents. She started a part-time job doing alterations for a local dry cleaner. With her daughter's prodding, she eventually started her own dressmaking business in her home. Her family and friends passed out fliers and cards advertising her business. Soon the doorbell began to ring. When Viola's family decided to put on a fashion show to demonstrate the quality of her work, business really took off. Today she's earning a good living from her own business.[67]

Given what's going on in our economy today, starting your own business might offer many advantages as an initial career. While most entrepreneurs gain some business experience as employees before starting their own company, some have decided to launch a business as their entry-level job. Brittany Rose, CEO of *More than Cheer*, started her business while an undergraduate at Virginia Commonwealth University. Her company specializes in upgrading the skills of cheerleaders through classes, camps, and coaching. Originally, she saw the company as an opportunity of supporting herself while staying in school. Yet the business was so successful, she decided to make it her full-time job upon graduation. She and her team are thriving while encouraging young cheerleaders and building a healthy profit margin at the same time.[68]

Starting your own business can be great fun and can produce steady income. If you are in need of work, don't spend your time moping and feeling sorry for yourself. Yes, launch an effective job search as we counsel in these pages. But also take advantage of what you have in your hands. It may be a need you have been asked to meet on a part-time or volunteer basis. Or it may be a skill or hobby you've developed over the years that could blossom into a business. It may be a talent in the kitchen -- like baking cupcakes. It may simply be an idea -- that's how Facebook got started. Launched by a handful of college students in 2004, this homemade business now has about a billion customers and is valued at roughly $40 billion. As long as you have the free time, why not take a risk. What have you got to lose? And the upside potential could really surprise you.

Section Two

Finding Work You Can Love

Chapter 10

Finding Your Unique Path

Finding work you can love is a process more than an outcome. Actually, the process is more like a journey—there's as much joy from the adventures you encounter on the way as there is from arriving at the hoped for destination. Consider the process of finding a vocation you enjoy, as an adventure you have the privilege of embarking on. It might be helpful to envision your search for work you can love as being like a quest—like Frodo's quest in *Lord of the Rings*. Beginning the trip is the first step on an expedition of discovery.

While many of us rush headlong into the vast maelstrom of career possibilities, we might be better served by slowing down to identify what makes you uniquely you. Your career will develop in stages, and it pays to be open and flexible as you move through it. We all need to expect changes in our career, and at times, to be willing to take the initiative to shift the paradigm. But underneath that, all successful and satisfying careers are built on the same foundation.

Perhaps the best analogy I can share is that building a career is a lot like building a house. The most important element is developing the foundation. Building a reliable foundation for a house takes a lot of time and effort, which sometimes goes unnoticed and is often unappreciated by the casual observer. Once you have an excellent foundation, framing the walls, rooms, installing windows and the roof, as well as all the elements of the finish and landscaping come relatively easily and in sequence. Yet, all of the superficial decorating touches that make a home beautiful, count for little when the storms of life hit. It's the foundation which determines whether or not the home will stand, in all kinds of elements and adversity, for decades, or centuries.

The bedrock foundation of every of fulfilling career requires a basic understanding of how humans are made. Each person is unique. That means you're unique! There's no one else like you on the planet. You cannot borrow someone else's career strategy to find a successful vocation for yourself. The foundation of your workplace success lies in your ability to find your own unique path. You've been designed for a special purpose. At the same time, it's critical to understand there are certain things you cannot do at all, and a great many things you cannot do well. Yet, there are also a few things you can do better than anyone else.

Jack Welch the legendary retired CEO of General Electric, tells the story of the son of a business acquaintance ready to graduate from Harvard, who came by one day to visit with one of his managers. The student had a list of questions about career opportunities in consulting or investment banking. He dutifully asked the questions and listened to the answers while politely taking notes. Yet the manager noticed he never seemed very curious about anything she said. As he stood to leave she noticed his folder was completely covered with intricate drawings of cars.

'Wow, those are amazing! Who did them?' she asked.

Suddenly, the senior was filled with energy. 'I did -- I'm always drawing cars,' he said. 'My dorm room is covered with posters and paintings of cars. I've been obsessed with cars since I was five years old. My whole life, I've wanted to be a car designer.'" The manager urged him to rethink his career plans and to seriously consider going to work in Detroit. She challenged him about his decision to go into consulting or banking when he seemed to have little or no interest in either.

"The senior deflated as quickly as he had come to life. 'My dad says the car business is not what I went to Harvard for.'"[69]

As you are planning for your career, self-knowledge will be your best ally in finding your sweet spot in the workplace. Everyone has a unique heartbeat, passion, and mission. You simply cannot find fulfillment and satisfaction in following someone else's dream. Very few people find success in a career which doesn't spring forth from their inner being.

Exploring the Process

Max Lucado has written a wonderful children's book called *A Hat for Ivan*. Like many excellent children's books, it also has a powerful message for adults. The story in this book is really a metaphor for the search to find our own individual sweet spot.

Ivan, the hero of the story, is coming of age. He's approaching the time when he'll find his own "hat"—symbolizing his special and unique place in the world. The story describes this journey of discovery. We're warned by the story not to try to imitate someone else's giftedness out of admiration. Ivan soon discovers other people may try to project their giftedness on to you, which almost never fits the unique person God has made you to be.

By the end of the story, we learn that finding your own special spot is a rite of passage. It's a process that takes time. It involves numerous steps. Most of all, it requires asking questions. In fact, Ivan is finally helped to his sweet spot by two questions his father asks him:

"Tell me Ivan, what do you really love to do?"

"And do you do it well?"[70]

Asking questions is one of the best ways we can begin to identify our unique design, but it's only one of several ways. If we are committed to doing our homework, we will find a variety of people with diverse insights to help guide us to a better understanding of ourselves. Your commitment to hard work, asking questions, and knocking on doors will go a long way to help you through what could be a convoluted journey. If you stick with it, this process can really pay off.

By the time he was 28 years old, Thomas Carvel found his career at a dead-end. A resident of New York City, he had bounced from one job to another without finding any sense of satisfaction or future. Carvel tried playing drums in a jazz combo in one of the better nightclubs in town. That fizzled out and he landed a slot playing semi-professional football. When that didn't work out, he found a retail position selling radios and appliances for a couple years. Nothing he tried seem to be a good fit. Yet he persisted.

Finally he decided to start his own business. He scraped together enough money to build a small trailer which he hitched to his car after loading it up with ice cream, hot dogs, and soft drinks. His plan was to drive north out of New York to Kenisco Dam where he would try to sell his merchandise to picnickers and tourists at a profit. Halfway to the lake one of his tires blew out. He had no spare, no tools to fix the tire, and no money to have it fixed. On top of that, the ice cream in his trailer was beginning to melt. But Tom Carvel was not a quitter.

He walked across the street and introduced himself to a man running a little pottery shop. After sharing his troubles with the elderly owner, the shopkeeper agreed that he could pull his trailer into the yard and hitch up his electricity. He opened up the stand right where he was, and began to sell refreshments, day and night. When the ice cream business was slow, he helped Pop Quinlan sell pottery. When business was brisk, he paid Pop what he could. Gradually business picked up, and Carvel began to discover the advantages of selling from a stationary stand. He used his free time to learn about the refrigeration business and invented several new devices for making and dispensing frozen soft ice cream. Within a few years he was able to market his own ice cream in Carvel stores. Later Carvel began to franchise his stores and by 1985 there were 865 stores which produced annual sales of over $300 million.[71]

A Process of Self Discovery

For most, discovering your unique design is much like an experience I had when I was in the 7th grade. My mother took me to an ophthalmologist, who sat me in front of a machine with a variety of lenses. The operator had me look at an eye chart on the wall, and I read the letters and numbers through various lenses. You may have gone through this routine yourself—one lens and then another are alternately flipped in front of one of your eyes, while the operator asks, "Is it better through this one? Or is it better through this one? Better with the first, or with the second?" This process of trial and error leads to the eventual selection of the appropriate corrective lenses for the new eyeglasses.

Discovering your own unique design is also a process of trial and error, where we try out different opportunities and evaluate how well they fit. It's an educational journey where we evaluate the things we like about a job or career field, and how well the requirements of that position fit our distinctive design. It's a process of self-discovery, almost like a writer working at discovering his own voice. You need to relax and be yourself.

When I was graduating from college I had a sense that there was one particular thing I was good at. I could even put it into words. My special talent appeared to be taking a concrete problem, moving it into the abstract, solving the problem in the abstract, and then bringing the solution back to the real world. I had no idea how this skill set connected to jobs people got paid for. The rest of my friends either were good at language, English, and had verbal skills, or they were good at math and science. They had some initial idea as to where to head to develop a career or find a job. I was clueless.

Max Lucado's advice in *A Hat for Ivan* is a good place to begin. Ask questions—lots of questions. We need to identify those things which motivate us. And that begins with recognizing the things we're interested in. Many of us have been so structured and pressurized by external forces (parents, social influences, educators, or our culture in general) we really don't know ourselves that well. We need to find out what's interesting and attractive to us in our own right. If we have free time, what kinds of things do we like to dig into? If we have a day off, what sort of things do we do for fun? When we were in school, what academic issues were most interesting to us?

Good Advice

When I was in my early thirties and wrestling with what direction to take in my career, a fellow sojourner gave me a good piece of advice: "Bruce, if you woke up tomorrow morning and you had $10 million in the bank and never had to work for a living again, what would you do? What would motivate you to get out of bed each day? What would you want to spend your time on? What are you passionately concerned about? If all your time was free time, what would you want to change in the world?" Then, after a significant pause, my friend added, "Whatever it is, that's what you should be doing. It's not about the money; it's about passion, it's about your dreams, and it's about your heart. If you follow your heart, your work will provide enough money to take care of your needs."

In hindsight, this turned out to be some of the best advice I've ever received. It reminds me of a comment by Frederick Buechner that in seeking our vocation in life we're "looking for the place where our passion meets the world's great need."

Buechner's own voyage of discovery is a great illustration of this principle. He relates, "By the time I was 16, I knew as surely as I knew anything that the work I want to spend my life doing was the work of words. I did not yet know what I wanted to say with them. I did not yet know in what form I wanted to say it or to what purpose. But if a vocation is as much the work that chooses you as the work you choose, then I knew from that time on my vocation was, for better or worse, to involve that searching for, and treasuring, and telling of secrets which is what the real business of words is all about."[72]

Born and raised in New York City, Buechner graduated from Princeton University in 1948 with a degree in English. He spent four years at the Lawrenceville School as a teacher of creative writing. In 1952 he gave up teaching to work full-time on his writing. His work includes fiction, autobiographies, nonfiction, and essays-- many of which have won both critical and commercial success. In 1958 Buechner again changed careers, being ordained as a Presbyterian pastor. For the balance of his career Buechner traded between ministry, writing, and teaching -- including stints at New York University and Exeter Academy where one of his students was the famed novelist John Irving. In short, his career, in all its manifestations, was built on his love of words and the work done with words.

Discover Your Inner Road Map

After reading Frederick Buechner's writing, it's fairly obvious he is introspective and quite good at self-diagnosis. This may explain why he was able to identify his life's career focus with such clarity at the age of 16. Many of us are not introspective by nature nor do we come with an innate capacity for self-analysis. But if a career is as much the work that chooses us as the work you choose, it is important to understand how you are wired. Getting honest feedback about who you are, what you do well, and those areas which are weaknesses in your life, is pretty difficult in these days of politically correct speech. This is where the tools and the process we want to introduce you to will prove valuable.

Whenever I have the opportunity, I am fascinated to watch the reality television show *American Idol*. Perhaps that's a bit ghoulish; watching this program is literally like watching a train wreck in slow motion. My favorite bit is watching the early auditions where the cast of judges travels to large cities around the United States and listens to thousands of young "wanna-be" musical stars belting out their best sample tunes on national television.

In the typical audition city, somewhere between 10,000 and 17,000 young adults turn up and wait for days to have the opportunity to sing a one minute acappella song for the panel of judges. In the average city the judges identify 50 to 75 supplicants who have at least a bit of musical talent. These individuals move forward to the next round of the elimination process in Hollywood, California.

It is not those with some musical talent who fascinate me, but the 9,900 musical prospects, out of the 10,000 applicants, who have no talent whatsoever. The vast majority of the first six or eight hours of this TV show consists of video clips of sad, deluded human beings who are willing to stand up on national TV and make an utter spectacle of themselves. Most of these not only have no musical ability -- they can't sing, they are off-key, they're off pitch, they can't remember the words, they create auditory manslaughter on any tune they attempt to sing. The key entertainment value of this portion of the *American Idol* contest consists of watching completely self-deceived individuals, who have no idea how badly they sing, making absolute fools of themselves in front of an audience of millions. Why do they do it?

The answer to that question, I believe, is the key to understanding why so many of us have trouble in shaping and guiding our careers and vocation. These tens of thousands of heartbreaking auditions result from the fact that no one has ever given honest feedback which helps these folks understand singing is not their talent. It may be the individuals have not sought honest feedback. Perhaps they have failed to do any of the analytical work to understand areas they are strong in and areas that are weaknesses (like singing). It may also be that they simply don't have the kinds of friends peopling their world who are upfront and honest enough to tell them, "You don't sing well enough to go on national TV." A real friend not only tells you when your zipper is down, they tell you to when you need to restrict your singing to the shower.

The foundation of a good career plan is understanding your unique design well enough that you don't waste your time trying to do things you're simply not wired to be good at doing. Every successful career is the result of carefully building on your strengths and working away from your areas of weakness. Not only do your strengths lead you to increasing levels of competence in the workplace, they also lead you into the kinds of work which result in personal fulfillment and satisfaction.

Please let me be honest, now that I've poked fun at the *American Idol* aspirants. I too have been guilty of being deluded about what makes me tick and how I'm wired. I obtained my first management position when I was about 27 years old. My company gave new managers the opportunity to apply some of these diagnostic tools that we're going to share with you. The first one I took was the Wilson Learning course on Social Styles. This diagnostic has you submit surveys to several people who work above you, several who are your peers, and several who work below you, to get feedback on how you relate to people in the workplace. The surveys are sent directly to Wilson Learning where they are popped on a computer and run through their analytics. When you arrive for the two-day seminar, in addition to a lot of training, they give you the feedback from your colleagues at work.

When I went to the seminar, I was excited to get my analysis back. Perhaps it was simply wishful thinking, but I assumed the feedback from my colleagues would say that I was a wonderful fellow – "Working with Bruce is like having Santa Claus around. He is such a great guy!" In fact, the feedback from most of my coworkers was that working with me was a bit like working with -- Attila the Hun. *What?* I was shocked! But I apparently had little insight about my own rough edges and how I came across to other people on the job. Evidently, I had some room to grow in the areas of people skills and management style.

The diagnostic tools will help you get under the hood and understand with real clarity how you're wired. This will not only point you in the direction of a career where you can be successful, it will help you understand the working environments, the work relationships, and even the corporate cultures which will help you find real pleasure in your work. After presenting a selection of diagnostic tools, we will also give you a process to use to sort out your unique strengths and your areas of weakness. Not every tool will be helpful to you, but as long as you find one or two tools that turn on the lights, you will discover this experience is highly rewarding. The process we share will enable you to manage the different diagnostic tools, the insights they give you, and will help you sort through the large number of other challenging issues which contribute to finding a job you not only can succeed at but one you can love.

Ask For Help

The most important step is to ask good questions, like Max Lucado suggests in *A Hat for Ivan*. Not only do you need to ask good questions, you need to find the right people to ask those questions. Some people's knowledge and insights about you are better than others. Even if you don't like what they have to say, you may learn a good deal if you're willing to listen. It pays to cultivate relationships with people who are knowledgeable about the fields you might potentially be interested in investigating. It's important to find good sources of honest criticism then to listen and reflect on the information you collect.

Solitude is a lost art which needs to be recovered. Take a long walk by yourself. Enjoy the flowers and the smell the roses. Sit by a bubbling brook and just think. Observe nature, its beautiful design and intricate relationship with the various elements that make up an ecosystem. Watch the waves wash in and out on the beach. Listen to the song birds and their different tunes. Marvel at the squirrels darting through the treetops and playing tag with one another in the flickering sunlight.

Then think about yourself. What are the things that give you the most pleasure in life? What kinds of tasks do you enjoy performing? What kinds of tasks do you dislike? What subjects or topics hold the greatest interest for you? What relationships work the best for you -- is it being given a task and the freedom to go off to do it on your own? Or would you rather be part of the team accomplishing a goal? Do you enjoy checking off each item on a list of tasks – or does the list cause an increase in your level of anxiety? Do you want to lead the team, or would you rather be a follower? We need to find out what's interesting and attractive to us. What skills do you like to use and what subject matter do you prefer to apply those skills against?

This kind of reflective thinking will help you begin to understand your own passion and inner wiring. Identifying this inner passion is what helped Tom Petty find his way into a career in music. Tom Petty, singer-songwriter and front man for Tom Petty and the Heartbreakers, found his career through discovering his passion. He struggled through a difficult childhood with an abusive father, and Tom found solace in music, writing his first original song at age 14. Success didn't come early nor did it come easily. For many years, Petty and his bandmates played in bars, honky-tonks, and small clubs. "Petty is amused by the impatience of today's aspiring singers on *American Idol*. 'They want to start at the top now,' he says, smiling. 'I just saw music as something I was compelled to do, something that made me feel good, and I wanted to do it.'" Since finally breaking out into success, Petty and his band have sold over 60 million albums and made it into the Rock and Roll Hall of Fame.[73]

A major diagnostic tool described in this section is to learn about your Motivated Abilities. This is the "inner theme song" in your life which ties together all the various strengths, talents, interests, and inclinations into a consistent pattern or direction. This is the overarching theme which runs through your life and ties together everything else about you. It is consistent and visible throughout your life from childhood through old age. It affects everything you do, and everything you are. It not only affects your work life, it describes how you will live in your marriage, your family life, and even how you will use your free time. Let's take a look at how your motivational pattern works.

Chapter 11

The Bent of the Twig

National research tells us the average person will spend approximately half his waking hours at work. Over the course of your lifetime, this means you're going to spend at least 100,000 hours on the job. As Mark Batterson wryly observed, "Better get yourself an ergonomic chair." In his book *Wild Goose Chase*, Batterson goes on to say, "Here is the mistake so many of us make: we start out pursuing a passion and end up settling for a paycheck. So instead of making a life, all we do is make a living. And our deep seated passions get buried beneath our day-to-day responsibilities."[74]

The voice you need to listen to is your own. Frederick Buechner once wrote, "The voice we should listen to most as we choose a vocation is the voice we might think we should listen to least, and that's the voice of our own gladness. What can we do that makes us gladdest? I believe that if it is a thing makes us truly glad, then it is a good thing and it is our thing." This is such a hard lesson to learn. We're so easily influenced by the values of our culture, and the things others hold in high regard.

Take my experience (Bruce) with letting peer pressure shape my vocation in the wrong direction. Early in my corporate career, I had an excellent job—my first management position. My title was Director of Marketing Research, which was somewhat overblown, given that I supervised two and a half people. Yet, it was a perfect fit for me. I had a small team and a healthy budget with which to do research. At the same time, this role gave me unprecedented access to leaders in the corporation, from the president on down. My position allowed me to have influence over many areas of the business, and other leaders sought out my insights and advice.

After three years in this ideal position, one balmy October afternoon, I was called in to my boss's office and given the opportunity to be promoted to Marketing Director. Now, I'd read *The Peter Principle* and knew all about people rising to the point of their incompetence, yet I was tempted. Honestly, I think I was attracted to the big increase in salary, responsibility, and status. But notice I wasn't drawn to the intrinsic demands of line management, in particular to managing these three product groups in our company. I had a good sense of how well-suited I was for a staff role rather than line management in the organization. My best fit was the dream job I already had. My current position allowed me to have responsibility for my tasks but also let me be an internal consultant to other areas of the company. In hindsight, it was clearly the allure of higher status which motivated me to yank my square peg out of a square hole and jam it smack dab into a round hole and a job that would never fit me.

Because of my lack of understanding of my own motivations, I signed up for an entire year of pain and suffering in this new position, before I finally made myself so miserable that I quit my job, moved my family 1,000 miles to the East Coast, and started in a new market research position in a different company.

In a commencement address at Stanford University, the late Steve Jobs, founder and CEO of Apple Computer and Pixar Animation Studios, shared some powerful advice from his life experience: "Your time is limited, so don't waste it living someone else's life." Jobs shared about how much he grew after he dropped out of Reed College and no longer had to take required classes. Being free to drop in on the classes that were interesting helped him find his own passion. Taking responsibility to pursue his curiosity and intuition is what led him to take the steps which ultimately resulted in the founding of Apple Computer. He concludes, "Don't be trapped by dogma—which is living with the results of other people's thinking. Don't let the noise of others' opinions drown out your own inner voice. And most important, have the courage to follow your own heart and intuition. They somehow already know what you truly want to become."[75]

Motivated Abilities

Arthur Miller, Jr., has probably done more than any other person to raise our understanding of the connection between the unique gifts and talents we have been given and our motivational pattern. Miller trained as a lawyer and entered the corporate world through jobs in the legal department. In spite of his training, his personal bent was to seek and resolve people problems in corporate life. Eventually his success in resolving these issues led to the suggestion he might want to leave off lawyering and take over the personnel department. Miller went on to prominence in the human resource field in several large corporations including Raytheon, the giant defense contractor.

In his early forties, as he reflected on his experience in the personnel field, he had one of those rare moments of illumination. Miller recognized that most human resource systems attempt to identify individual traits, talents, abilities, and gifts, and then from these try to predict job positions likely to produce success and satisfaction for this combination of attributes. Miller combined his knowledge of the human resource field—in particular, their efforts to get the right people in the right job—with new insights his study and experience had revealed and came to an interesting conclusion. Miller discerned that along with a person's natural talents, areas of giftedness, and developed abilities, each person appears to have a driving motivation to use all those attributes in a specific way. The empirical data in the field proved, beyond a doubt, every human being possesses both the gifting and motivation to accomplish something—that 1 to 2 percent I described earlier—better than anyone else in the world. *Our whole makeup drives us to use our gifts and our talents to achieve a specific purpose in the world.*

In explaining what he came to call our Motivated Abilities Pattern (MAP), Miller would say that if you want good job fit, you need to put people in jobs which fit their motivation because that's how they have been wired. Miller and his colleagues discovered the secret to finding fulfillment in both vocation and career: It is in using one's endowed giftedness to serve the world with excellence, and through that service to find your own unique place in the world.[76]

Arthur Miller went on to found People Management Inc., a global consulting corporation that applies the principles of S.I.M.A. (System for Identifying Motivated Abilities) to corporations, nonprofits, and a variety of organizations and their leaders around the world. (You can learn more about this system for identifying your motivated pattern by going to the website, www.simainternational.com.)

Identifying your own unique motivated abilities is both the simplest and the most complex of the various personality traits that we'll examine in this book. Finding your motivated abilities is merely a matter of looking back through your own personal history to identify achievements that have two characteristics: (1) it was something you enjoyed doing; (2) it was something you believe you did well. Such achievements may have occurred in your work, your home life, or your leisure time.

Finding Your Motivation

The process normally used to develop this personal history of achievements is to break your life into chunks of time. When I first took this test, I was in my early twenties and had only begun my working career. Therefore, most of my time slots were pre-career—junior high school, high school, college, and early working life. My task was to find two or three achievements for each of those time periods. Each accomplishment had to be what I thought was important, not what others might have considered impressive or noteworthy.

I've had this test conducted by People Management four different times over the course of my professional career, each time by a different analyst, and the result was always the same. It's as easy to recognize your motivational pattern in your childhood and early years as it is to see it over an entire professional career.

The core methodology is fairly simple. The difficulty comes in whether the respondent is able to come up with the right information from their personal history—the truly "relevant" accomplishments. Another intricacy is connecting the dots between the details of the different descriptions once you have them down on paper. People Management uses a highly sophisticated process and carefully trained analysts to do this work on behalf of their corporate clients. I'm going to give you a simple, do-it-yourself analytical process you can complete at home. My version owes much to an approach developed by Dr. Nick Isbister, who runs the S.I.M.A. practice in the U.K., and his colleague, Dr. Martin Robinson. You can find their entire process in their book *Who Do You Think You Are?*, which is well worth a read.

When I worked for the American Bible Society, I watched the People Management analysts do a motivational pattern for another vice president. This man had several Master's degrees, and had held a number of executive positions in large organizations. But the key to understanding his motivational pattern was an incident he described from his junior high years. Andy and his buddies lived in a New Jersey neighborhood with a lake about 15 minutes away. They would spend every summer riding their bikes to the lake—swimming, playing games, and enjoying themselves. One summer, Andy organized his friends to construct a bridge to a small island in the lake, about 20 feet from shore. Andy served as the "general contractor." He cast the vision, inspired his team, recruited individuals, and assigned them specific work to do. He made sure each boy gathered the materials and resources he would need for his part of the task. Then he continued to supervise and motivate until the bridge become reality. The process he describes as a 14-year-old boy, perfectly captures his current skills as an executive in organizing a large team to accomplish critical tasks in support of the organization's mission.

Do This Yourself

Identifying your own motivated abilities is actually both simple and complex. It's most helpful if you can identify a minimum of eight and a maximum of 16 achievements or accomplishments. Each achievement must be something *you* feel you really enjoyed doing, and that *you* believe you did well. Your perceptions on what to include on the list are what matters. If others praised you for accomplishments or activities that didn't really warm your heart, don't include them. *Your own perceptions* about enjoyment and success are what will help you identify the correct accomplishments.

Depending on your age, you might establish 4 to 6 time periods to represent your personal history. Someone in their early twenties might include a time block for middle school, high school, college years, and any work experience. That would give them four blocks of time with several accomplishments per block. Someone in their fifties might simply use decades of time. Begin with pre-college, then college, then 10-year blocks of time as areas to analyze. For each, you should come up with at least two accomplishments which meet the criteria.

I like to ask respondents to write at least a half page on each accomplishment. Describe why this experience made you feel successful. Talk about how you dealt with tasks, colleagues, and work responsibilities in this experience. Describe your relationships with others in this accomplishment—did you work alone, or did you lead part of a team, did you direct the team, or serve as the architect designing the project? Describe any specific kinds of activities or subjects that were important to this experience. Finally, talk a little bit about the kinds of organizations that made you feel positive or not.

Now comes the interesting part, where we begin to look for patterns. As Isbister and Robinson observe, this process is daunting for everyone. It's a little bit like staring up at the night sky full of stars and trying to pick out constellations.[77] As you read through your story and your descriptions about why these incidents were fulfilling and enjoyable, look for words that occur repeatedly. Look for themes which pop up in different accomplishments. Look for patterns.

When I analyze someone's accomplishments, I usually start simply by reading through their text one time. Next I re-read with a pen and circle words that seem to be important in their stories as a whole. Verbs are critical because they describe actions taken, and how results were accomplished. The next time through, I look for phrases, activities, actions, subject matter, and relationships which occur more than once, and I box those terms. The last time through I look for patterns, and I write those down on a separate sheet of paper.

You can interview yourself in the same way I would interview a colleague interested in discovering their motivations. Ask yourself follow-up questions: "What made this a pleasurable experience for me? What made me feel competent and successful?"

The more you think about each of these experiences and why they've risen to the top of your mental sorting deck, the better you'll understand why these achievements describe underlying core motivations.

When you're done, try to find an overall theme statement which describes the motivation and pattern you see reflected through most of your accomplishments. S.I.M.A. calls this "One Particular Result," and it explains the overarching thrust or theme that's identifiable for a particular individual. In my case (Bruce), my main motivational thrust is described as: "To engineer, plan or pull off the difficult, challenging or never been done before." In all my accomplishments you can see the desire to tackle complex, challenging, novel, and even daring kinds of problems. My approach to solving them is not simply by directing others, or to roll up my sleeves and do it with my own hands. Instead, I create a project type solution which includes analyzing the problem, finding better solutions, recruiting resources and people and then knitting them into the final resolution.

After you've got your main thrust identified, you can also go on and identify abilities you're motivated to use. These will appear among the frequently recurring words you circle in your analysis. You might also identify recurring subjects and circumstances you see repeated throughout your accomplishments. For example, in my descriptions, outdoor experiences are frequently mentioned. That tells me outdoor recreation, outdoor experiences, and contact with nature are critical to my health and well-being. If I don't have these as part of the intrinsic characteristics of my job, I need to have a balanced lifestyle which allows me to get time outdoors external to my work if I'm going to stay healthy. My MAP also indicates I love to package most kinds of work into projects. Even home maintenance work done on my own time, ends up being "projectized," with a beginning, middle, and end. Nothing thrills me like the satisfaction of completing a task and being able to check it off. Somehow, this fuels my sense of accomplishment and appeals to my engineering nature.

You should also look for patterns that describe how you relate to others. Emerging from most of your achievements will be a certain type of relationship you have with others. You may be the star, or the leader, or the helper, or part of a team, or a sole operator—but you probably have a preferred relationship that you seek in your accomplishments. That's not good or bad—it's simply the way you are wired. When you understand your need for that kind of relationship as you move forward into new opportunities, you'll find yourself being both satisfied and effective.

Seek Additional Help

I would urge you, if you want to understand your Motivated Abilities Pattern, to pick up a copy of *Who Do You Think You Are?* by Isbister and Robinson. This volume has a number of exercises to help you through the process and to keep you from getting stuck. This kind of diagnosis isn't easy to do on your own, unless you have a particularly analytical turn of mind like I do. Isbister and Robinson have done an excellent job of creating a do-it-yourself book that will help you gain deep insights into your motivations and abilities and how to apply what you learn in the process of developing your career and seeking your sweet spot.

You can also contact People Management (www.simainternational.com) about having a professional Motivated Abilities Pattern completed. I had my first MAP done while I was still in my early 20s. Although not inexpensive, the insights I gained from my pattern have been an invaluable guide to me in my career for the past 30 years. I've referred to it again and again while making decisions and choices about work. This experience has also allowed me to help many friends begin to find their sweet spot as well.

Once you understand how you are actually wired, it's as if the lights have suddenly come on. You will understand why you failed at some things you've tried in your career. You will also understand why certain things in your work give you great pleasure. Now you'll be in a position to guide your career in the direction of those things which are actually areas of giftedness in your life.

Strong Interest Inventory

Another tool that can help you take stock of your giftedness is the Strong Interest Inventory. The Strong Assessment is based on a theory largely championed by John Holland which suggests certain work environments, and those who choose them, can be sorted into six Types, or Themes: Realistic, Investigative, Artistic, Social, Enterprising, and Conventional. These themes are meant to provide a framework for matching people's interest with environments or types of jobs.

People tend to build skills in areas they enjoy, and conversely, they don't build skills in areas that do not come as naturally. Therefore, it's helpful to take stock of your particular interests and skills so you can complement them.

- **Realistic** refers to *Doers*, people who are hands on and product-oriented. These people prefer building, repairing, and hands-on activities. They like to work outdoors, and often have athletic and mechanical interests. They prefer to work with tools and machines.

- **Investigative** refers to *Thinkers*, people who are analytical and research-oriented. They want to know why things are the way they are—they are drawn to scientific, mathematical, and educational settings. They like to solve problems and prefer working with ideas over people.

- **Artistic** refers to *Creators*, people who are self-expressive and idea-oriented. They enjoy creating original work, have a good imagination, and prefer to work with ideas more than things. This is not restricted to the fine or performing arts, and can refer to an interest in broadly creative outlets.

- **Social** refers to *Helpers*, people who are helpful and service-oriented. They are interested in human relationships and like to help others with their problems. They prefer to deal with people more than data or things.

- **Enterprising** refers to the *Persuaders*. They are results-oriented and enjoy leading, selling, and influencing others. Comfortable with public speaking, they prefer working with people and ideas more than things.

- **Conventional** refers to the *Organizers*. They are orderly and data-oriented. They are good at following directions and paying attention to detail. They prefer working indoors and with clerical, arithmetic, and organizational tasks. They would rather deal with data, words, and numbers.[78]

Let me (Katybeth) give you an example of how these Themes might impact vocational satisfaction and fit. I work in an office with ten other colleagues, most of whom sought out positions in higher education because we had a desire to help students succeed. We are very collaborative and supportive of each other. Many of our projects are team-oriented, and almost all are explicitly tied to helping our clients in some way. We know each other's families, and people bring their partners and children to office get-togethers. We love to laugh and play games together, adding ice-breaker like questions to each staff meeting. This is a great environment for someone who identifies with the Social Theme, as I do.

Now imagine how someone who identifies with a Realistic Theme would perceive this same setting. It's entirely indoors and involves working almost exclusively with people. There are no machines or tools in this work, and most of it is inter-relational or intellectual, rather than hands-on. This would be a poor fit for someone with Realistic interests, and would likely lead to low job satisfaction and poor performance. However, working with the landscaping crew on this same campus might be a much better fit. A landscaper gets to work outside and uses tools and machinery to improve the aesthetics of the campus environment. Both settings are available at this one campus—knowing which fits you better is an important piece of finding your sweet spot.

In addition to helping you identify which Theme fits you best, the Strong Interest Inventory also measures Interest, Occupational, and Personal Style Scales. Each of these scales gets a bit more specific. Consider a geographic comparison. If you were to equate the Themes to the state where you live, the Interest Scales might represent your town, the Occupational Scales, your street address, and the Personal Style Scales, the way you decorate your house. There are 30 specific Interest Scales that are each associated with one Theme and relate to work leisure and educational activities. For instance, the Interest Scales associated with the Investigative Theme include Science, Research, Medical Science, and Mathematics. The Occupational Scales indicate how similar your interests are to satisfied workers in certain fields. For instance, if as a whole, attorneys tend to express interest in certain subjects and fields that are the same as your interests, Attorney might be listed in your Occupational Scales. The Personal Style Scales measure your preferred work style, learning environment, leadership style, risk taking and team orientation. Here you might learn that though you like working around people, you prefer to accomplish your task individually.

The Strong Interest Inventory is, in essence, a theme finder. It asks you a cluster of questions and looks for patterns in your answers, not unlike the process of the Motivational Abilities Pattern. When I use the Strong Interest Inventory with clients, it more often confirms what they already know at some level and provides a set of workplace vocabulary to seek out opportunities which match their interests.

StrengthsFinder 2.0

When Gallup, the creators of StrengthsFinder, surveyed over 10 million people over the last decade on the topic of employee engagement, only one out of three employees strongly agreed with this statement: "At work, I have the opportunity to do what I do best every day."[79]

Another Gallup survey reports that those who do not get to do what they do best every day are not emotionally engaged in their jobs. Those who do focus on their strengths everyday are six times as likely to be engaged in their jobs and more than three times more likely to report having an excellent quality of life.[80] This is great research to prove the very point —finding your sweet spot really matters.

StrengthsFinder is based on the idea that you will be able to make a greater impact on the world by identifying and building on your strengths, rather than obsessing over and trying to neutralize your weaknesses. Think about it. Perhaps you are incredibly technically savvy and can easily understand various programming languages, but have a hard time making conversation with people. It will take a lot of time, energy, and practice for you to become an average small talker, since you'll be swimming upstream against your natural talents and inclination. That same amount of time, energy, and practice applied to computer programming might create the next great technological revolution which could help improve medical care by making records easily accessible to all providers. Which seems like a better investment of your time and resources?

StrengthsFinder 2.0 describes 34 of the most common people talents Gallup discovered in their research. The book comes with a code which will allow you to take an online assessment to identify your Top 5 Themes of talent. Along with these Themes, you will receive ten action ideas for each Theme, resulting in 50 potential ideas for how to apply what you are best at doing.

I (Katybeth) found this to be very helpful personally—my Top 5 Themes are Connectedness, Belief, Individualization, Activator, and Responsibility. Most of these words are not on your everyday list of strengths and weaknesses. I never would have come up with the word "connectedness," but it helps me describe the fact that I love seeing and making connections—whether it's sharing an idea or resource with someone based on the conversation we're having, or it's connecting two people to each other for professional or personal reasons, or it's building a partnership because two groups are both working toward the same ends and would be stronger together. By knowing your strengths and having a language to share them, you will be better equipped to identify opportunities where you can make an impact.

The first and most definitive step in finding your way to your sweet spot is to identify your inner passion, your core strengths, and your motivational pattern. The three tools described above (Motivated Abilities Pattern, Strong Interest Inventory, and StrengthsFinder 2.0) can help you begin. But other details will assist in filling in the picture so you get a more complete sense of what makes up the unique you. After passion and motivation, the most powerful indicator to understanding your personality may be your temperament.

Chapter 12

Temperament

Early in my career I (Bruce) made a strategic blunder because I did not understand the role played by temperament in marketplace success and satisfaction. To some extent, this error may have been due to the Myth of Becoming I mentioned earlier (the notion that anyone can become anything he chooses if he simply puts his mind to it). One of my personality traits is that I'm an introvert. This doesn't mean I don't like people. I actually enjoy people, and I relate effectively to a wide range of personality types. Being an introvert simply means I gain energy by being alone. Extroverts gain energy from being with people.

My entry-level business positions involved market research and market analysis, which allowed me to spend significant time on my own when I was crunching numbers, creating questionnaires, or supervising research in the field. After diving into my first management level position, the thought popped into my head, "Maybe I should go into sales?" I rejected the idea out of hand because I (wrongly) believed a salesperson would spend all day face-to-face with people—not a happy thought for an introvert.

Later, I discovered the typical packaged-goods salesperson spends his day marching to a different drummer than I ever imagined. First thing in the morning, he hops in the car, drives for an hour, and then spends 15 minutes talking to a customer. After another hour in the car, there's another 15 minutes with a customer. Repeat. Then drive to the next customer and enjoy lunch together. The afternoon requires perhaps another four hours of driving and four 15-minute meetings. At the end of the day, a salesperson has spent three hours in face-to-face meetings and the balance of the day enjoying his own company. This is the perfect job for an introvert who likes people!

What did I choose to do instead? I decided to go into line management. From my first entry-level supervisory position and throughout my climb to executive roles at the top of the corporate ladder, I discovered line managers spend most of their days in meetings. Many days I was in meetings for 10 to 12 hours straight with barely a break to go to the bathroom. Whew! Talk about intense! As an introvert, I would come home totally brain-dead and wrung out from the constant din of meeting after meeting all day long. If I'd understood anything about the critical role of temperament in vocational satisfaction, I might have made very different choices in my career and found better outcomes over the long run.

Measuring Personality

Personality or temperament can be measured in a variety of ways. As early as 380 B.C., thoughtful Greeks noted the fact that people reflect a wide range of attributes and behaviors. Measures of personality or temperament try to find key variables to help us understand how some individuals react and respond to stimuli and environments and how those reactions differ from others.

Marketplace managers, particularly human resource personnel, often invest in helping employees understand temperament and personality because of its positive effect on the bottom line. The better people understand themselves, as well as those around them who are wired differently, the more effectively they can communicate with others in an organization. Typically, the better the communication in organizational culture, the better the ultimate outcome for the organization.

Each personality measurement tool tries to classify people according to several variables or combination of variables. My goal in this volume is not to teach you the details of each instrument. Each of these tools can help you unlock your understanding of what makes you tick, what fires your engines, and what you need from a job to move into your sweet spot. You don't need all of these tools--just one can give you the "Aha!!" that says, "This is me! This description crawls right inside my skin and describes how it feels to be me."

To get an in depth analysis of yourself on any one of these temperament diagnostic systems may require another textbook to work through all the elements. Our purpose is to give you a sampling or a taste of each of these ways of measuring personality. If you're interested in a particular style, I urge you to use the reference given to obtain the book, take a workshop or course, and get better versed in these tools.

Two-Dimension Tools

The simpler personality tools use only two dimensions. Wilson Learning, for example, has an instrument designed to measure social style or how we interact with others. It does so in two dimensions: *assertiveness* (putting ourselves forward) and *responsiveness* (showing emotions to others). Picture each of these variables as the X- and Y-axis of a graph. The population is simply divided into halves on each variable. So those who are more assertive than average would be counted as High Assertive. Those less assertive than average are classified Low Assertive. And you're either High Responsive or Low Responsive depending on whether you show your emotions more or less than average. This tool yields a classification pattern like this:

ANALYTICAL	DRIVER
(Low Responsive, Low Assertive)	*(Low Responsive, High Assertive)*
AMIABLE	EXPRESSIVE
(High Responsive, Low Assertive)	*(High Responsive, High Assertive)*

Each of these quadrants demonstrates a different set of social styles when relating to other people. *Drivers* are more assertive than most, and tend to be emotionally reserved. They like to get to the point, make a decision and move to action. *Expressives* are the life of the party. Being both high assertive and high responsive, they light up a room when they enter. They tend to be happy, good-natured, and fun to be with. *Amiables* are both warm and friendly and easy to get along with. Cooperation comes naturally to the Amiable. *Analyticals* are both emotionally reserved and less assertive. They like to have the facts, prefer to stick to business rather than get personal, and enjoy having the maximum amount of information when making a decision.

You can read about the details of each of these types in *Social Style / Management Style* by Robert and Dorothy Bolton.[81]

But the point isn't just to understand your particular pattern. The real value in understanding social styles is to identify the patterns of those around you at work and to learn how to be more responsive to their particular needs. Wilson Learning's research data shows that leaders come from every social style. There's no "best" style to have. Accommodation to the style or comfort zone of others is always required. No matter what pattern you reflect, three fourths of the people you work with have a different style.

Wilson Learning's research, conducted among hundreds of thousands of respondents, shows a high correlation between flexibility and vocational success. The better you're able to understand the social styles of others and move in their direction to make them feel more comfortable, the more successful you'll be in both communication and relationships.

The ultimate objective is to understand your personality, as measured by this or some other temperament tool, and learn how to modify your style to better mesh with those you work with in the marketplace.

The Adler Assessment

Another two-dimensional assessment tool was created by expert recruiter Lou Adler. Fellow executive recruiter, Scott Kauffman in Atlanta, is a big proponent of using assessment tools like the Adler Assessment, to help in screening candidates for positions. Look at it from management's point of view; if the research shows that two out of three management hires are a failure, an enormous amount of time, money, and effort get wasted in organizational life by hiring someone outside of their sweet spot. Recruiters, who get paid for their success in matching people to positions, have found that using a formal, objective assessment which uncovers attributes of the candidate's hardwiring go a long way towards minimizing bad hires and maximizing good job fit.

I'll let Scott Kauffman, a personal friend describe how he uses the Adler Assessment in his role as an executive recruiter. "Draw a horizontal axis (real or imaginary) that represents the speed of decision making. Label fast and instinctive on the right... slow and deliberate on the left. Those on the right prefer to make fast decisions with limited data. Those on the left are more cautious and would rather ponder a bit, collecting as much information as possible before deciding.

Then draw a vertical axis through the middle of the horizontal axis to create a "+" with four distinct quadrants. The vertical axis represents a focus on people or results. (Label *Results* at the top... *People* at the bottom.) Those who are very people-oriented are less concerned with getting things done on time and on budget. They'll tend to let things slide to ensure that everyone is okay. Those who are extremely results-focused will be less concerned with the needs of the people involved. They'll tend to push for results, even if it upsets some of those involved.

As a test, plot yourself and/or others you know well on the horizontal and vertical axes and see if you think it's accurate. Based on where you plot people on these two dimensions, they will fall into one of four quadrants. Each quadrant represents a general personality style (see description below).

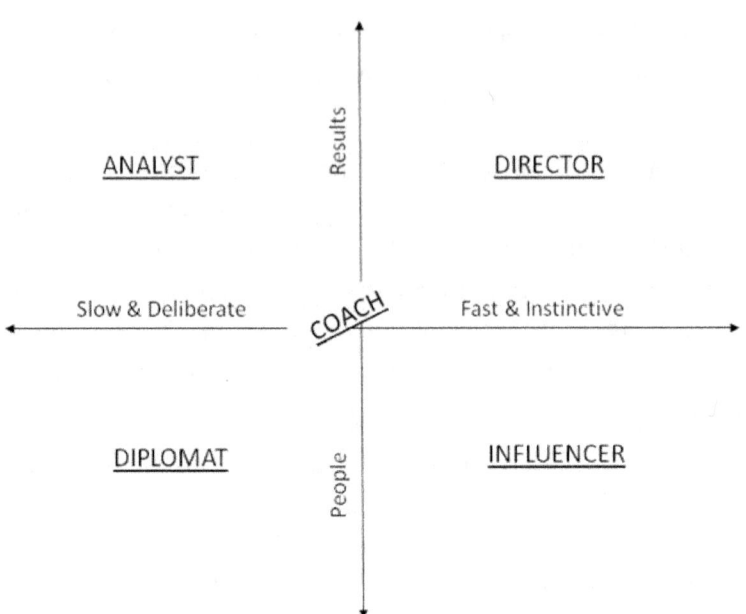

Top left = Analyst ('technical," detail-oriented, cautious, methodical, and conservative in their decision-making.)

Top right = Director (hard-charger, dominant, and fast-paced; less sensitive to the needs of others; delivering results is their number one priority)

Bottom left = Diplomat (proudly professes to be a "people person," Strong soft skills, gets along with everyone but sometimes doesn't get enough done)

Bottom right = Influencer (classic sales personality, tends to make instant judgments based on first impressions more than substance)

Near the center of both axes = Coach (often flexible and able to exhibit traits from all four quadrants as the situation requires)

People with each of these general styles have inherent strengths and weaknesses which will impact their fit with the job. Though this informal "assessment" is not precise, it can provide some valuable clues as to where to focus your efforts. According to Kauffman, you would likely have to work closely with someone for months to uncover what a good assessment can reveal it in minutes. From the hiring manager's perspective this is why analytical tools like the Alder Assessment are so helpful in getting the right person in the right job. From the perspective of a potential candidate, you should be delighted to take advantage of any assessment tool which helps you end up in a job that's a good fit for you in the long run.

Let me illustrate, again from my (Bruce's) career, where this kind of tooling can be very helpful. When I was promoted into my first marketing management position, I was working for a medium-sized, family-owned publishing company in Chicago. Their typical product took over two years to move from conception to hitting the market. The organizational culture was slow and deliberate and matched the product life cycle. Nothing happened in a hurry.

Every quarter I met with a senior accounting manager to establish the press run sizes for each product for the coming period. The accountant (probably an **analyst** on the Alder Assessment) would look back at the sales numbers for similar products in previous years and always suggest a very conservative print run. As the marketing manager (and a **director** on the Alder Assessment), it was my job to understand potential new markets, upcoming advertising and promotions, and to ensure we had enough product to satisfy any potential consumer demand.

Thus, my estimates of potential sales were always much higher than my accounting colleague's estimate. His job was to ensure we didn't print one single more book than we could sell. My job was to make certain we had every last book in inventory we might possibly be able to sell. Ultimately, the final press run was a compromise between these diametrically opposed positions. In this extremely conservative, tradition bound, slow-paced, family company culture, I was most often viewed as some kind of barbarian. My inherent desire to grow the business and focus on potential results caused most of my publishing colleagues to think I was the wildest and craziest guy they had ever met.

My next management position was a marketing job at Crayola Crayons which had recently gotten into the toy business. My immersion in the toy business, after years in a staid, Midwestern publishing culture, was like taking the polar bear plunge through the ice on New Year's Day. The toy business is very fast paced and aggressive. A typical toy company turns over a third of their product line every single year. A hit product will make money for three years in a row. Most did not achieve that standard. Thus, the corporate culture of the average toy company is a mad scramble to find 10, 20, or 30 new products every single year - hopefully a handful of which will be bestsellers and produce enough profit to keep the company alive for another 12 months.

My responsibilities included marketing research, new product development, and brand management. Most of our new products were created in a collaborative process which involved anywhere from a dozen to two dozen individuals. Many of my colleagues were delighted to take an idea, throw it against the wall like a piece of half cooked spaghetti, and hope something stuck. Of course, each half-baked idea which was actually turned into a product risked millions of dollars and the future of the company - on what was ultimately a hunch. In these product development meetings, I was always the guy who was screaming for some empirical data to show there was any consumer interest in this lame-brained idea.

It was amazing. Almost overnight I became more conservative than my former accounting manager back in the publishing business in Chicago. People formed the notion I was a data head, unwilling to make any decisions without strong evidence of some kind. My colleagues thought I was the most wooden, anal, uptight, rocket scientist they had ever met.

The change in corporate cultures between the publishing business and the toy business transformed me from an Alder Assessment **director** into an **analyst** without any actual change on my part. The corporate culture which you work in will have a major impact on how your unique strengths play out in the workplace. In finding a good job fit you must identify what makes you tick and the optimum environment to use your strength.

Multiple Dimensions

The Myers-Briggs Type Indicator is another popular tool used in workplace environments. It's based on four pairs of opposing attributes which are used to segment the population. These include:

- Extrovert vs. Introvert
- Sensate vs. Intuition
- Thinking vs. Feeling
- Judging vs. Perceiving

This measure of temperament has been found to be useful in a wide variety of marketplace settings. If you haven't already done so, it would be a great advantage to have your Myers-Briggs pattern identified. In many organizations someone in your human resource department can provide this test and score it. Any college or university can also most likely connect you to a Myers-Briggs test for about $15. Once you have the descriptors from a competent tester, the best explanations of each typology and what makes them tick can be found in *Please Understand Me* by David Keirsey and Marilyn Bates.[82]

Let me give you just one example of why this measure is critical for success in the workplace. If your boss has a J pattern ("Judging"), it means he likes to make decisions. As soon as a decision is made, he can relax even if he made a terrible decision. When you come to this manager with a problem, you'd better have done your homework, considered the alternatives, and decided on the best solution to the problem. By presenting it appropriately ("Here are three good alternatives, and why I believe this one is best"), you'll have no trouble getting a good decision from your supervisor. If you're not prepared, and you fail to present according to his needs as a J, you'll have a decision, even if it's crazy, before you know what hit you!

On the other hand, if your boss happens to have a P pattern ("Perceiving"), he or she will have great difficulty making decisions. If you bring a problem to her, it's better to have more options, rather than fewer options. The supervisor will need to feel that a wide range of alternatives have been considered before you focus down on the solution you believe is best in this particular instance. P's struggle with making decisions and always feel more comfortable not *after* a decision is made, but *before*, while their options are still open. If this is the kind of boss you have, and you need a decision from her before a certain deadline, you probably need to be proactive and run it by her a number of times well ahead of schedule, if you hope to stay on track.

In their various combinations the four pairs of attributes listed above produce 16 temperament patterns which endeavor to describe the differences between how various people in the population behave and make decisions. For example, my (Bruce) pattern (INTJ) is labeled "Architect of Change." My four attributes (Introvert, Intuition, Thinking, and Judging) combine to produce a person who looks to the future, is a builder (particularly of systems), and is an applier of theoretical models. This type is the supreme pragmatist who excels at brainstorming and discovering new concepts, and continually seeking strategies and tactics which have high payoff. Little wonder I gravitated towards a career in marketing research, new business development, and strategic planning.

My wife, Martie, falls into the ENFP pattern. Her attributes (Extrovert, Intuition, Feeling, and Perceiving) combine into a pattern which is labeled "Enthusiastic Innovator." ENFPs have great influence because of their extraordinary impact on other people. They're keen and penetrating observers, and they're capable of intense concentration on another individual. They tend to be hyper-sensitive and hyper-alert, while characteristically optimistic. They're warmly enthusiastic and successful in a wide variety of careers.

So Easy, Even Kids Can Do It

Dr. John Trent and Gary Smalley have developed a personality inventory so simple it can be used with children. Trent and Smalley, nationally known authors and speakers in the area of personal and family development, designed this tool to help parents and children learn how to get along with others who are wired differently from ourselves. We've used this tool, as described in the book *The Treasure Tree* by John Trent,[83] with our own family. Like many great children's books, this one has a powerful application for adults. The Trent/Smalley personality tool uses four animals as the labels for personality categories: the Lion, the Otter, the Golden Retriever, and the Beaver. Each typology has a slogan which captures the essence of this personality type. The Lion: "Let's do it now!" The Otter: "Trust me! It will work out!" The Golden Retriever: "Let's keep things the way they are." The Beaver: "How was it done in the past?"

The inventory test is quite simple. Each animal is associated with 19 words or phrases. The respondent goes through each list and circles those words which describe a consistent character trait in your own life. Circled items under each category are totaled and assigned points, from which a score is derived on the score sheet on the reverse side of this one-page test. Typically, a person is some combination of typologies rather than purely a single category. Even with these variations, you can normally see patterns in your own behavior which tend to place you primarily in one of the four categories of attitude and behavior.

The *Lion* is a person who takes charge and likes to make decisions, and who's confident, bold, goal-driven, and action-driven. This is the classic leader typology.

The *Golden Retriever* is loyal and calm, avoids confrontation, enjoys routine, and is warm and relational, sensitive to others, nurturing, thoughtful, and a peacemaker. This person makes a great follower and a great friend.

The *Otter* is associated with enthusiasm and risk-taking; he's energetic, verbal, fun-loving, and spontaneous. He enjoys change and he's a motivator and inspirational. Being married to an Otter, I can tell you they're great cheerleaders and always the life of the party.

Finally, the *Beaver* is accurate, consistent, reserved, orderly, conscientious, detailed, precise, and scheduled. This is the person you want in charge of your finances or doing the calculations for your trip to the moon.

These observed patterns can be highly predictable even at an early age. One Sunday afternoon, my wife and family were visiting friends with small children. While their girls, ages eight and eleven, happily played with my teenager daughters, their five-year-old brother Chad preferred to play alone. He quickly became engrossed playing on the floor with Lego blocks by himself. Rather than building structures with his blocks, Chad would take all the blocks and divide them into columns of red, blue, green, and yellow blocks. He would add them up as he divided the whole into individual categories. When finished, he would turn around and reverse the process by taking all the varied colored blocks and piling them into one "total" group, which he then numbered. Back and forth, Chad made his piles and counted up the numbers. For a couple hours he was quite happy repeating this organizing activity—the mark of a real Beaver. It would be easy to see him growing up to be an accountant.

Let me conclude this section on temperament and personality by pointing out that vocation is dramatically affected by your understanding of your own personality and how it differs from others. It doesn't really matter which typology you use; you may like one of the five systems I've described above, but there are also other personality assessment tools you might find more helpful to you. The goal is to find an instrument which helps you understand yourself. The objective is to gain insights about how you're uniquely wired and how you respond to circumstances and people. When your spirit resonates with a description and says, "Yes! That's me! That's exactly how I feel!"—then you're on the path to illumination.

Finding a personality or temperament assessment tool which sheds light on your inner workings will provide a number of benefits. You'll recognize your own strengths and weaknesses, how you like to operate, and the circumstances that most often lead to success.

Earlier I (Bruce) mentioned I've developed a 10-point checklist to use when people suggest I consider another position. Having learned what makes me tick, I know if at least eight out of ten of these items on my list are not strongly in play in a career opportunity, I won't be happy in the job, nor will I be very successful. These items include key temperament issues. Does the position allow me to be measured by results? Is there room for individual action and responsibility? Will I be able to lead a team? Is this an organization committed to change and growth?

Understanding your own temperament will help you see how you differ from others and will help you avoid the negative outcomes which so often come from the Myth of Becoming. Why pursue a career others would consider "successful" if it makes you miserable? Having a handle on your temperament will also be a major benefit in a multitude of relationships— not just at work, but your marriage, your children, and friends.

Appreciating how your temperament is wired will give you clear sign posts to guide you as you seek to find your sweet spot in the world of work. Yet, your own previous workplace experience can offer insights into your unique design which plays to your motivations. Understanding your past experiences may help you crack the puzzle of what to do in the future.

Chapter 13

Tap into Your Talents

While not as scientific as some of the personality tools we've just discussed, one of the best ways to focus in on your sweet spot in career and vocation is to analyze your own history. Life brings a wide variety of experiences our way; many of which appear to be random, spontaneous, and unexpected. Yet taking some time to reflect on and analyze some of our life journey may be the key to finding our way into a new future.

Wally Amos had always wanted a career as a big-time operator in the theater world. He had some early success as a theatrical booking agent in New York City. Then Amos moved to Los Angeles and set up his own independent agency. After 13 years of hustling business for his clients and struggling with finances, he was discouraged. In a moment of raw honesty, he had to admit his career had hit a wall. His marriage was gone. He was broke. And he knew in his heart that the fast-track he'd been trying to run on was the wrong track for him. Wally Amos packed his three sons into his old Rambler station wagon and set off to find a new life.

When he reflected back over the course of his life, he ended up thinking about cookies, of all things. As a boy he used to loiter in his Aunt Della's tiny kitchen in the Bronx waiting for her special chocolate chip cookies to pop out of the oven. They were a complete mystery—delicious in a way no other cookies ever tasted.

During his long sojourn in the theatrical booking business, or when times were hard, Wally would cheer himself up by making a batch of those chocolate chip cookies. As he stirred up the dough, he would experiment—dropping in pecans, coconut, extra chips, and other tasty morsels. At times, he made so many cookies he ended up carrying sacks of them around, handing them out to friends and business acquaintances. They were always a hit.

When Wally decided to reboot his life, one of his acquaintances suggested he open a cookie shop to sell his delicious treats. With the help of several friends and a little borrowed cash, he launched his first store in 1975. Emerging from this initial storefront on Sunset Boulevard, there grew a chain of over 3,500 Famous Amos Cookie stores.

Your History May Hold a Clue

Some of our earliest experiences in life can provide guidance as you seek to find your sweet spot in career and vocation. It's the "bent of the twig" that later becomes the shape of the tree—even in young children, you can begin to see indications that point to their ultimate adult career path.

My wife Martie has always loved children and has a special talent with them. Her first job as a teenager was babysitting five boys under the age of ten. While to some of us this sounds like a recipe for disaster, Martie loved it. In college she studied to become a math teacher, but after a teacher training stint at an inner-city high school in Pittsburgh, she jettisoned the entire notion of teaching as a career. Over the next decade she wandered through a variety of jobs, none of which seem to be a really good fit. She worked in ministry in her church for several years, worked as an executive assistant, did some other administrative jobs, and even sold bras to wealthy matrons in a prestigious Princeton department store.

When our children were old enough to go to school, Martie decided she wanted to home-school them. The process of leading our kids through their elementary school years motivated my wife to read, take courses, and learn a great deal about how to facilitate learning with children in this age group. After our daughters went to off to public school, Martie decided to volunteer in a local elementary school. The school soon recruited her— initially on a part-time basis, and later as a full-time employee. Working every day with young children, she discovered she has a special ability to help children learn to read. Even children with learning disabilities were able to find a door into reading with the help of my wife's coaching and encouragement.

After ten years of hands-on success, Martie went back to school and earned a Master's degree in reading and writing. She now works full-time as a specialist in this area and loves her job. She tells me she would pay for the privilege of working with children every day and helping them discover the joy of reading.

Experience is a Great Teacher

My experience (Katybeth) working in the career counseling area of university life tells me college students often haven't had enough work experience to understand where their talents might lie. As young adults, we frequently find we haven't had a wide enough array of experiences to tap into those particular things we're good with. We grow up in a home or a family system with a specific set of values or interests, and it may not be until after we leave home that we begin to discover latent talents which no one in our family ever noticed or encouraged.

My own (Bruce's) family was composed primarily of engineers and mechanical geniuses. My father was an industrial engineer and spent his workdays designing integrated manufacturing systems that could solve more problems than you could shake a stick at. At home and on weekends he continued to express his technical talents. My brothers were gifted mechanics. They were constantly building go carts, rebuilding antique cars, rigging up rocket launchers, and generally impressing all the kids in the neighborhood. I was so "mechanically challenged" I could barely change the tire on my bike. I always felt like the black sheep of the family with my lack of hands-on skills.

It wasn't until I was in college that I began to discover I had talents no one else in my family possessed. I was actually pretty good at working with people. I excelled in organizing and motivating teams of people to accomplish various tasks. With everyone at home busy building rocket launchers, mechanical slingshots, and go-carts, how was I ever supposed to discover my people skills? Fortunately, I became involved in a large college youth group at my church. I began serving as a volunteer and eventually was asked to join a committee planning a week-long off-site retreat for 500 collegians. As you can imagine, this was quite a logistical feat for a dozen 20-year-olds to pull off. Our committee worked together for about six weeks and then, two weeks before the retreat, our chairman— a grad student at a local seminary—quit.

Much to my amazement, the church leadership team and the retreat committee nominated me to take over leadership of the event. Through this I discovered I have a natural talent for administration. It's easy for me to break large operations into small tasks and assign people and resources to accomplish each component.

The result was the best retreat this college group ever pulled off. This incident helped me discover more about the sweet spot I am designed to fit. Leadership, planning, administration, and team building are all activities I do well and enjoy. I simply had never before had any life experiences which allowed me to identify those talents.

Get Involved

If you're young, or feel your experience has been limited, I would strongly recommend you begin to stretch yourself. Immerse yourself in new experiences. There are lots of ways to gain experience. Consider volunteering at local community organizations. Lots of organizations need volunteers: candy stripers at the hospital, students helping coach younger students after school, workers in the food pantry for those in need, helping build playgrounds for inner-city neighborhoods, distributing blankets to the homeless, and teaching literacy skills to adults. For opportunities to serve, check out the local YMCA or organizations who work with youth. Investigate rescue missions and community service agencies, or perhaps local churches. If there's a high school or college nearby, they'll often list community service opportunities in your immediate vicinity.

If you're still in school, try some of the student activities that are offered. Go on a trip to the opera or ballet. Take a day trip into the nearest big city. Participate in a beginners snowboarding class. Most colleges offer dozens of extracurricular activities and clubs. Try one out. Try a new one every semester. If you don't like it, you don't have to keep doing it. But if you've never had any experience with tennis, sailing, chess, or water polo, how can you possibly know whether this is something you might enjoy? Be brave!

If you're a bit shy, take a friend with you on these ventures. Maybe you'll make some new friends, even if you don't discover any experiences that excite you. Broaden your horizons—you may find an experience that opens up a whole new view of life.

You've heard the story of Bill Gates and the development of Microsoft. What you may not realize is that Gates stumbled into his success because of his willingness to try a new experience. In 1968, he was an eighth-grader at a private school in Seattle. Every year his school's mothers' club had a rummage sale. One year they invested the proceeds in a funny little computer called an ASR-33 Teletype. This unit was parked in a closet and the sign was hung outside identifying this space as the computer club. Now in 1968, most colleges didn't have computer clubs. Bill Gates, a precocious but bored eighth-grader, ended up practically living in the computer room. He and several friends taught themselves to program. "It was my obsession," Gates says of his early high school years. "I skipped athletics. I went up there at night. We were programming on weekends. It would be a rare week that we wouldn't get 20 or 30 hours in."

Because of his willingness to take advantage of this niche opportunity at an early age, Gates gained thousands of hours of practice time. "By the time Gates dropped out of Harvard after his sophomore year to try his hand at his own software company, he'd been programming practically nonstop for seven consecutive years. He had way past 10,000 hours of experience." The willingness to try a new experience and the persistence to practice it until he developed a high level of expertise were the critical foundation stones that resulted in the development of Microsoft and its long-term success.[84]

Hard Experiences Can Be Valuable

Early in our marriage, we had a friend make a cross-stitch sampler featuring this statement: "When life gives you lemons, make lemonade." That statement has always stuck in my mind. As I've seen our economy go through periods of boom and bust over the course of my career, I often find myself reflecting on that statement. Frequently our vocational and career plans don't work out as expected. We may find ourselves in a difficult relationship with a supervisor and come to work one morning only to discover we've been fired. We may work for a company that finds itself as part of a downward trend in the economy, and we're laid off.

Our country has recently been recovering from a deep recession which has resulted in unemployment and financial hardship for millions of workers. Historically, these economic downturns happen with startling regularity. What's important is not the present unemployment rate, it's the fact that you will go through a number of bad employment markets during the course of a 40 year career.

Jim Clifton, the CEO of Gallup Research estimates about one in six working Americans can't find a job or the right job. Tough things happen to people in the workplace. When it happens to you, it may in no way be your fault. Life sometimes does give you lemons. The relevant question is whether you can learn how to make lemonade out of it.

Lee Child joined a television production company straight out of college. He enjoyed 20 years of success and had every expectation of sticking with this job until retirement. When new management came in, they decided to increase profits by cutting costs. "I was a cost. I got cut," Lee says. While his first reaction was anger and a sense of betrayal, Child became scared as he thought more about being a middle-aged guy with no other job skills and a mortgage and family to support. Ultimately, Lee was able to channel his anger into determination. He decided to try his hand at writing thrillers. His main character, Jack Reacher, was downsized out of the U.S. Army, just like Child had been downsized out of television. Child's books (13 to date) have gone on to become international best sellers. One of his novels was recently released as a major motion picture starring Tom Cruise as the title character. If the success of this first movie is any indication, Child may have launched a block buster book and movie franchise.[85]

Not everyone is going to become a bestselling novelist. But when you find your vocational life hard aground, look at your own past and see if there is not a recipe for lemonade in your history. I was in a career support group with a fellow who was in his 50s when he lost his job as the Executive Director of his college fraternity.

For a year after he was laid off, Chris foraged around trying to find a new position similar to the one he had lost. The fact that he and his family loved Richmond, Virginia, and had no desire to relocate was a handicap. As a form of self-therapy during his unemployment, he started on a series of home remodeling projects. Earlier in his life, woodworking had been a favorite hobby. He figured he could use his down time to refurbish the cabinets in his kitchen and remodel a bathroom. An excellent craftsman, Newcomer found the work relaxing, refreshing and it gave him a sense of pride. Soon friends and neighbors who saw his work began to ask him to do improvement projects on their homes. Finally, after about 18 months looking for an office job, the light bulb turned on! Craig realized he loved home remodeling work and was making excellent money doing it. He went on to get his contractor's license, hung out his shingle, and what was once a hobby is now a prosperous and rewarding business.

Child's and Newcomer's experience, and that of many other workers, is that the outcome of a bad experience can actually be quite positive.

Analytical Hindsight

They say hindsight is 20/20. Before you dismiss this as an obvious but somewhat useless mantra to get you through tough times, consider this: When the freight train of your career goes off the rails and you can't figure out what's gone wrong or how to fix it, it may help to resort to some analytical hindsight. Use this form of developmental thinking to review your experience and history and identify positives and negatives without any reference to where they point. We often start with a hypothesis, and then keep only the data that supports our particular hypothesis. Sometimes collecting random points of data from our own work experience, while holding off on any hypothesis, can give us a totally different picture than the one we've been using to guide our career. This process lets the old facts tell you a new story.

In his early 40s, Brett Fuller lost his position as a regional manager for a chain restaurant in Texas. Honestly, he wasn't heart-broken; the restaurant business paid well, but had become a dismal grind. Fuller knew the passion was missing, but had no idea what to do next. Unemployed for over a year, he and his family cut their budget, sold their house, and moved into a smaller rental, downgraded to a used car and were still feeling the pinch of a shrinking budget. Yet when the chance came for Brett to join four friends or a short-term mission trip to Uganda, his wife insisted he go. During the course of the trip, he was introduced to a pastor in Kahudu who had organized a group of about 70 women, most of them widows, who made baskets and beads out of varnished recycled paper to sell to tourists. Unfortunately, there wasn't much of a local market for these products.

Fuller was blown away by the quality and beauty of the finished products. He eagerly asked the pastor if he could take some necklaces home to share with his family and friends. When he returned to Texas and unloaded his suitcase full of necklaces, everyone who saw them reacted with delight and wanted to buy some. Soon his phone was ringing with requests for beads. He sent the money for the beads back to the pastor in Uganda, and before he knew it, he was running a business, ordering beads and baskets from the widows' cooperative and selling them to jewelry and craft stores in Fort Worth. Over the months the business blossomed and grew until Fuller finally realized that this wasn't some side project while he was looking for a real job. In fact it had become his job. Not only did he provide enough income to support his family, his business provided a job for the poor women of Uganda.[86]

Reflection may prove to be one of the most powerful tools in your career development toolkit. Take some time to reflect on your own experiences with a truly open mind. Consider your personality and temperament, and listen to what your experience says about environments that bring out your best. Consider your gifts and how they may impact your career as well as your personal life. Finally, listen to the voice of your own gladness, to the dreams and the passions that set your soul on fire.

In the previous chapters we have considered your **motivations** and **passions**, your **temperament** and your **experience**. Each of these are different levels at which you can conduct an analysis of your special design. Some of these are going to prove more helpful than others. And there are other ways to get insight about what makes you tick and what satisfies your soul. Our job is to at least consider each of these elements. If we invest some thought, a bit of study, and time for reflection, we may be surprised at what directional pointers pop out of the process. One insight may be enough. Or perhaps you will see a number of items begin to come together like viewing a constellation in the night sky.

Chapter 14

Putting It All Together

Over the course of the last 13 chapters we've explored a variety of approaches for helping you find your sweet spot in career and vocation. At this point we want to help you see where we are headed and enable you get a perspective on how you can integrate the diverse elements in your search process.

While we've given you a number of tools, this process isn't about techniques or methodologies. Each of these instruments is a building block which you can use to gradually erect a model of the unique you – the special combination of passion and strengths which together create a three dimensional image of the distinctive person you are. No particular building block or method or process is vital to the recipe. Only if that specific technique is helpful to you, only if it yields insights which make it possible to know yourself better, then you should add that methodology to your individual procedure.

In the journey of building your career, the foundation – your analysis of what makes you unique - ultimately determines your long-term success. If you're going to become all the person you were meant to be in the world of work, it's going to require some trust. **You need to trust the design of your unique person.** You have been made like no one else—and you have been designed with excellence and with a purpose. You're not a mistake! You're unique, you have high value, and you were made to do something better than anyone else. Building your career on any foundation other than trust in your unique design is foolish.

It's a Process, and It Takes Time

Discovering your unique design, your purpose in life, and connecting it to a real-world vocation is a process which takes time. We live in a day when people are often looking for an easy, quick, shortcut to get things done. When we see the Staples Office Supply "Easy Button" commercial, we laugh, but that cuts awfully close to where many of us live. You and your career are worth investing in. Shortcuts are only going to lead you into dead-end roads and disaster. Unless you want your work life to be a sequence of disappointments, be prepared to be patient with the process. Be patient with investing in yourself, step by step, until you find work which really makes you come alive. It may take a number of steps, and you may have to adjust course along the way, but if you patiently keep after it, success in the marketplace can be yours.

Orville Redenbacher was raised on a farm near Terre Haute, Indiana. When he was a kid, each night his dad would pop a batch of popcorn in a long-handled wire popper over the fireplace. At the age of ten, Orville planted an acre of popcorn as a 4-H project. Year after year he tried to improve this strain of popcorn. After attending Purdue University, he and Charlie Bowman founded Chester Hybrids, a farm that produced fertilizer and hybrid seeds. He spent most of his adult life doggedly pursuing his dream, trying to improve his Red Bow variety of popcorn and trying to get retailers to buy it, without much success. At the age of 63, he was ready to give up. God may have given him the talent to grow better popcorn, but he didn't seem to be able to sell it.

Before quitting his life-long dream, he made one last attempt by seeking help from a marketing counselor in Chicago. The consultant told him to call the popcorn "Orville Redenbacher's Gourmet Popping Corn" and to package it with his face on the label. Redenbacher thought he'd wasted $13,000 on bad advice. But before he threw in the towel, he packaged a production run exactly as the consultant had advised, and shipped a case to Marshall Fields Department Store in Chicago. The rest is history—his unique premium brand of popcorn took off! Within six years the brand had captured a third of the popcorn market in the U.S. It's still the number-one selling popcorn brand in America.[87]

While you're engaged on this journey to find your sweet spot, it is imperative you remain open and flexible. Don't get stressed out about hitting the bull's-eye on every effort. Especially in the first half of your career, you will find a significant number of jobs that teach you a lot more about what you don't like than they teach you about your sweet spot. Whenever you run into a dead end, or you learn something you don't like about a particular kind of job or workplace, you need to remember you've taken an enormous educational step closer to where you will be working in your sweet spot. We simply need to relax and enjoy the experience. Even when we make a mistake, what we learn from that mistake can be used for good purpose.

Don't let your ego get in the way of finding your sweet spot -- that place where you are really happy and productive. Not everyone could or should grow up to be the CEO. Some of us, unfortunately, are prone to seek positions which will make us look better in other people's eyes. In a culture that's enamored with fame, it's easy to be blinded by the flashy, high-profile positions around us. Others of us are simply competitive—we envy the success and positions of others, and we aspire to be like them. Yet each one of us as a unique person. We don't need to compete; we need to seek to become our unique self, thereby finding success and satisfaction.

Build on Your Strengths

Identifying and understanding how to use your strengths is a critical step to appreciating the unique competencies nature has built into you. Your personal strengths—whether they're gifts, a natural talent, a unique experience, an area of interest, or your particular personality—are all vital components of what gives you the ability to excel in a particular field or a specific kind of task. You can only build a successful career on the unique strengths you have been given. If you're not building on your personal strengths, you're probably headed in the wrong direction. Build on your strengths.

The Hedgehog Concept

In researching how companies move from being good to becoming great, business professor and author Jim Collins discovered three overlapping areas that produce what he named the Hedgehog Concept. This is simply a fresh term to identify the focused place—your sweet spot—where you can be most productive and have the most impact. To quote Collins, "A Hedgehog Concept is a simple, crystalline concept that flows from deep understanding about the intersection of the following three circles: what you can be the best in the world at, what drives your economic engine, and what you are deeply passionate about."[88]

Collins suggested this concept could be used by an individual as a guide to their work life, so long as it meets these three tests.

First, you are doing work for which you have a genetic or God-given talent.... Second, you're well paid for what you do.... Third, you are doing work you are passionate about and absolutely love to do, enjoying the actual process for its own sake.... If you could drive toward the intersection of these three circles and translate that intersection into a simple, crystalline concept that guided your life choices, then you'd have a Hedgehog Concept for yourself.[89]

I like to start with *passion*. If you don't love what you do, then even if you make a lot of money at it, you'll find it to be a soul-sucking experience. It's all too easy to pick a career because it pays well or is highly respected, then after 40 years of hard labor end up "successful" but empty. As Collins points out, "You can't manufacture passion or motivate people to be passionate about something. You can only discover what ignites your passion and the passions of those around you."[90]

As you'll discover in the next part of this book, unless you're able to develop a high level of excellence in the requirements of your particular profession, you'll have little lasting impact in the workplace. Mere competence is the enemy of finding excellence in your career. Don't let your ego get in the way of an honest evaluation of those things you're really able to excel at. Be brutally honest with yourself. We're not shooting for adequacy, but *superiority*. Ask others in your circle of influence to help you be objective in pinpointing your strengths.

One of my good friends is a guy who has bounced around and tried a lot of professions. He began with an excellent education. Upon graduation, he tried the family business, finance, but got bored with it. He returned to school for an MBA and went into a management training program in a large corporation. At the age of 30, Tommy felt led to leave the business world and launch a non-profit ministry to work for social justice in his home town. While the seven years he ran the non-profit were quite successful, after a spell he was burnt out from all the intense people demands. He took a couple years off to hang out in his basement and write. Then he spent several years launching a new consulting firm. By the time Tommy was in his early 40s, he found himself with a wife and two teenaged children and no real idea what he wanted to do as career for the rest of his life.

Tommy took the courageous step of e-mailing about 35 people he had known over the time since he graduated from college. Some were friends, others work colleagues or people he just knew fairly well from community connections. Tommy asked this question. "As you look back over the time we have known each other, could you tell me how I have added value to our relationship? Do you see any particular strengths in my life which you feel stand above everything else?"

That takes real courage. But asking friends how he adds value and asking about his top strengths really paid off. Tommy got some great feedback and most of it pointed him in one consistent direction. His friends' honest guidance got Tommy off to a fresh start, and he is now enrolled in the top academic program in the country training to be a leadership coach.

The last component of the Hedgehog Principle is the issue of economics. If you happen to be independently wealthy, then perhaps there's little need to worry about how well your work pays. If you're single, Spartan, and able to live frugally, conceivably you can get by on a very low income. Many of us, however, find ourselves in a position of needing to support ourselves and other dependents, and thus we require a higher level of income. In most instances you'll discover a combination of your passion and your best skills can be applied in a variety of ways, each of which produces a different level of cash flow.

If, for example, your giftedness lies in the area of teaching, there are multiple applications for that skill. You could drag your soapbox down to the Boston Common on Sunday afternoons and climb up and preach your heart out. There's no financial remuneration, but perhaps some personal satisfaction. Or you could teach an adult Sunday school class in your congregation. Like my wife, your passion could be for children; teaching in an elementary school classroom may best suit you. If your skillset allows it, and your economic needs are higher, you could get a day job as a marketing manager and teach evening business courses as an adjunct in a community college. A variety of positions are available in corporate human resource departments as a trainer, which would allow you to use your teaching skills and perhaps make better money. Some have found both high income and the ability to control their schedule by going on the road and teaching seminars for an assortment of corporate or academic concerns. A good friend of mine has built an excellent consulting business going into corporate environments and teaching staff personnel a range of skills. This last application provides high dollars and great variety in work environments.

As we strive toward finding a hedgehog concept for ourselves, we need to look to the intersection of these three elements—our passion, what we can do with excellence, and the economic opportunities where we can use our gift. One of the beautiful things about our country is that we have a plethora of potential opportunities for numerous skill sets. If your passion is helping to heal people, and your giftedness led you into nursing, there are many ways you could find unique applications of that gift mix.

You might choose to work as an elementary school nurse. A different personality might feel that an urban emergency room setting is a better fit. I have a friend who's a laboratory nurse, which gives her a higher dose of analysis and a lower dose of people time. Another friend works in a retirement community caring for geriatric patients and their nursing needs. She finds great satisfaction caring for individuals and their families during the last years of life. One of my wife's good friends has turned her nursing into the teaching profession—she works in a college teaching young nursing students.

Remember, it's not just a question of money; it's about the opportunity to find a good fit for your passions, your personality, and your strengths. Any particular set of giftedness and passion can be applied in multiple environments to yield personal satisfaction, career success, and significant impact in your community.

Enjoy the Journey

Remember that all this is a progression, a journey. It takes time. There are no shortcuts or easy answers. James Collins found in his research that for the few corporations who were able to identify a Hedgehog Principle, which helped them break through to greatness, it took an average of four years of hard work to do so. He reminds us, "It took Einstein ten years of groping through the fog to get to the theory of special relativity, and he was a bright guy."[91]

We need to be willing to persist. Keep asking questions, and keep asking for feedback from those who know you best. Revisit, review, evaluate, analyze, boil down, and summarize your thoughts. It's a lot like making maple syrup: it takes 40 gallons of sap to boil down to one gallon of maple syrup. In the same way it takes a great deal of time, questioning, reflecting, and evaluation to find your sweet spot.

Once you have some notions about what makes you tick, the second part of this puzzle is figuring out the specific kind of environments which are receptive and even hospitable towards your unique strengths and passion. In the following section we are going to dig into the practical -- the actual, concrete steps you can take to land a job that moves you toward your sweet spot. We're going to look at corporate culture and show you how organizational culture can make or break your experience in the workplace. The better you can anticipate and understand the culture before you accept a job, the fewer mistakes you'll make by placing yourself in an inhospitable environment. Once you've landed a position, your attitude and its manifestations in your day-to-day work situation can make or break your ability to grow a successful career.

In addition, strong careers are always built on relational capital -- so we're going to lay out strategies and tactics for you to maximize the people connections you have in the marketplace. Finally, a successful career is only one component of a fulfilling life. Work needs to be integrated in the context of the rest of your life to achieve balance, both personally and professionally.

Section Three

Finding a Job You Can Love

Chapter 15

Landing the Job -- Part I

Now we want to dig into the practical question of how you can land the job you want. Let me assure you, everything we have covered so far is necessary if you're going to land a job you love. The foundational issues we have covered in Chapters 9 through 13 are critical for you to be able to identify, obtain and fully develop a job or career which gives you the fulfillment you desire.

If you are just dipping into this book at this point hoping to get some action points for your job seeking strategy, I would urge you to go back and begin your reading at Chapter 9 so you don't end up landing a job which leads you in the wrong direction or proves painful and disappointing. Nothing is truer than this little slogan: "If you aim at nothing, you're sure to hit it."

This past week I had the disconcerting experience of having lunch with a friend who told me this story. "Early on in high school, I decided I wanted to be a doctor. I've invested four years in medical school, four years in residency, and now I'm seven years into private practice, although this is essentially my first real job out of school. At the age of 37, I find myself with a wife, three kids, a mortgage, two car payments and a job which I am not convinced is a really good fit for my skills and temperament. I'm thinking I need to get some serious career counseling." Wow! This just emphasizes the point that it is much better to begin the self-exploration process, as early as possible, and not just assume, "Oh, everything will work out."

The place to begin in your strategy to land the job your heart longs for is with the Hedgehog Principle. If your life had a strategic plan like a corporation, your Hedgehog Principle would be the Mission Statement of "Corporation You." In a corporate strategic plan, the Mission Statement is the end result the organization hopes to obtain by its efforts in the world. In a similar vein the Hedgehog Principle serves the same purpose in organizing and focusing your vocational life. The intersection of the three elements of the Hedgehog Principle: your passion, your key strengths, and your economic goals, is where you hope your career will take you. Each job you obtain during your career should take you incrementally closer to this missional end described by your Hedgehog Principle. As the late business guru and author Steven Covey taught in *Seven Habits of Highly Effective People*, it is critical to begin with the end in mind.

The Practical Results of Passion

Christoph Eschenbach is the world-class conductor who leads the National Symphony Orchestra in Washington DC. As you would expect, Eschenbach has a passionate attachment to music. Not simply because of his vocation, but because he believes it saved his life. Born in Breslau, Germany, in February 1940, his mother died giving birth to him. His father was killed several years later for resisting the Nazi regime. A grandmother took him in and moved out of Germany when the Russians took over. They bounced around refugee camps in Central Europe where his grandmother died of typhus during the worst winter of the century. Of 60 refugees sharing the room with Christoph and his grandmother, all but the 6-year-old boy died from the disease. When a distant cousin rescued him from the camp, he was "sick with typhus, suffering from skin diseases, and lice and was too traumatized to say a word. He did not speak for more than a year."

His adoptive mother was a piano teacher, and Eschenbach remembers lying in bed in his new home hearing his mother play the piano and sing. Bach, Beethoven, Rachmaninoff, Chopin, and Schumann. "I was just mesmerized," Eschenbach says. His new mother taught him to play the piano. He also took violin lessons at the Hamburg Conservancy. While he became a prodigy as a concert soloist on the piano, Eschenbach found the piano left him feeling lonely. Wanting to be in dialogue with other musicians musically, led him into his career in conducting.[92]

Not everyone has as dramatic a story as Eschenbach. But even people with a normal background can have dreams which lead them to extraordinary accomplishments. Tom Fatjo, for example, was a prim and proper graduate of Rice University. To the outside observer, Fatjo seems like a fairly typical, quiet, patient, you might even say pedestrian accounting executive. His 9-to-5 job allowed him to live a predictable, but perhaps boring life. He and his family resided in the Willowbrook development in the western suburbs of Houston, Texas. But Tom had a problem -- it was this reoccurring dream. A dream he could not seem to shake. Residents of his development had been wrestling with the city government for years over garbage pickup at the back door of their homes. While numerous solutions had been attempted, none succeeded and the garbage was starting to pile up, as were the flies, and the smells in the East Texas heat. Tom kept dreaming this crazy idea that he could solve the problem.

Eventually, he acted on the dream and purchased a garbage truck as a side business to supplement his day job as an accountant. That decision led to a 10-year adventure which is an unbelievable story in itself. Eventually, Tom's solution to his neighborhood garbage problem evolved into the largest solid waste disposal company in the world, Browning Ferris Industries, Inc., which today has annual sales of in excess of $500 million dollars.[93]

Knowing Your Strengths

It's not enough to know your dreams. According to the Hedgehog Principle, great careers are also built on a unique set of strengths which you possess and can happily contribute to your vocation. For example, lots of young adults decide to become lawyers. Why? It pays well and is prestigious. That flawed thinking is probably why there are so many unemployed lawyers and poorly paid lawyers in the United States today. There are lots of ways to practice law – only a few of which may fit your strengths.

If you like to make an argument, are quick on your feet, and good with your gab – then litigation might be an appropriate line of work. Researching deeds would drive you batty. My father-in-law was a history major at Princeton before he became a lawyer. He practiced family law – lots of real estate closing, wills, and estate settlements. Sounds boring, but he enjoyed the work. Researching the history of a property was just another history puzzle for him.

Perhaps you have an exceptional gift of reading clues about people from observation. That being your unique strength, you would be happier as a jury consultant, rather than some other path in the legal field. It may be that you enjoy managing the nuances of public policy and how legislation affects people in various industries or walks of life. Perhaps a career in government service in the bowels of a policy making unit, would be a good application of your key strength. As you can see, every line of work has a multitude of types of positions and applications of skills which may or may not fit you. It's up to you to figure out how you are wired. What are your top five strengths and how might those be used in any field you are interested in? If you don't figure it out, no one will do it for you.

Knowing yourself can empower you to resist unwarranted influence from others who may try to push you in different directions from where your heart really wants to go. Kate Carrara grew up in a Philadelphia family where everyone was a lawyer. Kate says, "My father's a lawyer; my grandfather's a lawyer; so I'd went to law school and spent six years working as a trial lawyer for my family's firm....I found the work was insanely boring." Kate began to plot her career switch. In July 2009 she gave up her high-paying job, sold her house, her car, and her diamond engagement ring, and started *Buttercream*, a mobile cupcake shop. After a year Carrara's growing business has one vending truck, five employees, and is making a profit of $100,000 a year. Kate not only loves her job as Philadelphia's *Cupcake Lady*, but is now looking into expanding the business into kiosks, retail, and wholesale outlets.[94]

Economic Engine

The last element of the Hedgehog Principle is the economic engine which drives or supports your career. Passion is great and being able to use your unique strengths is tremendously fulfilling, but if you have not identified vocational opportunities that actually pay you to apply your strengths and passion, you might consider making it a hobby.

I (Bruce) love the outdoors. I am passionate about being afield. I love nature, hiking, and canoeing. I enjoy many forms of fishing, hunting, and trapping. Camping thrills me as much today as when I was a kid. I think it's wonderful to sleep out under a starlit sky. I find even home based outdoor activities like gardening or watching birds fascinating. Recently, I read an article about becoming a professional woods bum. The author describes how simple it would be to quit your day job, move back into the woods, build a simple tar paper shack, and live off the fruit of your recreational activities. He suggested growing a large garden, hunting & fishing for your food, running a trap line and selling the furs for cash income. These and other tactics are proposed to enable you to get off the grid and live in harmony with Mother Nature. Then the author proceeded to give examples of people who had done just that.

I considered this possibility (for about two minutes) and decided it would never work for me. The truth is, I am simply not that proficient at my outdoor activities to support myself with them. For example, last time I went small game hunting I took 18 shots and managed to collect a rabbit and a woodcock (a migratory game bird a little bigger than a morning dove). Okay, that was worse than usual, but I still had an enjoyable afternoon afield. The last three times I went trout fishing, all I got was cold and wet. Reality therapy tells me I'm much better off to keep my day job as a management consultant and limit my outdoor activities to pleasure trips. I'm quite happy to simply take my gun for a walk in the woods; why try to turn it into a job?

If you love the outdoors and you are serious about earning a living at it, there are a variety of economic opportunities which will allow you to chase a living outdoors. Fishing guides can earn anywhere from $20,000 to $35,000 per year. Hunting guides make a little less, $15,000 to $20,000, perhaps due to shorter seasons. Outdoor writers, taxidermists, and gunsmiths all start out at the low end of the range ($15,000 - $20,000) but depending on success, have more long-term potential. Working as a game warden or forest ranger both require significant education, but typical starting salaries are higher - between $30,000 and $45,000.[95]

Target Your Prospects

Once you have a firm grasp of your passions, strengths, and potential economic opportunities, you have the core around which you can begin to develop a career strategy. Understanding yourself and what elements need to be part of your vocational future are the bedrock upon which to begin to refine your search for specific jobs. As Ralph Waldo Emerson once said, "Self trust is the first secret of success."

Now that you understand something of your own uniqueness, it's time to begin researching potential opportunities. You need to get to work identifying industries that hire potential variants of the job you're looking for. If your goal is to be a wordsmith and work in some area of writing, there are literally thousands of different firms and organizations that you could let do that and earn a living. Your research should look for industries that hire the skillsets you see as part of your strong suit.

While our country is showing signs of recovering from the Great Recession of 2007 – 2009, the recovery is uneven. Some industrial sectors, like telecommunications and utilities, are continuing to decline and reduce their head count. Over our recent history, small businesses, those with fewer than 100 workers, show the most job growth and account for two thirds of job creation in the US. For example, large businesses (500 or more employees) hired 17,000 workers in March 2011. Mid-sized businesses accounted for 82,000 new hires and the smallest firms (fewer than 50 employees) produced 102,000 new jobs in the same time period. In general, smaller, younger, newer companies are producing the most job growth, so don't be afraid to research and target these companies.[96]

Once you've identified industries, next you should begin to target organizations, specific companies, or even geographic areas which have a high number of these kinds of opportunities. If you've decided that your one true love is writing country ballads, it may make sense to target Nashville, the home of country music in America, as a geographic location which would tend to have more of the specific kinds of jobs you are interested in. Interested in working in an American vineyard? Then you might take a look at Napa Valley, California. Find yourself attracted to creative hardware developments in the field of electronic information technology? Seattle, Washington, San Jose, California, or Austin, Texas, might be good locations to focus your research. Have skills in petroleum engineering? You might want to focus on the explosive growth produced by the fracking of natural gas supplies in the Marcus Shale Belt across portions of Ohio, Pennsylvania, and western New York.

Location is a factor you ought to consider during this research phase. Particular types of jobs might be very difficult to find in one location, and quite abundant in another. For example, teaching positions in elementary and secondary school systems are very difficult to come by in the greater Pittsburgh, Pennsylvania, area. I'm not sure why, perhaps it's because of the large number of universities and technology firms which bring extra spouses into the teaching market. Whatever the reason, this was the case even before the recent contraction caused by the Great Recession of 2007–2009. If you live in Brooklyn, New York, or in any other major urban center on the East Coast, you know that many school systems are contracting and laying off teaching staff rather than hiring new teachers. If you have your heart set on teaching you might want to look at North or South Dakota, two states that offer a wide variety of open teaching positions, a very affordable quality of life, and many of the community amenities American families' desire.

National data about your area of interest is just that – a large generic picture which may not prove true in your section of the country. The national research claims there is soaring demand for high school teachers of math and sciences. A good friend graduated from college with a burning desire to teach high school biology. In spite of wonderful educational credentials, Jackie discovered the areas of the Northeast where she lived were over populated with teachers and had few openings for new biology teachers. Being a person of real courage and firm conviction, Jackie widened her search. Eventually she landed a plum position teaching sciences in a private school in China, a country she had always wanted to visit. Over the course of eight years, she taught Biology and several other subjects to an academically advanced population of high school students in two different schools in central China. In addition to learning the Chinese language and culture, she was able to travel extensively throughout Asia and Europe on weekends and holidays. When Jackie decided to return to the States, she discovered, much to her surprise, that certain prestigious public high schools in the Washington, DC, suburbs actively recruit science teachers who have significant experience teaching international students. Instead of a scarcity of jobs, she found herself the subject of a bidding war between schools anxious to recruit her to their staff!

Specific business organizations often provide multiple job opportunities in particular kinds of disciplines. That's why it's critical to look at individual companies during your research phase. If you're interested in consumer packaged goods marketing, Procter & Gamble, Johnson & Johnson, General Foods, H.J.Heinz, Kraft, Gillette, Colgate-Palmolive, and Nestlé's would all be business organizations which would offer a wide variety of these type of positions. Many of the classic consumer marketing departments in these blue-chip businesses have internship programs and entry-level training programs which are used to develop large numbers of beginner marketing staff for these companies. If you can get in on the ground floor, you learn the basics of this profession from some of the best people in the business. Even if you don't earn much money in one of these entry-level slots, having a couple of years of marketing at Procter & Gamble is the equivalent of having an MBA from Harvard Business School to hiring managers looking for marketing staff.

Organizational culture matter…a lot! As you are researching companies, you may find individual organizations with values and organizational culture that are so attractive to you to decide you would like to work for them in any position. Focus on the interests you have identified as strengths, but keep applying even if there are no posted positions in your area. There was a time in IT where Microsoft or Hewlett-Packard would be that organization. Currently Apple or Google might be the business of choice to invest your career in if you want to be in a strong culture company that provides a unique working environment in the IT industry.

Strong culture companies can be exciting places to work. Stonyfield Farms, for example, located in Londonderry, NH, began 25 years ago with two friends and seven cows. Today it is the third largest yogurt company in the US with sales over $400 million per year. Stonyfield, which sells organic yogurt, was a green company before going green was hip. Over the years it has continued to innovate on many fronts and have been real trailblazers for the healthy production of dairy products. It's a brand noted for innovation, for charitable giving, for ethical business practices, and I'm sure it does not hurt that it's located in beautiful New Hampshire. If you ever wanted to apply your business skills in a progressive, green company which shares many of your values – Stonyfield would be the place to dig in for a long and satisfying career.

If you're in college, use your school's Career Center to help you with your research. Even if you're not a student or graduate, a local university may allow you to use the research database systems on campus for free or for a modest fee. Your local library may also have resource tools to get you into databases which will help you with this research. Online tools like CareerSearch or Vault may be useful in this task. If a government agency offers workforce training or resources, they also may be a good source to use to leverage your research into broader pools of information about jobs, companies, and industries. Check out the Occupational Outlook Handbook at http://statsbls.gov/oco/.

"Majoring in the field that you're targeting isn't enough," says Leslie Mittler, president of Priority Candidates, which helps prepare graduates for the job hunt. "Few graduates even pick up a newspaper," Mittler says." They should be reading newspapers, periodicals, relevant books and watching cable TV shows which address issues in areas of their interest."[97] These additional steps in the research process will not only expand your network of potential opportunities and put you in touch with other people and organizations who can help you land a job, they will prepare you for the interview process. Being conversant with current events in the business or field you're interested in will show potential employers you have a passion for their industry.

This background research is one area where the Internet can truly be helpful. When you come across the name of a company, go online and find that company's website. You can learn a lot about the organization and the people who work for it. The company website, Facebook page, Twitter updates and the profiles of employees that appear on LinkedIn will tell you a lot about the organizational culture of the company. They may also provide up-to-the-minute listings of new job openings. You should also check comments by past and current employees on job oriented websites for more background information about relevant issues. Glassdoor.com is one such resource.[98]

Job search websites like (www.indeed.com) can be helpful in the research process. Don't however rely on them to turn up a job for you. Over half of all positions are never posted, let alone advertised on a job search site. Look for companies who might offer the kinds of jobs you are seeking. Target that company – build a network of contacts inside the company who can introduce you to others and alert you to pre- advertised positions. Then you need to keep shaking the trees in your networks until an appropriate job falls out.

Databases and search engines can be very useful for finding organizations that may hire people in the job categories you're interested in. Use the Web for preliminary research. Many of these search engines are geographic in nature so you may turn up businesses in your target market you simply weren't aware of. Who knew Scholastic Books was headquartered outside Richmond Virginia? Who knew Johnson & Johnson had a major facility in Manchester, New Hampshire? Database searches can open up myriads of companies and employment opportunities that might have real potential for your search. The websites of the local Chamber of Commerce can be a great resource for identifying major employers in the region.

Crafting the Resume and Cover Letter

The research you've been doing on the line of work you're interested in, the industries in which it's used, the locations in which it's most prevalent, and the specific companies which have multiple opportunities in this specific line of work – this work is much like the consumer market research used in positioning a brand. Our objective is to get a coherent understanding of what our potential employers' value, what they are looking for in employees, and finally what attributes they seek in the position you hope to fill in their firm. Combine this intelligence about potential employers with what you've learned through your Hedgehog Principle exercise.

The result is a focus on your essentials as a brand, which you are offering employers. An exercise that can help you focus on the fundamentals of your brand (and a good job fit) is to put your resume on a 3 x 5 card. By way of example, here is mine:

Bruce Dreisbach

Strategic Business Builder
- Identifies key leverage points to grow the business. Creative strategies / tactics.
- Recruit people / resources to implement.
- Manages effective execution of the plan.
- Produces 30% increase in sales, 20% increase in profits, 15% reduction in costs.

Once you have your index card-sized resume, you're ready to write your full-page version. It is absolutely vital that you start with the job you hope to land in mind. What skills does it require? What experience and education? What length resume is acceptable in this industry for your level? The majority of employers prefer a one-page resume. Education is the main exception to this rule. I have seen professionals with 20 years of experience adequately represent their skills in one page. The key is to focus on your accomplishments rather than a litany of each responsibility. Think about it—you and the guy next to you were assigned the same job, you did it well and he did it poorly. You could both write the same phrase about "responsible for x, y, and z." This does you no favors—you want to distinguish your resume from his. Consider how you can convey the impact that you made and the value you added in each setting.

Based on your knowledge of the job and the industry requirements, take stock of your experiences to date. Look for groupings—perhaps professional experience, community involvement and education. Or if your work history in the field you are targeting is limited, you might organize your resume by relevant and other experience, which allows you to include non-paid involvement in the relevant experience section, furthering highlighting what you can offer your potential employer. Select a consistent format being sure to include the name of the organization, your title, and the dates you were there in the same place relative to the next entry.

Using bold, italics, underline or capitals can help set off this important information. An entry might start like this:

Project Manager, **Tutenkaman, Inc.**, July 2010-present

Writing the job descriptions may be the most difficult part. Focus on accomplishments, rather than responsibilities. Start each phrase using an action verb and avoid using "I," "me," and "my." Ask yourself questions like: How much? For whom? Why? How? To what end? What timeframe? What happened? Whenever relevant, quantify and qualify. For instance, let's say you wrote a report. A bullet that reads, "Responsible for writing a report" doesn't tell me much. Instead write:

Project Manager, **Tutenkaman, Inc.**, July 2010-present

- Independently wrote a report on quality management teams to update senior leadership team on latest developments in the field
- Researched latest developments in quality management teams using journals and 15 interviews with project managers
- Conducted one-hour oral presentation of findings to senior managers
- Report persuaded management to begin using new team design that increased efficiency 15% during the first six months of its implementation

Be sure the accomplishments you highlight demonstrate the skills the employer is seeking for that position. If you have not stated it in your resume, the employer does not know you have that skillset. It's even okay to adjust your phrasing to reflect the terms used in the job description or industry jargon. Be sure to have someone read over your resume once you've written it—watch out for typos! That's the first place an employer will look to see if you pay attention to detail. They are trying to find reasons to throw out some resumes. Don't give them a reason!

Your resume is your one-page advertisement of skills and abilities, specifically targeted toward the job or industry you seek. Whenever you have the opportunity, take the time to write a cover letter as well. The resume is all about you—the job description is all about your potential employer. A well-written cover letter builds a bridge between the two, demonstrating why you are the perfect fit for this position at this organization. Typically a one-page business letter, this is your chance to say what you might want to if you were meeting this employer face to face. Do not repeat your resume or the job description—they already have both of those. Tell them why you are interested in this position at this company and what you have to offer. The letter needs to show the employer what's in it for them, not what's in it for you. When they finish reading, you want them to want to meet you and hear more about what you propose. Remember, the employer has a problem. The company has a job that needs to be done, and they don't have anyone to do it. Present yourself as a solution to their problem. Above all, your resume and cover letter are crafted to get you an interview. It's the interview that gets you the job.

Networking

Of all the things that we share with you in this chapter on landing the job, this section on networking is one of the most important. Once you clearly understand your Hedgehog Principle and you have strong insights into what your potential employer is looking for, networking is the major bridge between where you are and where you'd like to be vocationally. If you only take one piece of advice away from this chapter, the value of networking is the one I suggest you capture.

Networking is critical simply because most jobs are filled through networking. Career professionals estimate between 70% and 80% of all jobs are filled through networking. Tapping into your circle of friends, family, professors, previous employers, civic organizations, alumni of your university, a job club, the Chamber of Commerce, and other sources of relationships is most often the means of landing the position in which you are interested.

Think about finding a job being a lot like finding a date. Pretend you're about 25, single, and you're interested in settling down. You'd like to meet a nice person and explore a long-term relationship that is mutually beneficial. Where would you start? Many people meet their significant others through friends or friends of friends. Your best friend knows you're interesting and meets someone who they suggest you might be compatible with. They invite both of you to an event to meet each other; one thing leads to another, and down the road is happily ever after! This is networking. Most people meet their partners through friends because there is a vetting process automatically built in. If your friend knows this person, you already know you have certain things in common. You have someone to vouch for the character of the person. You are pretty sure they aren't an axe-murderer.

The same is true for networking in a professional context. An employer would much rather hire someone who is somewhat of a known entity. After all, you will likely spend more time with your employer and co-workers than with your partner in any given week. You will all be happier if it's a good match.

Unfortunately, the convenience of the Internet has led many job searchers to the false conclusion that the best way to find a job is to use appropriate search engines or online sites. Richard Bolles, author of the perennial bestselling career guide *What Color Is Your Parachute?*, thinks the Internet can encourage laziness, especially in people who are not inclined to work hard. "You are rescued by the thought, 'I'll post my resume and while I sleep, they'll match it with a vacancy and the next morning I'll get up and there's a job,'" Bolles said. He believes there are always job openings, though they turn up more often through face-to-face conversations than on websites. He encourages people to knock on doors and visit old friends to find out about potential openings. Bolles lists "the least effective ways to find work -- including responding to an ad in a professional or trade journal, which he calculates as having a 7% chance of success. For Internet ads, it's 10%, according to his calculation."[99]

The vast majority of positions are simply never listed in typical media. This includes the Internet, but also newspapers, professional journals, radio, and other common listing agencies. Approximately half of all jobs are filled before they even get posted. Many positions are discussed, shaped, and advertised in the manager's mind before pen is ever put to paper. During this phase of developmental thinking, the job creator is often searching his mental file cabinet for potential candidates to fill the position.

Or this process takes place verbally in discussions between people who are involved in the hiring decision. At the end of the job development process, only about a third of open jobs are actually posted anywhere.

Even when jobs are listed, you have to recognize there is an enormous amount of competition for each publicly listed position. Donald Asher, a career and education consultant based in Nevada, calls "pursuing posted openings a waste of time: no matter how perfect you think you are for that job, someone who is more perfect already has it," he says. "It's hard to stand out in a pile of thousands of resumes," Asher writes with bluntness. "You need to get out of that pile." To show you how difficult these public listings are, Asher once made a bet with a colleague and ran an ad that said, "Hard work, bad boss, low pay. Fax your resume." Seventy-two people applied for this job before he ran out of fax paper according to Asher. [100]

In this day and age you often have to fill out the online job application to be officially hired, as companies must comply with certain legal guidelines regarding employment. However, if you can couple your written application with real-live relationships, or networking within the organization, you are far more likely to be pulled out of the pile and offered an interview. In the interview it's up to you to make the case for why the company should choose you for the position.

Powerful Communication

Perhaps one of the most powerful aspects of networking is the fact that face-to-face relationships do a much better job of communicating who you are as a person. Researchers have determined that 55% of communication takes place through the body language of the two people who are relating. Another 38% of the message is delivered through your tone of voice. Only 7% of communication is delivered by the content of your message. Think about the implications of this! If I send you my resume through the Internet, via an e-mail, or even in a typewritten form on paper, you're only getting 7% of the message that I'm trying to deliver about who I am and my interest in your organization's position. So when you search for a job on the Internet, you not only have to deal with the intense competition from thousands of others who are searching online, you must realize that the employer is getting a very little impression of who you really are and what you can offer his organization.

When an acquaintance hands your resume to a potential employer, they are standing in as a witness to your character and capabilities. In essence they're saying, "Hey Jack, you ought to take a look at my friend Stan. He would be a great addition to your team." You cannot get that kind of recommendation from an Internet application.

When an employer is considering a person as a potential hire, one of the major factors in considering your application is that they like you. It's that simple. This is the reason most commercial sales are made -- the buyer likes the salesperson. And part of that process of liking you involves trusting you. The best way for an employer to figure out if they like you and if they think you could be a good fit for their culture is having a face-to-face conversation. During the process of networking, the better known you become in a wide circle of relationships, the more likely you are to find a good connection. Richard Bolles says that this is one of the two most important things in actually landing a job. He agrees that objective measures and skills count, but he thinks just as important are your personality, emotional connections, charm, and other intangible factors.

By having accurately described your job and career objectives, researched the desires of potential employers, and begun working your personal network of friends, you are now in a position to see things really begin to happen in your job search. The tactic that unleashes your strategic groundwork is a simple but profoundly powerful method known as the informational interview. It's not a job interview, but it is the interview which produces the best jobs, for the majority of seekers, most of the time.

Chapter 16

Landing the Job -- Part II

Informational Interviews

The most powerful tool in your networking arsenal is the informational interview. Richard Bolles popularized this concept many years ago in his best-selling book *What Color is Your Parachute?* Think about the time when you were considering colleges or other schools you might want to attend. Perhaps you went to visit the campuses of the schools you were considering. Do you remember some of the perceptions you formed from the print materials or websites before you went? Once you arrived on campus, did your perceptions shift? Did you start to get a sense of whether you would fit in there, feel comfortable, and be able to succeed? Informational interviews are to jobs what campus visits are to college.

On the surface, an informational interview is designed to elicit more detailed information about a particular kind of career or company. It consists of getting the name and phone number of an insider in an organization who may be in a company you're interested in working for, or who works in the specific type of industry or career you're interested in. You call, introduce yourself (and your referral source if there is one) and ask if you could have 20 minutes to interview them about working in their field. You emphasize their acknowledged expertise in this field and your interest and enthusiasm to learn more about this field as a potential career. Everyone loves to talk about themselves. People feel important, like their work matters, when you call and ask to hear about their journey. And remember—when you find the job you love, people will call you to ask how you got there too!

Let's say you've just earned a Master's degree in Communication with an emphasis in Sports Public Relations. You would love to land an entry level job as a PR person for a college sports program. Your Aunt Bessie knows a guy from church who knows somebody at Harvard University who works in the Human Resource Department for Athletics. Your Aunt gets you a name and number and you place a call out of the blue. It goes something like this.

"Hi, my name is Geoff Hines, and I got your name from David Miller (the friend of the friend from church). He says you are one of the most knowledgeable people in the field of collegiate athletics and suggested I call you. I recently graduated from Midwest University with a Master's degree in Communication. During my undergraduate days at Duke, I played Division I basketball and club lacrosse. (Add anything else that might make you appear to have qualifications to go into this line of work.) My interest is in working in the public relations and communications side of college athletics. I was wondering if you would spare me 20 minutes to meet with you and ask some questions about working in collegiate sports. I'd be happy to stop in your office whenever it is convenient for you."

Most people will be happy to grant you 20 minutes of their time. For one thing, they are flattered that someone considers them an expert in their field. Secondly, they are touched because some bright young person, who is interested in their field, bothered to call them to learn more. Assuming the tone of your voice communicates encouraging things about your personality, most people will respond positively to the opportunity to help someone else. We are wired to want to help others, especially if all it takes is 20 minutes of our time and expertise.

When you arrive for the informational interview, come dressed as you would for a professional interview and follow the rules of etiquette for interviewing described below. Bring questions which show you have researched what they do in particular, what their organization does and other industry issues that reflect on the position you are seeking. Good questions on your part will stimulate good conversation; bring a list you are prepared to ask. You don't have to stick to the list, but it will help you if you're nervous and make you look prepared. Be ready to answer questions about your own background, skillsets, and interests. Ask if your contact knows of any positions you might be qualified for? Solicit their advice about where and how you should conduct your job search. Think of this technique as a form of the game of leap-frog. You only need one contact to start, but you need a lead from them to continue the game. Ask if they know anyone else in the field who you might speak to? If there was a particular area that was more interesting to you, mention this and ask for suggestions of people who do such work. Offer to leave a resume and cover letter detailing your search interests.

When you are preparing for your informational interview, create a resume and cover letter based on what you think this person or organization might be looking for in a new hire. These are the documents you ask for feedback on or offer to leave at the end of your informational interview. Suggest that if anyone comes to mind who might be potentially interested in what you have to offer, that your respondent could pass the information along to them. Thank them profusely for taking the time to speak with you. Ask if you can follow up at some point in the future. Remember, there is a basic human impulse to want help a fellow who needs a hand up. People will surprise you with their gracious support and encouragement. It never hurts to ask for help.

Follow Up

When you finish with your informational interview, you should send a thank you note to the respondent. I'm often asked, "Should I send an e-mail or a hand written note?" Do both – an e-mail as soon as you leave the location and a hand-written letter within a week. In both pieces you want to reinforce some of the things you learned from the informational interview. Review some of the strengths you would bring an employer, and ask them to e-mail you any future ideas or leads they may generate. Also take the input from each session and use it to refine and improve your resume, cover letter, and potential search. If they gave you any other contacts in the field, follow up with these folks and seek additional informational interviews.

Feel free to stay in touch, unless they ask you not to. When you're reading newspapers or other periodicals and see items about their organization or their profession, clip them and send them along with a short handwritten note saying, "Recently I read this piece about _____, and I thought you might find it interesting." Best Wishes,

Geoff Hines. If you had a positive informational interview, you might give them a call once a month. Update them on your search and ask if they know of any job leads or people you might contact.

Persistence is critical. While in my (Bruce) first management position, I received an unsolicited resume from a young woman named Katja Beam, a recent college graduate. She was interested in working in publishing, in particular on the marketing side of publishing. I read the resume and cover letter and thought, "This person would make a terrific hire, if I had a position available. But I don't." So I crumpled up the resume and tossed it in the circular file. About a week later I received a phone call from Katja, who again left me with a very favorable impression. However, I told her, to my knowledge, we had no openings in the firm. Yet, I confessed I had "lost' her resume and asked if she would send me a replacement so I could circulate it to other managers.

When her materials arrived, I circulated them to other managers without discovering any entry-level vacancies. After a couple weeks she called again, and I had to relate my lack of success in identifying any openings. This resume also ended up in the trash. Four weeks later Katja called once more. We had an excellent conversation where she filled me in on what she had been doing in her job search, on her continuing interest in working in publishing; particularly in marketing or marketing research. As we concluded, I mentioned to Katja that I had again "mislaid" her resume and was not able to lay my hands on it – would she mind sending me another?

I actually took her next resume and used it as an illustration for a proposal I created for top management about developing a management training program. I suggested hiring a few bright college graduates every year (like Katja) and putting them to work doing the kinds of things we typically hired high school graduates to do and paying them the same rate. Over two years we would assign trainees to each of our three divisions for six months and the last six months of the two-year program they could work for a specific department they were interested in. This program would cost virtually nothing, and would allow us to screen potential long-term recruits for the company for two years. At the end of that time, we could either decide to hire them full time or simply let them go at the end of the program. Our "win" would be excellent junior staff members who had been tested and mentored for two years. Those who washed out of the program would have their obligatory two years of experience in an entry-level job, which would help them move forward in their future careers.

I thought this management training idea was brilliant. However, my management was unwilling to take the risk investing in something new. So the third resume went into the trash. A month later Katja was back on the phone giving me a cheerful update on her job search.

Now truly embarrassed, I again asked for a fourth resume, which proceeded to sit on the corner of my desk, letting it gather dust, for about three months, while I dithered about what to do with it. Finally, I was having lunch one day with the manager of the Advertising Department, and I again found myself describing the attributes I thought someone like Katja could bring to our company. My colleague was so impressed by my pitch, that he went back to his office, created a new position, called up Ms Beam, gave her an interview and hired her. This was over 25 years ago and my sources tell me Katja has steadily climbed the management ladder and has enjoyed a long and successful career in the firm. Be persistent – it is the key to success.

Richard Bolles also claims persistence is essential to landing a job. He insists the jobs are out there, that there are always job openings. Finding these openings requires face-to-face conversations. He encourages people to knock on doors and visit old friends to find out about potential openings. Develop new friends and keep expanding your network. Bowles claims that if you devote enough time to your search, you will find the job you're looking for.[101]

Career consultant Donald Asher determined that "even if you have the worst job hunting strategy in the world, you'll find a job soon enough if you spend 40 hours each week on your search." Asher asserts, "Even though most people know looking for a job should be a full-time job in itself, most job seekers act like they are on permanent vacation, devoting a mere six hours a week to finding work."[102]

Informational interviews are the key to finding the job you're looking for. If you haven't had 100 informational interviews with key targets inside of companies that could potentially hire you, you haven't been looking hard enough. On an average day you can probably do three informational interviews with different people. Use the rest of the day to do research to expand your pool of leads -- people, organizations, and creative ideas. Convert those leads into the names of people who could hire you to do the kind of work you're interested in and then work the phones to turn those leads into appointments for future informational interviews. You'll also need time to handle the follow-up work with those you have interviewed -- both correspondence and telephone calls. All of this will take you at least eight hours a day, five days a week. This should be your full-time job until you land in a new position.

Successful Interviewing

Here are a few practical pointers to help you with your interviews. Preparation is critical -- the more you can learn about this company before you go and interview the better. It will help you to converse intelligently about the issues that are of concern to them. It will also help you develop sharp questions so the interviewer knows you have done your homework and are up to speed from the employer's point of view. It doesn't hurt to practice your answers to the questions you think you might be asked, or the way in which you would phrase questions when and if you get a chance to ask. I wouldn't suggest working from notes in the midst of your interview, but the more you practice before hand, the more comfortable and natural you'll be responding during the stress of the interview.

Jack Welch, the famous retired CEO of General Electric, reminds us that interviews are two way conversations. Not only do you want them to learn about you, it's critical that you learn about the people and the organizational culture before you commit to working there. Welch says, "Everything else about the job can be perfect -- the task, pay, location -- but if you do not enjoy your colleagues on a day-to-day basis, work can be torture. This may seem obvious, but I'm surprised at how often I meet people who have taken jobs in companies where they do not share the organization's overall sensibilities. If you join a company where your sensibilities don't fit in, you'll find yourself putting on a persona just to get along. What a career killer -- to fake who you are every day."[103]

While all of us desire to put on our "best selves" during the interview, it is in your long-term interest to be yourself. Be real and be honest. It's a bit like dating. Sure, we put our best foot forward in hopes of making a good impression. It would be nice to "win" the girl or the guy, but then think of the consequences! If you win the guy or girl (or the job) you're going to be married to them for quite some time. That being the case, you would hate to wake up in a long term relationship with buyer's remorse. Both parties really need to be convinced this is a good fit for you to end up with a "win-win" outcome.

Jack Welch shares the story of a recent MBA graduate, "who tripped over the doorjamb on her way into an interview with three executives at a prestigious consulting firm. After scrambling back to her feet, she shook hands with her interviewers, saying, 'And I'm Grace, the ballet teacher.' While the candidate responded with remarkable poise under pressure, the interviewers were much less compassionate. 'None of them cracked a smile, nor did they try to put her at ease after what was obviously an embarrassing moment. She ended up being offered the job; she declined.' 'They saw the real me, and I saw the real them,' she recalls."[104]

Interview Don'ts

There are several things you might want avoid if you hope to have a successful interview. While these might seem obvious to some, clearly not everyone has thought through the implications of their interview behavior. Columnist Michelle Singletary relates a number of faux paus committed by applicants turned up in a recent survey by CareerBuilder.com.

One applicant sat and ate all of the sweets out of candy dish on the manager's desk while trying to answer interview questions. Another person blew her nose and lined up the used tissues on the table in front of her -- perhaps she was just being meticulous? One young man wore a hat to the interview that said, "Take this job and shove it!" - perhaps he was demonstrating his sense of humor. Another young man brought in a copy of his college diploma with a large smear of liquid white out used to add his name to the document.

Other unique approaches to the interview include: One woman arrived with her mother in tow (so she would be sure of arriving on time). Another prospect brought confidential documents from his previous employer. A candidate answered every question only after referring to a detailed binder of notes. One woman revealed her favorite pastime is to walk around in her pajamas all day and do nothing. A young man provided a comprehensive listing of how a previous employer made him mad. Another guy hugged the hiring manager at the end of the interview.

CareerBuilder asked hiring managers what they consider to be the most common interview mistakes: 71% said answering a cell phone or texting during the interview. This is incredibly rude. Sixty-nine percent said dressing inappropriately. Sixty-nine percent don't like it when an applicant appears bored. Sixty-six percent said appearing arrogant is a real turnoff. Sixty-three percent cited talking negatively about a current or previous employer. Finally 59% said chewing gum was unprofessional - an interview turnoff.[105]

Humility May Help

We've given this advice before, but it bears repeating. In a tough job market you may have to start lower than you expect. Kevin Holt, a recent honors graduate with a bachelor's degree in communication has been looking for over six months. He says, "It's daunting. You feel like you're going after everything, and soon there are no more opportunities to even look for." In a case like this where you've applied for hundreds of jobs without success, you might consider applying for an internship. Many firms hire interns who are college graduates. "But Holtz, who had an internship with a marketing director for a pharmaceutical company when he was a student, is now applying for another one while he looks for work. 'Recent graduates are looking for internships to break into an industry and start their career,' says Carolyn C. Wise, senior education editor at Vault.com. 'There are thousands of internships across the country, and they are so diverse.'"[106]

New Mexico State assistant football coach Mike Rutenburg is a Cornell University graduate like his parents. He is hyper smart, highly organized, and driven to accomplish. These traits have earned him the nickname "Stockbroker." And yet, Rutenberg's paycheck ($30,000) is the lowest among the 900 assistants in the NCAA Football Subdivision according to

USA Today research. Growing up in Bethesda, MD, football was all Rutenberg ever wanted to do. He realizes he could make more money working on Wall Street, but his true love is football and he is willing to start out on the bottom to succeed. So now he works about 112 hours a week during the season which works out to $5.58 an hour -- nearly $2 less than New Mexico's minimum wage. His annual salary is $7,402 less than the median household income in Las Cruces County where he lives.[107]

Temping is another alternative strategy to breaking into a tough job market. Professional and blue-collar temporary jobs are being added more quickly than permanent hires in our sluggish economic recovery, according to labor experts. Manufacturing and information technology are two of the areas with the strongest demand for temporary workers. While it's true these jobs offer less stability, the wages tend to be lower, and there are fewer benefits – yet this is chance to get into a company and demonstrate the skill sets that you might bring to their team on a full-time basis. While businesses will continue to be cautious about adding full-time workers, managers are more likely to select new full-time employees from the ranks of temporary workers serving in their firms. Another benefit of temping is the modest positive cash flow it you provides while you continue looking for a full-time job.

The best executive assistant I ever hired was a temporary worker in my company. I (Bruce) had started a new job working as the VP of Marketing for a firm in mid-town Manhattan. One of my first tasks was to find and hire a high level executive assistant. Jacqueline was recommended by the VP of another division, who knew of her work as a temporary secretary in her department. Honestly, this woman had the worst resume I had ever seen! It consisted of job changes (even career changes) every 9 to 10 months for 10 years straight. She had attended 4 colleges (over 10 years) and still had not completed a bachelor's degree. I used to joke with her that she had one year of experience repeated 10 years in a row. Her job history was working against her, but her actual performance in the organization over the past three or four months was outstanding. I took a risk and hired her, trusting her recent performance was the more accurate reflection of her true potential. She not only developed into the best administrative assistant I've ever had, she finally went on and finished her bachelor's degree in marketing (four colleges, 15 years). With four or five years of steady work under her belt, and her college degree completed, Jacqueline landed increasingly responsible positions in marketing management for several blue-chip brands in the New York City area.

Volunteering is another potential way into full-time employment opportunities. Whether you are a stay-at-home parent returning to your career in the workforce, a recent college graduate looking for your first break into the world of work, or a mid-career worker struggling through a period of transition, you might want to think about the role volunteering can play in helping you find your new job. There are lots of organizations, both non-profit and for-profit, that seek volunteers to help their organizations. While volunteering doesn't pay, it does offer a number of benefits. You can have the opportunity to develop functional job skills, experience, and accomplishments you can use to bolster your resume in looking for a paying job. The organization you volunteer for may eventually offer you a full-time paying position. Volunteering is also a great way to expand your network of friends who can help you in your job search. The more people you get out and rub shoulders with every day, the more likely you are to ultimately turn up the paying job you desire.

Suggestions for Mid-Career Transition

If you're in a mid-career transition rather than being at the beginning of your career, should you use a different strategy than we've articulated above? Well, yes and no. Because you already have experience in the workplace, you're really beginning at different place. Our recommendation is that your entry into this job search process is going to be somewhat different, but many of the steps that you take and the actual search will be very similar to what we've described above.

The first thing you need to do is to look at your attitude. **It's important to accept the fact that crisis and change are normal in life.** If you are not changing, you are not living. Think back to when you were graduating from elementary school and being promoted into middle school. You come off the high of being the top dog in the school for a whole year and now you're moving into a new school environment where you are the lowest form of life in the building – mere dirt to be squished between the toes of upperclassman. Sure, that's a scary feeling, but if you survive the process, you too will eventually become an upperclassman. And who would want to spend their entire life living fifth or six grade over and over again? Change and crisis are normal, and they produce good things in your life.

Next, I would recommend that you do a mini strategic plan for your career. The classic SWOT analysis is a good template. Evaluate your career to date. List your **S**trengths, **W**eaknesses, **O**pportunities, and **T**hreats. Is this really the career that you want to be in? Does this type of work or industry have a positive long-term future? Are there other things you'd rather do? Would the investment in additional education or training improve your career prospects?

Retirement writer Kerry Hannon suggests you might try VocationVacation, a Portland, Oregon company that allows paying customers to vacation with working mentors across the country. Clients pay between $500 to $2,000 plus out-of-pocket travel expenses to shadow private investigators, sports announcers, fishing guides, and other "dream job" holders. Research specific areas you have an interest in, if that's different than what you've been doing. Developing a list of wide-ranging alternatives can't hurt during your mid-career transition.[108]

Part of your strategic planning should be an honest evaluation of the long-term prospects for your particular kind of work and the industry that you're in. If, for example, you're a machinist working in the automobile industry, given much of what's been happening over the last few decades, you might want to develop a Plan B. You might decide to get additional training in orthopedics and building artificial limbs. This is a growing industry which uses advanced technology to build and fit artificial limbs and other prosthetic devices. After some education and an apprenticeship you could successfully convert your mechanical skills into a new career with a bright future.

Polly Bangs worked as a social worker until she found herself in a career transition. Her analysis of potential opportunities uncovered an interesting observation. Having worked as a youth counselor in a Portland outreach organization, Polly realized that schools simply didn't offer any job-readiness training classes. In 2007 Holly launched Urban Opportunities

(UO), a work-placement project aimed at low-income, high-risk kids ages 14 to 20. Her non-profit organization partners with a local homeless youth shelter, and Polly leads after school programs at multiple high schools. Her students are referred by counselors and teachers. In cooperation with local businesses she developed her own curriculum and launched a successful fundraising program to support this outreach.[109]

Another sage piece of advice is to "look at what's in your hand." No, we are not going touchy feely on you, we are simply suggesting that you look closer to home for potential opportunities to springboard your new career. When Joe and Amy Sharp of Columbus, Ohio, had their first son, they found themselves dissatisfied with the typical cheap plastic toys that were available in big box stores. Joe, a carpenter, began making simple wooden rattles and blocks. Not only did their son find these toys that fueled imagination fascinating, many of their friends asked for the unique toys for their children as well. When Joe's construction income dropped off, the Sharps decided to open a wooden toy store online through Etsy, a portal designed sell all things handmade. Launched in 2007, within two years, the sales of their handmade wooden toys had risen 600% and is now their full-time occupation.[110]

Hobby to Side Business to Career

Sometimes a hobby you enjoy may turn into a side business and eventually, into a full-time job. Clive Mulley had a good job as an insurance actuarial working for a large company in downtown Baltimore, Maryland. He enjoyed the mathematical aspects of the number crunching in his job, although, when he was honest with himself, he had to admit his work life looked much like the cartoon strip Dilbert. It entailed going in every day to an expansive floor of generic cubicles, sitting in front of your computer screen grinding out numbers, hour after hour, and sat through long boring meetings with generally incompetent managers.

His hobby was renovating buildings. Mulley's twin brother Nigel also lived and worked in Baltimore. When Nigel bought a two flat in a rundown section of town, he convinced Clive to go in on the deal with him. Every evening, after work, the brothers got busy stripping out the old and replacing it with new until their duplex home was not only beautiful, but highly functional. When the triple-decker next door came on the market, Clive and Nigel bought it, fixed it up, and rented it out. This project was so successful they began to look for other buildings which had upside potential. In a few years, they owned and managed a half dozen rental properties in downtown Baltimore. When Clive lost his actuarial job in a company downsizing, he ran the numbers and discovered that he was actually making more money renovating and renting properties than he'd been making in his day job. Delighted with this discovery, he abandoned his career in insurance and became a full-time developer – buying, rehabilitating, and renting urban properties.

Evaluate if Necessary

Evaluation is critical for a mid-career job transition. Clinical psychologist Jessica Schairer suggests you ask, "Do I need a total change of scene, or do I just need a vacation? Do I need to change my whole entire career, or do I just need to change the company I'm working with? Many times, people think the whole industry they are working in is terrible, but it's not. Sometimes you don't have to change your career, you just have to change your company."[111]

Some people do need a radical change. After years of corporate monotony as a database specialist for a large conglomerate in Northern Virginia, Marisa VanDyke was going out of her mind with boredom. "Every day was the same: wake up, go to work, eat dinner, go to the gym, go to bed." So VanDyke tossed a dart at a map of the US. It landed on Montana. She quit her job, sold her condo, packed her car and drove off to Montana. When she got there she decided it wasn't far enough and kept driving until she got to Cooper Landing, Alaska where she snagged a job as a waitress. A few months later she heard about a job at a research station in Antarctica. Marisa applied, was accepted, and two weeks later was landing on an ice strip in minus 80-degree temperatures to start her new career.[112] We are not advocating this approach as a good career search strategy. But in some cases, you have dug such a deep hole in the wrong direction that it is useful to push the clear button and start with a fresh sheet of paper.

Others simply need to "reinterpret" the career they are presently in. Audrey Schafer was vice president of corporate communications at a telecom company in Reston, Virginia. When she was off work, she was addicted to music -- seeing up to six bands a week to quench her thirst for alternative musical sounds. Eventually, she walked away from her high-paying job to start Schaefer Company Communications, her own music marketing firm which she runs out of her home. While she makes a lot less money than she used to, she now goes to concerts for work and sees her kids and her husband a lot more than she did when she was a corporate slave. She says, "When you get to the point where it's more frightening to stay and do the same things over and over again than it is to leap, then it's time to go."[113]

Let me conclude by offering this perspective: Landing the job is not that hard. It involves hard work, but that is different than being intrinsically difficult. If you do your research on yourself and work at it until you can easily articulate what assets you bring to the table, you are halfway there. Then you have to do your research on who is hiring and what they are looking for in your field. If you generate enough leads to do a hundred informational interviews, you will be well on your way to finding a job with real potential.

Think of these informational interviews as being sales calls. Every sales professional knows you have to go out and shake the tree before any fruit falls off. Get out there and hustle. Knock on doors. Have informational interviews. Get the "Nos" out of the ways and soon you will have found a "Yes." You only need one. But before you go out to shake the tree, let's talk about organizational culture.

Chapter 17

Bridging the Gap – Academy vs. Workplace

If you are leaving the academic world for the real world – you have been living on an alien planet. The real world is different. Brace yourself. Evel Knievel, the American stunt rider and daredevil, once attempted to jump the Snake River Canyon in the Skycycle X-2, a hybrid contraption merging together a motorcycle and a steam rocket. He failed in this attempt but survived the jump. For a man who made a career out of insane jumping stunts, who is in the Guinness Book of World Records for having survived the most broken bones in a lifetime (433 to be exact), the Snake River Canyon jump could have been much worse.

For many young adults, the transition from college to the workplace feels a bit like Evel Knievel's attempt on the Snake River Canyon. There is a yawning gap between the world of the academy and the world of work. When you get to the end of your college career and you're about to launch into the adult world of work and individual responsibility, it can feel like you're headed towards the edge of the cliff -- the other side is impossibly far away and the potential drop to the bottom of the canyon is so deep you can't even see it.

There are a number reasons why those who are just entering the workplace, or those who've been on the road of a career for some time, look back at the world of education and wonder if it's an alternate alien universe from the one they're currently living in. There are multiple environmental elements of these two worlds which are dramatically different. Different doesn't mean better or worse, it just means they're different. The shock to the system when transitioning from one world to the other can be a bit like leaping into the northern Maine ocean on a hot July day. The contrast between the 90-degree air temperature and the 50-degree water temperature produces distress on many fronts.

Your introduction to the adult world includes new responsibilities, different lifestyle issues, dramatically dissimilar kinds of relationships, and new social patterns. None of these issues are things the educational process is particularly designed to address and equip you for. My sense is very few parents or families work at preparing their offspring for their introduction into the adult world either. This traumatic transition appears to have been overlooked by most of those who are supposed to be preparing us for adulthood.

We think it would be helpful to alert you to some of the issues which impact your transition from the world of study to the world of work. Being aware of these factors, and preparing yourself for the transition, can enable you to better navigate the rugged terrain as you seek to enter the workplace and independent adult living.

Environmental Differences Are Dramatic

The consistent presence of structure is one of most the most common characteristics of the world of education. Your schooling, beginning in pre-school, through 12 years of elementary and secondary education, and through all levels of study at university, we see a process which is highly organized, guided by adult leaders, and characterized by many discrete and measurable steps. Even the objectives of the schooling process are spelled out clearly. It's to complete assignments, get good grades, and be promoted to the next level. There are numerous rules and expectations, and accountability generally takes place in fairly short cycles.

Then you graduate and prepare to enter the world of work. Facing you is a vast sea of opportunities, choices, and potential decisions which could lead to success or failure. Usually there is very little structure. In fact, you're expected to create your own structure. Unlike all the rules, standards, expectations, guidance and accountability of the educational process - you're left pretty much on your own. Your job is to write the Great American novel with your life, and you've been given a blank sheet of paper. So much for guidance.

"For Olivia, a 22-year-old in Raleigh, North Carolina, the proliferation of opportunities for her career, geographic location, and studies make it more difficult for her to settle any one aspect of her life. 'Some people feel anxious after graduation because they can't think of anything they want to do. If anything, I'm anxious because there are so many things I would like to do,' Olivia says."[114]

You can't predict the future, although you know choices and decisions you make at the beginning of your career may have long-term implications. This underscores a second difference between the worlds of education and work. In college there exist multiple support systems and mentors to help you chart your academic chess game from the beginning of your education until you graduate with the desired degree. As a freshman, you were probably assigned a faculty advisor who helped you through the thicket of courses, choices, sequence, pre-requisites, timing and all the details necessary to help satisfy the requirements and earn the degree of your choice. Academic advisors, deans, faculty members, career counselors, peer counselors, resident assistants, and many other people lend a hand during your college experience to ensure you graduate in a timely fashion.

As Joanna, who graduated from Bucknell University with a Master's degree discovered, the world of work is not a particularly supportive environment. She says, "The difference from college I encountered in my first job was the environment was sterile, not nurturing, and full of people who didn't care about my welfare or happiness or well-being, partly because it might be in their 'best interest' to do better than me. At the same time, I found myself walking into a den of hostility day after day, I also realized the bottom had dropped out of my social world."[115]

The workplace generally doesn't provide leadership advisors, peer advisors, or mentors of any sort. And as Joanna discovered, the social environment is dramatically different as well. If you're going to succeed in most workplace environments, you will need to seek out and develop mentors of your own. The organization will normally not provide a mentor, and even if it does, it may be fairly superficial.

In most of my jobs (Bruce) I had to seek out and develop relationships with others in my place of work. Even peers can help you learn a lot, avoid mistakes, and learn the culture in a new organization. Folks who are higher in the organizational chart can become mentors and can provide a great deal of support and wisdom to help you develop your career, but these you will have to solicit and recruit on your own. When you dive into the world of work, you will have to develop your own network of friends and support. It's not an environmental constant like it is in college. Living in a dorm and taking classes provides many opportunities to make friends with peers in the university. Most work environments provide neither the circumstances nor the right kind of individuals to build social support.

Welcome to the Adult World

A third element of making the leap from the world of study into the world of work involves a number of peripheral issues outside the workplace. It is all too easy to be overwhelmed with practical details of living such as finding a place to live, living on a budget, being responsible for your own life and choices, and building a social life from scratch.

When my youngest daughter landed her dream, entry level job in Washington, DC (ok, that would be any entry level job that let her live and work in DC), she found the gritty details of survival pressed her to the limits. Her first housing was a basement "apartment" (two dark, dingy concrete block rooms and a small bath) she found through family friends. Her Dad affectionately refers to this phase of her life as 'living in the Bat Cave.' With kitchen facilities of a hot pot and a microwave, she subsisted on Ramen Noodles and Pop-Tarts. She constantly worried about money, knowing her income was too low, her meager budget too high, and there were no margins for mistakes. Her Dad kept slipping her sums of cash instructing her to buy at least one hot meal a day. The stereo entertainment consisted of a screaming infant upstairs, accompanied by a constantly yipping miniature dachshund. No wonder the rent was so low!

Her commute, by car, bus and subway, was wildly unpredictable. It took anywhere from 45 minutes to an hour and 45 minutes; so most days she arrived at her desk at least an hour early. She was the youngest person at work, by a decade, so it was hard to make friends at the office. Six months later she got promoted, which allowed her to move into a real apartment. True, the Metro subway ran right outside her basement flat rattling the windows, but it shortened her commute to a predictable 40 minutes. When she found a roommate, she could finally afford to buy and cook real food. Of course, each successive roommate provided enough drama for a first novel, the furniture was regularly stolen from the balcony, and the drug addicts across the street kept breaking into her car to steal stuff to sell for their next fix.

There can be an enormous learning curve in adjusting to the realities of living on your own as an independent adult. Add on top of that the rigors of adjusting to a new job and a new career; it can produce a good deal of stress. It's much different than life at a residential college where there are built-in systems to care for many of your needs. This transition can make you anxious, depressed, or just rattle your sense of self-esteem. Relax. This is normal, and we will give you some effective coping strategies for adult living in Chapter 21.

Translating the Transition

Success in college doesn't automatically produce success in the workplace. Nor does a poor performance in academic subjects predicate a poor performance in the world of work. In all honesty the translation process between these two worlds is very uneven.

Carly, a 28-year-old from Atlanta found the transition didn't translate at all. She'd been highly successful in school having arrived with an athletic scholarship and worked part-time as a waitress during school. In college she never worried about money, and she never thought about how she would earn a living after she graduated. "I thought I was very important in college and that I would go on to do great things, like write the Great American novel. And then I really got very depressed - knowing I don't have the maturity for it (adult living). I don't think I knew what that all meant. I was totally unprepared for life after college."

After graduating, her first job was to live on an Indian reservation in Oregon. But she found living in a shack in the middle of the desert with no car and no phone, wasn't what she had hoped. She moved to LA and went to work in the film industry. Talk about whiplash... here she found a much faster pace of life, extremely competitive coworkers, and difficult living circumstances; all of which produced a much higher level of stress. "I felt like who I was before I moved to LA and graduated from college was sort of lost. I was an English department geek who loved going to teas and readings, and then all of a sudden I had no way of knowing how to apply that to my real life," she says.[116]

Some people have the experience of struggling through the educational process and never finding success at school. Yet when they hit the real world of work, they take off and do spectacularly well. A good friend of mine had trouble learning to read in early elementary school. He was finally diagnosed with dyslexia and was given additional help, but he always struggled with school. Frankly, he told me by third-grade, he felt like a loser and had trouble shaking the feeling. As a teenager, Dick focused on athletics. He was always good with anything that involved a ball. Somehow, he scratched and clawed his way through his class work. While Dick had trouble maintaining a C- average, he managed to graduate from high school and actually finished a four-year college degree.

When Dick landed in the world of business, an amazing transformation took place. It was like watching an otter dive into water for the first time. Dick was a natural. He understood people, could read relationships, and handled office politics with the grace of someone 15 years older. He had an ability to catch the nuances and read between the lines that far surpassed many of his elders in the firm. Nothing in his 16 years of education gave even a hint of the strength of his relational skills. Within a year, he decided he wanted to be a stockbroker, went through the training, earned his licenses and opened an office in Colorado. Within two years he was not only earning a good living, but he was chosen to be the trainer for all of his firm's personnel across the state of Colorado. Within five years he was a star - pulling down an annual income that many corporate CEOs never attain.

The feeling of having dashed expectations is not uncommon after the transition from college to the marketplace. Greg, a graduate of Georgetown University, ended up settling for an uninspiring job because of the pressure of finances. His original plan had been to go from college to graduate school, but he wasn't accepted in any schools. Not knowing what else to do and never having developed a resume, he turned his summer job into a full-time position – an unintentional career. "I went through some hard times because I wasn't ready for it. I got myself into some budget trouble the first couple years. Things got kind of out of control. I went back to some of my high school friends and discovered I really didn't have much in common with them." At times Greg felt so lonely he would drive back to his old college in the fall because he missed it so much. After a few years he found he didn't really fit in there either. "I was disappointed with the real world. There were so many things when I got out of college that I wanted to do. And they were all superseded by financial things that needed to be taken care of first, such as school loans, rent, getting a car, and paying for fun things I wanted to do."[117]

Relevant Preparation?

How relevant is the academic preparation you receive in college for the real world of work? There are actually so many variables in the equation that it's somewhat hard to answer the question. Sometimes there is a pretty clear correlation between the subject matter you study to prepare for a particular field--like accounting--and the actual work you do in the marketplace. In many other cases there is a huge disconnect between the things that are taught at the university and the expectations once you land a real job in your field.

Even among educational experts, there are many doubts about the relevance of the courses in degree programs to the real world job they're supposed to prepare you for. Author Charles Murray says, "The B.A., which has become a requirement to get a job interview, often has absolutely nothing to do with what the job requires. But the reality in today's world is that having the B.A. makes a difference."[118]

My wife, who spent the last several decades teaching reading and writing to elementary school students, is amazed at how little preparation most elementary school degree programs give to teach reading. She regularly encounters young teachers who are "highly qualified" graduates of well-respected, accredited universities, who have survived the student teaching process, and been certified to teach elementary age children. Unfortunately, during four or five years of college-level preparation, they only had one course in reading. These new teachers are put in charge of a classroom full of first, second, or third graders with absolutely no idea how to teach children to read. The educational research is conclusive about a child who is unable to read at grade level by fourth grade -- they have a very low chance of learning during the rest of school and a high likelihood of dropping out of high school before graduation. Clearly, there is a disconnect between those designing the curriculum and the realities of the classroom.

A significant number of adults enroll in college and never complete a course of study. Perhaps that's because they find much of the academic course load difficult to relate to the real world, or the particular field they're interested in. And many college dropouts do quite well in the world of work.

Harvard dropout Bill Gates was able to scratch together a living by building Microsoft. Fellow Harvard dropout Mark Zuckerberg and several of his roommates left school after founding Facebook, currently the most used social network in the world. Even though he just turned 30, Zuckerberg is now in a position to give $100 million gifts to charity, like his recent investment in the schools of Newark, New Jersey. Steve Jobs, the co-founder and CEO of Apple Computer, enrolled in Reed College, but then dropped out after the first six months. Over the following 18 months, Jobs was able to stop taking required classes that didn't interest him and begin dropping in on the ones that looked fascinating. Much of what defines the design and functionality of state-of-the-art electronics today originated in those interesting classes Jobs was able to sit in on during this period of non-enrollment.

Conflicting Cultures

I (Bruce) began my research career doing social science research in the bowels of John F. Kennedy School of Government at Harvard University. Frankly, I thought I was pretty hot stuff -grinding up 64,000 tons of data and analyzing it to explain the behavior of United States Senate campaigns. Yet when I left Harvard and went into marketing research in the business world, I found I had to start all over again at the very bottom. Business researchers have absolutely no respect for academic research work. My new colleagues found my former association as a social science researcher at Harvard about as distasteful as if I had arrived after falling off a turnip truck.

There was a good reason for this: the world of the university and the world of business have vastly different cultures. In many ways these cultures conflict with one another. The Academy values knowledge as an existential good in and of itself. Whether it has any practical value or application in the real world matters little. The business world values pragmatic experience. They care less for theories and ideas and more for empirical proof of practical value and predictable performance in the real world.

Part of the gap is caused by the universities' lack of familiarity with actual conditions on the ground in the world of business. One of my (Bruce) previous clients was a prestigious business school in the Southeast. As I got to know the faculty of the school, I was impressed with how bright these people were. At the same time, I realized they seem to be fairly ignorant of basic operating conditions in business. Then it dawned on me– in a faculty of over 20 individuals, not a single one had ever had a job in the business world. They obtained a Bachelor's degree, a Master's, and then a PhD and went to work teaching "business" in the university where they stayed their entire career. A major cultural difference is that the academy values *credentials* and the business world values *accomplishment*.

Promises, Promises

In many fields there are significant variations between the promises and expectations provided by the university and the actual realities of working in that field. Early in your academic career, you should make it a priority to immerse yourself in the actual day-to-day work of the field itself. Do your own research; don't just assume the sales pitch by the powers that be is actually true. Invest a summer in an internship as soon as you can. If you're thinking about moving into a particular career, find a professional in that field and network with them or shadow them for a day or a week. We're not trying to insinuate that academic authorities are lying to you, it's just that in many disciplines the perception of the field among academics and practitioners is vastly different.

Before you invest in more education, you would be wise to investigate alternative educational vendors. When my wife decided to go back to school to get a Master's degree as a Reading and Writing Specialist, she found one program at a lesser-known State University with a 14-month degree program whose graduates are certified to teach reading in any public school grades K-12. **Cost: $11,000.** She found a similar degree program at the premier State University which took two full years to complete. **Cost: $28,000.** Upon graduation, you were qualified for absolutely nothing. You had to go elsewhere to get the needed credentials to teach.

Even law school, which historically has always been considered the fast track to a remunerative and respectable career, is no longer considered a safe choice. In the last decade, particularly during the Great Recession, applications to law school have been on the increase. The number of LSAT takers climbed 20.5% between 2007 and 2009. At the same time, a number of current or recent law school students claim they've been ripped off! They went to law school and now are underemployed or jobless, in debt, and three years older. Internet sites resound with complaints from unemployed attorneys that law schools "have become nothing more than tuition sucking diploma mills." Others are suing in court claiming their degree and job promises constitute fraud.

The job market for lawyers is terrible, particularly for young lawyers. Approximately a third of law school graduates can't get jobs at all. [119]

Is College for Everyone?

In the American education establishment there is an unstated assumption that everyone should go to college. High schools across the country measure their effectiveness by how many warm bodies they can ship off to college. But many educational experts say we do a great disservice to a good proportion of these students. These experts agree that almost all young people need some training after high school, but it's not necessarily a Bachelor's degree. Encouraging someone to attend college who is not ready to do college-level work is a disservice to those who can't handle it and flunk out. These students end up without a diploma and a pile of debt.[120]

If you are a kinesthetic learner, you learn best by working with your hands. You probably enjoy things you do with your hands, and you learn more when there is physical contact involved with the subject matter.

Focused training in a technical or trade school might be perfect for your learning style and interests. Becoming a dental hygienist, a veterinary assistant, a computer technician, a building contractor, a machinist, or an electrician might be an excellent alternative to a four-year college. There are many technical colleges which provide practical training for readily available jobs with good pay, and they won't leave you swimming in debt.

These career alternatives may better fit who you are while paying well. Remember the $60,000 a year machinist jobs outside Pittsburgh (see p.96,97)? That may be a better alternative. My two next door neighbors when I was growing up were a plumber and a wallpaper hanger. While my Dad had a Master's degree in engineering and was a white collar manager, the neighbors on either side probably made just as much money as he did and enjoyed comparable lifestyles.

Don't fall for the myth that the longer you stay in school, the more money you make. While historically it was true that a Bachelor's degree would increase your lifelong earnings and grad school would increase it more, this is no longer the case. "Today the gains from going to college have stagnated for certain groups and occupations," reports Richard Vedder, an economist at Ohio University. "The problem may be that 70% of high school graduates are now going to college, most of them to get a piece of paper they think will let them lead an upper-middle-class life," says Vedder. "It's becoming mathematically impossible for that to happen. We cannot all earn more than average."[121]

Others who find difficulty in landing a job after graduation, such as during our current recession, revert to grad school in hopes of improving their prospects. Often this is simply putting off the 'day of reckoning.' What the myth of higher education fails to recognize is that all the education in the world will not help if jobs do not exist. Many people today obtain graduate degrees simply to end up waitressing. The number of PhD's driving taxicabs in New York City is absolutely astonishing.

Perhaps the best advice comes from financial columnist Michelle Singletary. "The answer to this problem isn't to discourage people from attending college but to challenge them to go with no debt or as little debt as possible. Generally, a college education does lead to greater employment opportunities, plenty of data show. But there's a point at which the amount of debt accumulated is too much to handle for college graduates starting out."[122]

Consider beginning your college education at a less expensive community college. You can often complete general requirements for a four-year degree at a community college for a lot less money. Consider obtaining a focused Associates Degree, at that community college, which will actually help you get a job. Once you start working, you can continue your education to finish getting a four year degree while your job helps support you and pays for your college education. One advantage of going to school while working is that your employer will often help foot the bill for your education. Another major advantage of this route is that your work experience in your field can motivate you in your studies and make you a better student – knowing the real world value of what you are learning.

Not only is there a great cultural divide between the academy and the marketplace, depending on what career you pursue, you may find astonishing cultural differences among potential employers of your skill set. These culturally-induced variations can make or break your career success and your ability to locate and build on your sweet spot at work. In order to find a job you can love, it is vital you find the right corporate culture for you.

Chapter 18

Corporate Culture: Context is Everything

The environment in your particular workplace has a great deal to do with your ability to find your sweet spot and grow a career. In this chapter we discuss how to evaluate which growth medium is best for you. Every organization develops a culture. These are both visible and invisible manifestations of how people in the organization relate to one another, address their work, and perceive the outside world. Culture is the way a group of people in an organization solve problems and reconcile dilemmas.

The first marketing research company I worked for was a family-owned firm with about 35 employees. Relationships between employees of all levels were warm and friendly. I had equal access to the president and owner, as well as to the lowest level housewife tipping research ads into magazines. Except for the two partners who were usually out with clients, we all ate our homemade lunches sitting around the same table in the staff break room. People had different job responsibilities and higher or lower levels of compensation, but everyone was on an equal footing in terms of social level and value. The corporate culture was much like an extended family.

Later on I worked for a company that placed a high value on hierarchical status and the perks that came with it. All the officers of the corporation had offices on the top floor of the building. The most important officers had corner offices with huge walls of windows on two sides of their suite. Only these officers and their secretarial staff were allowed on this floor. Each Vice President was issued a corporate car, a top-of-the-line American luxury car with specified features, trim, accessories and paint scheme. The President/CEO's car was larger, more expensive, a more prestigious model. Each officer had an assigned parking spot at the front entrance of corporate headquarters with his name stenciled in bold black lettering. This obsession with outward signs of rank filtered all down the organization. With every level of promotion there was an assigned size of office, window placement, office furnishings, even the assignment of artwork from the corporate collection. Looking back on this workplace experience, I admit it was the nicest office I ever had, although the competency of my colleagues left a lot to be desired.

M&M/Mars was the most unique, strong culture corporation I ever labored for. I worked in the US headquarters with about 4,000 other people. Not a single reserved parking spot on the campus. The rule was "First Come, First Served." Even the President of this $2 billion a year unit of Mars Inc. had to compete with the lowest line worker for a parking spot in the morning. Every worker in the firm, including the owners, Forrest and John Mars, clocked in on a time clock each morning. Everyone in by 8:30AM got a 10% punctuality bonus for the day. The idea was to keep senior executives from dragging in late, delaying meetings and thus lowering overall productivity.

I had a beautiful office, with glass walls overlooking the scenic splendor of a wooded piece of North Jersey. True, I shared my office with 400 other associates. Known as the bullpen layout, no one had a private office. In fact, the President was right out in the middle of the floor, surrounded by his six Vice Presidents. Each had a desk, a credenza, and a file cabinet. With luck, their Executive Secretary was within hailing distance. I was fortunate. My entire staff of 12 was within the sound of my raised voice. All in a space about the size of my former office in the "status conscious" firm. If you wanted to talk to an accounting guy or a brand manager, all you had to do was look across to see if he was in, pop over and chat, then get on with the job. Mars' organizational culture has a great many attributes which demonstrate an egalitarian outlook, a focus on efficiency, and a desire to be highly successful in their chosen business.

The Petri Dish

In high school, college, or whenever you took your last biology lab course, you probably got to use a Petri dish. This shallow round dish contains a blob of organic medium, used to grow various kinds of macrobiotic life for experimentation. If you have good medium in the dish, you generally grow better specimens in less time. This same principle holds true for corporate cultures and your career. If you pick jobs in firms with an organizational culture which is hospitable to your unique personality, you will find your career growing deeper and stronger in less time. Pick the wrong corporate culture, and you could stunt your career growth for a long time.

The right culture will be one that provides a hospitable environment for your passions and unique strengths to make their optimum contribution. I am an excellent teacher, and I have been able to use my teaching skills in many different settings. But when I began my career, I tried to use those skills teaching at a private high school outside Boston. Meyers-Briggs shows I am an INTJ also known as the Architect of Change. When I teach, I want to help my students push the boundaries and discover new innovations. The school I worked for was hide-bound with tradition, committed to long held habits and deeply stuck in a rut. They had no interest in innovation, only in having everyone follow all the rules. This was not a good fit for me.

Later in my career I became VP of Marketing for a large nonprofit organization based in New York City. I discovered that many nonprofit organizations in New York City have a unique, shared organizational culture all their own. Every week I would post sticky notes on my office door reciting the most recent increase in gross sales, net sales, and profits for our newest product line. It took me about six months to realize I was the only one who cared about sales. The prevailing attitude ran like this. "Who cares about the customer? As long as the donor support is there, it doesn't matter what we do for our constituents."

One of the organization's primary products was a book which cost us $9.00 to manufacture and which we sold for $2.50. Donors' contributions covered the difference. We had a customer service department with 35 people doing the work of five, while delivering horrid customer service. When I suggested we outsource this function, the reaction was, "We can't do that. These people are so bad no one else will hire them." When a clerk was caught depositing customer checks into her own bank account, she was removed from that department. Eventually they transferred her to the group that counted loose cash customers sent in. Hello? Raising the issues of honesty, ethics, efficiency, and being good stewards of our clients' money only garnered me uncomprehending stares. It simply was not part of their culture.

If you are in the right kind of company, you will enjoy the work ethic, the attitudes of your colleagues, and the mission of your organization. You will have room to grow. You will probably feel affirmed and encouraged by others at work, both your supervisor and peers. On the other hand, if you feel like you have to put on a fake persona to get along at the office, you are probably in the wrong company. If your sense of urgency and striving for excellence is not matched by others, you may want to consider alternatives.

Nationality Influences Culture

National culture has a powerful influence over business organizations. Edgar Schein teaches at the Sloan School of Management at MIT and is the leading expert in the field of organizational culture. Schein consults with leading international and domestic firms and is always amazed at the contrast in culture and how it can be driven by the nationality of leaders. One client Schein worked with was Ciba-Geigy, a huge Swiss-based multi-national chemical corporation. From the front door inward, Ciba-Geigy is formal, authoritarian, rigid, and highly structured. Employees always address each other by title and surname –"Dr. This" or "Dr. That." Ciba was highly conscious of rank and status, invested in much structured planning, had little or no cross-function dialog, and indulged in many protocols in their interaction. All these elements are typical of the Swiss culture of the founders.

By contrast, Schein also worked with Digital Equipment Corporation (DEC), an American computer company launched from one of the labs at MIT. It became the most successful manufacturer of mini-computers and employed a worldwide force of over 100,000 people with over $14 billion in sales by the mid 1990s. In contrast to Ciba-Geigy, DEC's culture appeared relaxed, informal in dress and manner, with a fast-paced dynamic of interaction of employees at all levels. One of the best known traits of the DEC culture was the freedom to debate decisions at any level by staff of any rank. No private dining rooms, no reserved parking places, no special offices. Furnishings were inexpensive and functional. In many ways this multi-billion dollar firm retained much of the organizational culture of the small lab of scientists and engineers from which it grew.

If you take a job in the automobile business, you will run into cultural differences determined by nationality, even if you only work in the United States. American-led firms tend to have high structure and much underlying conflict between the "doers" and the "deciders." Management vs. labor conflicts often inject a great deal of tension, redundancy, and inefficiency into the manufacturing process. If you work for a Japanese firm, you will not find the "Star Culture" players in Design and Marketing that you find in American firms. Decisions are always made by teams, in a way that includes many diverse points of view and most decisions lean toward limiting risk to the firm. Japanese firms are so committed to including everyone in the process, that line workers can push a button and stop the line to correct a problem or deal with a quality defect. Finally, if you work for a German firm, like BMW or Volkswagen, in America you will find unique differences in their US-based operations. How they organize themselves, how time is managed, the status of those with higher titles and education, and many other features of German culture crop up even in US-based manufacturing units producing cars for sale in America.

When I worked for Mars, Inc., I was responsible for much of the consumer research from the east coast of the Americas to the east coast of the Pacific Rim. My counterpart, who handled the research for Europe and the other half of the globe, was based outside of London. Our teams met regularly, and we traveled back and forth for meetings almost monthly. One of my American team colleagues was a sensory researcher who had been born and raised in Scotland. At the age of seven, she and her family immigrated to the United States. One day I asked her to explain the essential difference between Brits and Americans. Here's what she told me:

"The best way I can explain it is to tell you a true story. A few years ago, there was a British Airways 747 jet sitting on the runway at Heathrow Airport getting ready to depart to New York City. About half the passengers were Brits and half Yanks. All of a sudden, smoke started leaking out of the ceiling. The BA flight attendants came though the cabin and told everyone to stay in their seats until they were told to queue up. The Brits obeyed. The Americans said, "What! Are you nuts? I'm getting out of here!" They pushed and shoved, climbed over the seats, popped out the exit doors and slid down the chutes to safety. How rude! …all of a sudden, there was a whoosh, and flames shot out of the plane's ceiling. When it was all over, every British passenger on the flight died and every American lived. That is the difference between Brits and Americans."

Understanding Corporate Culture

If you are willing to dig deep enough, you will find that almost every organization has a unique corporate culture. Rather than focusing on the minute details which set each culture apart – perhaps better left to those who diagnose organizational life it may be more helpful to recognize there are certain kinds of cultures which share similar themes, core values, behaviors, and expectations. Often industries will share similar corporate cultures. Education tends to be a *Process culture* which values activity rather than results (which are hard to measure). Advertising tends to be a *Star culture* where key individuals go out and land accounts, or where individual creatives come up with a groundbreaking campaign which puts the client on the map. Retail stores tend to be *Work Hard, Play Hard cultures* – environments which have lots of small risks and very quick feedback. Those who manufacture nuclear power plants, airplanes, or who put astronauts into space likely have *Bet Your Company cultures*. It takes years to find out if you've succeeded and if you fail, you are likely to go out of business. This creates deliberate, thorough, and careful decision making.

Certain disciplines within a larger company often have differing corporate cultures. I worked at a publishing company, which probably had the Work Hard / Play Hard culture as its primary or overall corporate culture. The Accounting and Human Resources departments were more Process cultures. Sales and Marketing looked much more like the Star culture (also called the *Tough-Guy, Macho culture*). The Editorial staff fell into the mainstream Work Hard/Play Hard culture.

Banking tends to produce a Work Hard /Play Hard culture. These folks make many small decisions every day. These are low-risk decisions, but over time, they accumulate into success or failure. I have a Mission Statement brochure from my local bank, and it puts the first emphasis on their employees. They want to treat them well because good employees are the source all those decisions which ultimately determine the success of Tower Bank. Next, they focus on customers and how to treat them right. Later they talk about producing a good return for shareholders and managing interest rate risk, but it's clear from this document that people are the means to the end (good financial results).

When I worked at M&M/Mars, I was responsible for interviewing and hiring many staff members. I might interview 150 potential hires over the course of a year. I took a good deal of trouble explaining the unique corporate culture at Mars. My favorite metaphor was that Mars was like "slightly controlled anarchy." If you would not have been comfortable strutting down Main Street in the Wild West 100 years ago with only your six guns and an attitude, you might not be comfortable at Mars either. Mars liked to hire the best and the brightest, but they also gave kudos to those willing to take risks to pursue aggressive growth. An eagerness to push the envelope and a tendency to encourage the troops to charge almost always resulted in rapid career advancement. Even if your risk produced a colossal failure, you were not dismissed. Your career might plateau, but Mars continued to value those willing to gamble to help the company grow. These are the traits of the Tough Guy, Macho culture.

Zappos is another example of a company with a strong, distinctive culture. Zappos, the e-retailer, has built a billion dollar a year business on its reputation as a company obsessed with customer service. Zappos offers extremely fast shipping free to every customer. If you are unhappy with a purchase, the return shipping is also free. Service reps are given great latitude to go to extremes to make sure customers are happy.

Each new customer service rep goes through a four-week training program where they are immersed in Zappos' unique culture, beliefs, and practices. This company is so convinced its unique culture gives it competitive advantage, it is willing to put money behind that conviction. A week into their training, every new recruit is given "The Offer." Recruits are offered a week's pay plus a $3,000 bonus to quit today. *Business Week* reports only two to three percent accept the offer. The other 97% reject the offer. Overwhelmingly, these recruits buy into the uniqueness and high value of the Zappos culture. Those who don't, take the offer and disappear before they can do any damage to the firm's reputation. What a cool idea![123]

There are several ways to analyze and describe corporate cultures. The classic work on corporate cultures, *Corporate Cultures*, was originally written by Terrance Deal & Allan Kennedy and to this day remains perhaps the clearest typology of American workplaces. If you are considering working overseas or working for an American company owned by a foreign organization, you might take a look at the corporate cultures template developed by Fons Trompenaars and Charles Hampden- Turner in *Riding the Waves of Culture*. This typology is more complex but does a better job of explaining the diversity of cultures in organizations all around the globe. Deal & Kennedy, however, do a better job of explaining the American workplace. If you are planning to work in America, this is a good book to delve into the details of this topic.

Variety is Good

The fact that there are so many different kinds of organizational cultures is good. For most careers and skills sets, there are a variety of places you can apply your talents. Within any particular discipline, the specific corporate culture of the workplace you select may offer widely differing opportunities for your personality and talent. Your long-term happiness and fulfillment in a job have a lot more to do with picking the right corporate culture than selecting the position with the highest pay and best benefits. It is critical to achieve a good fit between your gifts and personality and the culture of the place you choose to work.

If you graduated with a law degree, there are a number of possible types of organizations where you might land a job and grow a career. You could look for an entry level position in a prestigious, 'white shoe' law firm. This probably will pay the most money. If you don't mind grinding out 80 to 100 hours a week of the dullest grunt work in the law profession for years on end; if you can survive the cut-throat competition; you may just end up becoming a partner in the firm and becoming wealthy. Or, not.

There are many alternatives you might consider before you fall victim to the siren call of big money. One attorney I know chose to open a practice offering defense services for adolescent offenders. It was one way he could give back after surviving a troubled adolescence. Another attorney friend teaches at Taylor University in rural Indiana. He runs a program where he travels to Brazil one week each month and teaches a course on ethics and corruption in international law to classes composed of half American and half Brazilian students. Fascinating work. My own attorney went to work for his family's law firm. He works with his uncle and his dad and does wills, estates, home closings, and small business law in the town he grew up in. Perhaps not the most glamorous or remunerative legal work, but he is well known and well respected in the community and is able to enjoy a sane lifestyle with much time for family and fun.

Perhaps going to work in an urban law clinic might appeal to you. While the pay isn't great, the work offers enormous variety and challenge, and you can invest your legal talents in changing people's lives. Another lawyer I know wanted to combine his law degree with his concern for environmental issues. He moved back to his home state of New Hampshire and became a land use litigator. Over ten years he has worked to keep inappropriate development out of the North Country and in the process has become the best land use litigator in the state.

Medicine is another example of how the corporate culture of the workplace you choose will impact your professional experience. Graduating with an MD and completing a residency is only part of the process. Take a moment and think about the day-to-day workplace environment of your job as a doctor, depending on where you decide to practice. You might work in a veteran's hospital in the United States and care for returning soldiers with serious injuries. You could decide to apply your skills in a rural clinic where you are the only medical help for hours around. You might join a group of ten highly-qualified physicians in a suburban practice outside one of the nicer cities in the US. Alternately, you could work as an ER doctor, specializing in gunshot wounds in a busy, inner-city public hospital. Conceivably you might choose to become a plastic surgeon to the stars in Hollywood. Or you might want to serve in a field hospital on the forward lines in Afghanistan. All potential choices for a doctor – every single one with dramatically different outcomes based on the corporate culture of the organization of your choice.

Many fields offer a similar range of options. Information technology, nursing, accounting, computer security, retail sales management, law enforcement and numerous other fields present an array of contrasting work environments depending on the corporate culture of the firm where you decide to use your skills. Is this a good fit for you? The employer won't tell you. It's up to you to do your research and find a good match between your sweet spot and a specific organizational culture.

Identifying Corporate Culture

It is critical for you to prepare yourself to diagnose an organization's culture from the outside. It is easier to do cultural diagnoses from the inside. But as the jungle explorer found, once he was in the cannibals' stew pot, it could be too late, once you are inside. Let's look at elements of culture you can identify during the process of researching, interviewing, and following up with an organization which might potentially employ you. You may not be able to pick up everything, but you can certainly learn enough to determine if this company is a good fit for the unique you.

First, begin by using your eyes. Look at how people dress, how they walk, how they talk to each other. Do they look tense? Or relaxed? Is anyone laughing or looking like they might burst out laughing? As you walk through the halls of the organization, are the office doors open or closed? All closed doors indicates this may be a place with a lot of people who are introverted, prefer solitary work, feel isolated, or even threatened by others. How are you treated in reception? If people are warm, friendly, courteous, offer to take your coat or bring you coffee, this is a reflection of how this company treats people in general. If they are formal, distant, distrustful, and painfully awkward, this is telling of the general atmosphere.

Look at the employees. How they dress is a clue. When my daughter moved from a college in Washington, DC, to a college in Boston, the first thing that impressed her was how her new boss dressed. In DC everybody was dressed up, very formal--probably a result of the powerful influence the Federal government has on the culture of Washington. Her new manager in Boston wore khaki slacks, a blue oxford cloth button down shirt, and a fleece LL Bean vest. *Ahh...* Having been raised in New Hampshire, she knew she would enjoy this new culture.

Observe *how* people work. Do they seem nervous, frantic, like their boxers are on fire? Some corporate cultures exist in a permanent state of crisis. Everything is always a rush job! Everybody is expected to drop their regular work and address the crisis of the moment. This is ok if you are going to work in a fire station, but if it's a manufacturing plant, or a school, beware. I've been told that the culture at PepsiCo is very competitive. There are two people competing for every seat in the place. One wins, thus promoted, and the other gets let go. This makes for a tense work environment. If you're highly competitive, it may be a good fit for you.

Perhaps you observe that people in a prospective workplace are calm, relaxed, paced, seem to know what they are doing. If you worked for me, I think this is what you would experience. The reason is simple. I am a big picture person, a strategic planner. I honestly believe that inside a 3-month timeframe there is very little you can do to affect the outcome of your work. So my subordinates plan very carefully for three months out to three years, stick to the plan, have monthly reviews for adjustments, and simply skip the daily or weekly crisis. I just don't believe in them. Also, you will find my subordinates laugh a lot. If your work isn't fun, why do it?

You can learn a lot from observation. Yes, it is helpful to read through a company's website and see what that says about the organizational culture. But beware, the folks in Public Relations indulge in describing "espoused values," as anthropologists call them. That's where we loudly proclaim our commitment to a cultural value we do not actually practice. In one client's organization I read all the usual talk about being an equal opportunity employer. When I started meeting with management, I noticed there were no women in management. Puzzled, I finally pulled their organization chart and counted. You had to go down about 35 positions into the organization before you found the first woman manager. They plainly did not practice the equalitarian standards their website preached.

On another client engagement, I was given a tour of the company campus. The literature described the "friendly community" experienced in Company X's workplace. As the tour guide was telling me what a "friendly, collaborative" company this was, I noticed as associates passed each other on the walkways, they looked down and did not speak to each other. Very few people were in conversation anywhere on campus and the lower level people seemed allergic to high ranking staff members as they passed. No one was having casual conversation over the water cooler or in the hallways. Hmm… when there is a conflict between stated values and your own observations, believe your eyes, not the company PR.

Next, ask questions. This is a critical discipline to diagnose corporate culture. You can learn a lot about the values of a company by asking questions. When I, (Katybeth) was interviewing for professional positions towards the end of my grad school training, I received an invitation from a very prestigious university. I was so excited to even interview with this school. While the formal parts of the interview process were pretty much what you would expect, I learned the real juicy stuff about the corporate culture in the "informal" parts of the interview.

Over lunch, the person who would have been my boss mentioned that although she and her husband met while working at this university, they now only saw each other on weekends because they both worked very late every night. I asked a single member of the staff about what kinds of social activities were available in the area, a pretty typical question for one single person to raise with a peer. This employee acknowledged that even though she had been working at University X for over 18 months, she had no idea what kind of social life might be available. Frankly, she had done nothing but work since she got here and could shed no light on the topic of life outside of work.

Later in the day, another employee told me I better not suggest any ideas I wasn't willing to spearhead to completion. This department wasn't exactly built around teamwork. From her experience, it sounded like everyone was overworked and kept their heads down in fear of getting more assignments. God forbid you actually make a suggestion! When I considered all of this information I gleaned through casual conversation, I began to see a pattern. This was a corporate culture that valued workaholics. If you wanted nothing in your life, but work, stress and pressure, this would be a great place to work. From the final analysis I decided that even though this school had a great reputation, I was not at all interested in living in a pressure-cooker workplace.

When you are interviewing, or if an associate is assigned to take you to lunch, ask, "Who are the heroes in the company and why? How do you measure success here? What is the typical workday like? What causes people to get promoted? When do they get fired? How much turnover is there in the typical year? What do people do for fun?" These kinds of questions can reveal a lot about the 'real world' environment of this specific workplace.

I ask these questions in many different companies. You never know what you will turn up. In a large, well-known food manufacturer on the West Coast, I discovered that market research data was always analyzed out to four decimal places. That tells me they are meticulous, make decisions with empirical data, can be a bit fussy, and have a high aversion to risk. At Mars, Inc. they *like* typos in papers, correspondence and presentations. This tells management you are not wasting time polishing papers but are focused on productive work that builds the business. Efficiency and productivity are everything in the Mars culture.

Another client organization had so many meetings, it consumed all the productive time of the top leaders. So the business went out and hired "shadow" Vice Presidents for every Vice President in the organization. The job of these Associate VP's was to do the functional area work of each VP (say Marketing, for example) while the Official VP (always called the "functional area expert") spent 90% of his or her workday in meetings. Now that's a great culture if you like meetings and don't care if anything ever gets done.

Even dropping casual questions can help. Ask the receptionist, a secretary, any ordinary person you bump into in during your time in the office. "What's it like to work here? What's the driving value of this place?

What is this company all about?" I know these seem like vague questions, and they are. Deliberately so. If you get back dramatically different feedback than you got from the official interviews, beware. Something isn't right. If everyone you ask those leading questions to gives different answers, it means the corporate culture is muddled, confused, perhaps conflicted – not a good thing. If everyone gives the same kind of answer, and it matches that of the official contacts, it indicates this is a strong culture corporation with a consistent and unified team.

Let me summarize by saying that trying to identify corporate culture is a bit like trying to pick a single puppy from a litter of eight-week-old dogs. It's intuitive and subjective, but if you think carefully about your goals and needs, you'll make the right choice. Want an aggressive hunting dog? Pick the biggest male pup that chases all the others. Want a dog that's good with children? Pick a pup that is more laid back and seems to get along with others. Want a quiet dog who will lay on your hearth rug for hours looking at you with eyes of adoration? Pick the runt of the litter.

Picking the right corporate culture for you works the same way. Know what you want and need. Keep your eyes open, ask lots of questions, and do your research. Think critically about what you learn. You may not always be able to articulate your thinking, but if you do these things you will know the right culture for you when you see it. Remember, it is better to take a lower paying job in a company whose culture you respect. You will have more potential to grow in such a firm, and you will enjoy almost every day you work there. Having done the research to identify your own unique strengths and passions, and finding an industry and corporate culture that suits you – you are now well on your way to launching a successful career.

Chapter 19

Attitude Determines Altitude

Good news! You have finally landed the job you wanted. It may be your first entry level job out of school, your first promotion, or maybe a big step up into management. Perhaps you are mid -career or have finally gotten back on the horse after a voluntary or involuntary layoff from your old job. Possibly you are further along in your vocation and you are striving to "re-career" your work life for any number of reasons. Whatever the case, the good news is you have finally been invited on board to begin a new voyage into the marketplace.

That's the good news. Unfortunately, landing the job was the easy part. I know it doesn't feel like that, after spending months and perhaps years beating the bushes to land this particular spot. Your first day at work is the beginning of a long process in which you will have a great many opportunities to nurture a happy and healthy career or to sabotage your work life, make yourself miserable, and guarantee an unhappy ending. The choice is yours.

Your attitude, in its many manifestations, can make or break your ability to grow a successful career, once you've begun that new job. We would like to use this chapter to walk you through some very practical advice so, no matter what line of work you choose, you can grow the positive and rewarding career we all want. If you are new to the world of work, these issues will come as a bit of a surprise – we are seldom taught about our attitudes and how they impact our daily experience and our long-term success at work. If you've been in the workplace for a while, you may discover attitudinal mistakes in your past, which undermined your growth in previous positions. No matter what line of work you are in, the issues we discuss in this chapter can either fertilize the expansion and development of your career or cause it to become the victim of stunted growth.

Nurturing a career is a lot like growing a garden. At first, you must prepare the soil – digging to loosen the dirt, pulling up rocks, blending in organic compost, and incorporating appropriate nutrients. With your career, this is the prep work of identifying the unique you and finding the appropriate corporate culture environment in which to grow your profession. Having done that, the seed is planted, and your job is launched. Is that the end of it? No way! With your garden, you have months of hard work ahead of you before you reap a harvest. You must faithfully pull the weeds, add fertilizer, water, prune, thin, support and care for your plants before you get the bountiful harvest you desire.

In the garden of your career, you face the same situation. A successful career is built a day at a time. It is carefully cultivated through good times and bad. It involves a number of details which must be vigilantly and consistently attended to. You will need attitudes, skills and habits which get you over the hurdles of a difficult supervisor, contentious peers, and circumstances beyond your control. If you adopt the perspectives, strategies and tools we will share in this chapter, carefully cultivate the garden of your workplace situation over time, you too will reap the bountiful career harvest you hope for.

Expectations

Often college graduates leave school with over-inflated ideas of their real worth and value in the marketplace. I'm not sure this is always their fault. Sometimes it is the result of excessive focus on self by adults in the pre-work universe. If everyone around you is always saying 'you are going to be a star,' pretty soon you believe it. Often, I see the university painting overly rosy scenarios for students so they graduate thinking they are just a short step or two from being a CEO. I don't care if you have a PhD in Business, when you first go to work in a business, you know next to nothing. You don't know the industry or how that particular business operates. You have a lot to learn. If you want to lead a business one day, you'd be wise to learn those basics from the bottom up. Even then, you don't have experience or sound judgment – the two elements leadership is built on. It will take you years to learn these before you ever potentially qualify for a leadership position.

My friend Blaine Rummel graduated from college with a BS in Economics. I'm not sure what he thought he was going to do with this degree, become the next Chairman of the Federal Reserve? It took him six months to figure out no one was going to pay him to mess around with economics based on his degree. Most of the positions he qualified for involved various administrative tasks, typing, answering phones, filing and running errands. He spent two or three years duffing around in low level administrative jobs of this sort.

Meanwhile, Blaine found he had a growing interest in computers. He enjoyed fooling around with them and writing various applications. He liked seeing what they could do and picked up some experience doing small projects for his employers. When Blaine decided to see if he could switch into a career in computers, he found his sweet spot. It turns out his curiosity about computers taught him enough so he could communicate with computer geeks. His academic background and a business internship in college gave him basic knowledge of business operations. Blaine also possessed good people skills. He found he could talk to clients and vendors, organize a work flow, prepare a budget, and keep the project on track. Soon he was working as a systems designer for a major computer company installing network systems. Within five years of starting this new line of work, he made Vice President.

Flexibility

Blaine's story introduces a second issue: the need to be flexible. Often we don't really know what we want to do for work when we choose a major in college. If you graduate and can't figure out what to do with your degree, keep an open mind. Like Blaine, there may be a hobby or an interest which can transform your search for your sweet spot.

Change is a constant in the world of work. Don't fight it – embrace it. Most people resist change, feel threatened, and are tempted to fight change. But change is a good thing. It is also inevitable. Spencer Johnson wrote a parable about dealing with change entitled, *Who Moved My Cheese?* First published in 1998, this handy little book is an international bestseller and today remains on the top ten list of business books. In it Johnson describes various ways people often deal with change and the outcome of each strategy. In short, he recommends we anticipate change. It is going to come, so keep your eyes open. Look for it. I suggest at least once a year you take a half day to monitor the change happening in your workplace, and think about how to respond. Prepare ahead and adapt to change quickly when it comes.[124]

When Chris Meidt, offensive assistant coach for the Washington Redskins, surveyed his workplace in 2009, he realized changes would come. While the NFL lockout was more than two years away, Meidt realized the owners' desire for more revenue might shrink the coaching pool. With about 600 coaching positions in the NFL, 2010 saw that number cut by 30 positions. Meidt was one of those left without a job, in spite of rave reviews. Through a contact from a previous college coaching job, Chris was recruited to become a market manager for Wal-Mart in Wisconsin. He said he still sees himself as a coach, just offering a different kind of leadership to the people of seven Wal-Mart retail stores north of Milwaukee. Meidt loves his new job which allows him to use his skills as a communicator to build and encourage people. And Wal-Mart is thrilled to have the coach's talents on their team.[125]

Enthusiasm

Your attitude plays a big role in being able to be flexible, adapt to change and rise above difficult circumstances in your job. As a dear friend used to tell me, "Gratitude is the key to a new attitude." If you have a job, of any kind, in today's economy, you should be grateful. It may not be all that you would like it to be. It may not be what you want to do for the rest of your life. But be grateful you have any job at all. If you invest a positive attitude in your current job, instead of whining and complaining, you may be able to see your present circumstances transformed into something much better.

Enthusiasm is one of the traits that set winners apart from the rest of the pack. Most people prefer to work with those who greet each new day with a smile and a warm welcome. Don't be half-hearted at work. It will set back your career. Of course your job has a lot of tedious grunt work. That's why they call it work, and pay you for doing it! Did you think you were being paid to attend an afternoon garden party? Every trade and profession has difficult thankless tasks that are part of the process. Grin and bear it. Find the fun in the midst of the pain. Don't take yourself so seriously. If you attack each day at work with a cheerful attitude, soon you'll get promoted, and somebody else will get your old grunt work.

In the beginning of my career as a market researcher, I was working on study after study about new sanitary protection products. Our client was a large manufacturer of various feminine hygiene products made from paper and plastic. My job was to field the complaints from consumers who had a bad experience with a test product. The lowest I sank was when I was analyzing women's complaints about these products, and they would mail in the used product along with their complaint.

I also had the privilege of analyzing complaints about a new line of nursing pad liners, which apparently had a tendency to rip the sensitive skin off the nursing mother's breast. Ouch! In the end, those of us who could laugh, went on and became serious market researchers. Those who could not see the humor and use the pads for drink coasters, well, those folks ended up going into another line of work. I laughed. So I was promoted to the toilet paper study, which I enjoyed immensely. Believe it or not, within ten years I held one of the top jobs in my field. Laughing all the way to the bank.

Make Your Boss a Success

No matter what you do for a living--no matter where you are positioned in the organizational chart, one of your key responsibilities is to make your boss a success. This is not always easy to do, but it is a critical performance objective, no matter what you do. When you take a myopic view of your job and just think about the requirements listed on your job description, you make a serious error. Every organization has politics, and the politics of any organization make it incumbent on you to support your boss and make him a winner. It is simply not acceptable to say, "Well, that's not my job." If your boss is seen as a loser in your business, everyone who works for him will be seen as a loser. That includes you.

You can't possibly be an outstanding employee if your boss and department are taking a lot of heat for whatever reason. It may even be your boss' fault, like the idiot manager who appears in the Dilbert cartoons.

It does not matter. Be creative and find ways to help your boss, even if he/she is a blob. Think like your boss's boss, and take the extra effort to help your department perform well, even if it is not well led. Find ways to take work from your boss' plate. Then your boss can take work from her boss. Doing this proves you know how to add value and are worthy of promotion.

We all want to have an inspiring supervisor who sets a great tone, mentors us, equips us, and supports us to succeed. Yet, this will not always be the case. If you put in the extra effort to make your boss a winner, eventually you will be selected for a promotion, and you will have earned yourself a better ride with a stronger leader.

What if Your Boss is a Bad Boss?

What if your boss is a real stinker? It does happen. If you spend any time in the workplace, eventually you will have a boss that just makes you grind your teeth in frustration. Sometimes, bosses, and their subordinates, are simply victims of the Peter Principle. You remember – the cream rises until it sours? People tend to rise to their level of incompetence. Good staffers are often promoted once too often, and we can't see the mistake until it's been made. These folks have good intentions, but they are in over their head. Rarely will management (or the manager) confront this one, so make the best of it. Find ways to support and help the boss with things they don't do well. Coping strategies can often improve the overall health of your work experience.

The micro-manager, control freak boss, is another common variant of the bad boss. This person's behavior is often motivated by fear. They don't even realize they are over-controlling people. They are so terrified of making a mistake, or of having someone else's mistake reflect badly on them, that they indulge in micro managing. As they view it, they are preventing terrible mistakes from being made on their watch.

The best way to cope with this boss is not to confront them or challenge them, but to offer reassurance. Ask lots of questions when he lays out a project and take plenty of notes. Restate his directions and confirm in writing the measurable result to be achieved. As you do the work, give the boss progress reports. Excess information will allay his fears that you are not on top of the assignment. When he tries to control your work, repeat back the measurable objective (from your voluminous notes) and ask if this means he is changing the end product. Interpret any attempt to change the process as instructions to change the outcome. If you repeat this process multiple times, and deliver the goods on each assignment, eventually his confidence level will rise and he will give you some latitude.[126]

On occasion, I come across a boss who is terse to the point of rudeness, demanding, demeaning and treats both staff and customers like dog doo on her shoe. This harsh approach generally dispenses so much hurt and pain that it may bring out the teenager in any of us. The temptation to hit back at unreasonable and arbitrary demands can bring an overreaction on our part we may later regret. My suggestion; bite your lip and don't respond at all. Count to ten or one hundred or whatever it takes for you to get control of your temper. Resorting to your fists won't help anything.

When you get behind the façade of this type of boss, you often find a person who is broken in some significant way. They have been rejected in relationships, they are lonely, isolated, emotionally wounded, or have excessive fear of being taken advantage of. Often they have an over-inflated fear of failure. They feel their tough guy (harsh) approach will prevent anyone from thinking they are soft and taking advantage of them. You can pray for them, offer random acts of kindness, say thank you a lot, and always be positive in the face of their assaults. These steps may not do anything to modify their behavior or heal their hurt, but it will keep you from spiraling down into the same pit they are living in.

Then there is the bad boss for whom there is no explanation. When you get beyond the causal factors which you can potentially address or even just understand with a modicum of sympathy, there are still bosses who are just BAD. These people injure those around them on a daily basis, they cause significant damage to the team, set back the department's objectives and harm the relationship with the customer. Don't spend a lot of time asking why. You may not ever know why. Try to develop coping strategies to accomplish two things. First, do what you can to help the team achieve the departmental objective and serve the customer. This falls under the umbrella of making the boss a success. Second, begin to network in the wider organization to seek alternative opportunities. Don't be negative or disloyal in how you talk about your present position. Simply express your interest in growing and developing so you can better help your firm succeed. If you have to look outside your company to find new opportunities, do so.

If you wait patiently, the bad boss may be removed. But you may also have to secure your own exit strategy for self-preservation. Many bad bosses are never removed. At some point, a bad boss can produce harmful impacts on your overall health and wellbeing. Ulcers, stress, sleep disorders, or heart palpitations come to mind. Or even worse, you gradually find you are becoming more and more like your bad boss. Look at the school playground. Bullies are often the result of bullying. Before this happens, you need to find a way out.

Toxic Management

In some organizations you can see a consistent pattern which indicates the whole management process is toxic. This does not mean the leadership has bad intentions. Often their intentions are wholly good. But as they say, the road to hell is paved with good intentions. What happens in these organizations is that the decision making process becomes so dysfunctional, it cannot help but produce bad decisions and have a negative impact on everyone involved in the organization.

My hometown NFL football team is a prime example of this syndrome. For many years it was a storied franchise with three Super Bowl wins to its credit. Then the team was purchased by a brash young entrepreneur, who for ten years has produced losing seasons most of the time, a constantly revolving door of coaches, a demoralized and discouraged corps of players, and a sea of unhappy fans. Fans are consistently frustrated when great coaches and players are hired and then undermined by a meddling owner and his minions.

The owner goes around the coach to cut sweetheart deals with players directly. In one case he offered a $100 million dollar contract to a 27-year-old lineman. After a year, and a coaching change, the star lineman decided he did not like the new formation so he refused to play. He is now the highest paid pain in a coach's butt in the league. On another occasion, the owner hired two new assistant head coaches before he hired the head coach. Then he discovered no head coach would take the job without the freedom to pick his assistants. The owner had to promote a quarterback coach to the head coaching position where, surprise, surprise, it turned out this poor guy was way over his head.

In another quarterbacks and coaches brouhaha, the team drafted an Auburn standout quarterback in 2005. Suffering under a constant change of coaches and offensive strategies, this young college standout rose to be "one of the league's elite quarterbacks" and then collapsed with his team into the worst team record in their history by the end of the 2009 season. In 2010 under a new coach, the team drafted a veteran quarterback who had led his former team to four NFC division championships, five NFC championship games and one Super Bowl appearance. Unfortunately, the new coach never told the new quarterbacks coach (his son) of this inspired trade. The young quarterbacks coach did not want this veteran and played him very reluctantly. Two thirds of the way through the season, he simply benched his All Pro quarterback for the balance of the (losing) season.

This kind of management fiasco is brutal on the players, creates incredible negative pressure on the team as a whole and makes forward progress impossible. No wonder fans greeted all the changes of the new season with placards reading "Fire the Owner!" An organization suffering from toxic management simply cannot heal itself. If you are in a toxic organization, your best and only choice is to get out as soon as you can.

Teamwork

Let's go back to more positive advice about the things you can do to build a successful career in any organization and industry. Our advice is to learn to be a good team player. Don't hog the ball, don't dominate the spotlight, don't run your mouth in excessive and arrogant praise of yourself. How well you get along with your peers, and even with a wide range of subordinates, will have a significant bearing on your ability to be promoted. Your co-workers regard will also have a significant impact on your ability to perform your work well.

Even in a competitive environment, it pays to have allies. Make friends with others. Secretaries and maintenance staff can prove to be sources of important information and can help you accomplish tasks you can't get done on your own. Be gracious and kind to everyone. Be willing to ask for help. No one thinks you are all knowing – don't pretend to be. Actually asking for someone's help is a good way to make them your friend and ally. Often you will need others' help to accomplish your job. Remember your boss knows more about what is expected in his assignments. Solicit help from the boss. When others are involved in your success, be sure to share the credit with them. Praise is rare enough; it's always good to spread it around.

Work on your listening skills. In general, you should ask more than you tell and listen more than you speak. Those who pontificate verbal baloney in hopes of convincing others of their competence, generally come off looking like a blowhard. There is a reason God has given you two ears and one mouth. You need to learn to be an effective listener. One expert who has conducted over 6,500 executive assessments, coached thousands of leaders and surveyed millions of employees, claims the number one shortcoming of leaders is mediocre listening skills. You can learn to be a better listener, to be an active listener. Reflect back what the other person has said in your own words. Dialog until you really grasp what they think and how they feel.[127]

Always Be Alert To Personal Development

As you go about doing your job each day, you should always be asking, "How can I do a better job? What skills could I develop which would make me more valuable to my team, my employer? What areas do I struggle with? Can I get more training to improve my performance?" Sure, it would be nice if someone in your chain of command took an interest in your personal development. You need to take the initiative to stimulate your own growth and progress, whether or not you have a mentor or a supportive supervisor.

In this vein develop openness to accepting feedback. When people offer criticism, it's quite natural to defend ourselves. Don't. Ask questions instead, and try to learn as much as you can from your critic. Sort through what they have to say, and see if there isn't a kernel of truth in the critique. Perhaps this insight will help you identify areas you can work on to become a better performer. We would go so far as to suggest you solicit feedback. When you complete a major assignment, ask your boss (or the client) "Was there anything I did that was particularly helpful to you? Was there anything I might have done differently to improve the final outcome?"

The whole notion of deflecting criticism rather than defending yourself seems counter intuitive to many, but it is one of the most important tools I (Bruce) have learned during my many years in the business world. When someone attacks you, "You screwed up the numbers on the Kleinfeld Project!!!" Our normal response is to defend ourselves. We attack back, and our colleagues defend themselves. Here's how it often goes. "I feel like I may have been 5% at fault, but its clear Harry is 95% in the wrong, so there's no way I'm backing down and accepting any blame!" The other party to the conflict feels the same way. Like a dog chasing its own tail, this scenario goes nowhere. Thus starts another World War, which is not an effective way to get business done or to solve problems.

Here's my alternative approach. Give it a try. When Harry attacks, I respond, "Gee, Harry, maybe you are right. It's probably all my fault." Now what exactly can Harry say to that? He can't fight. He just won the fight. I offer no defense for him to shred nor do I attack him so he has to defend himself. After a long pause, I then follow up, "Let's take a look at this problem and see if we can't find a solution for it." Now we are on the same side and are working to resolve the issue. No war required.

My first year at M&M/Mars, I had the head of the Accounting Department attack me in just such a fashion. Apparently, my predecessor had screwed up some inter-departmental billings to the tune of $2 million dollars. Targets were missed, and the senior accounting folks were not going to get their annual bonuses. I could see why they were irate. Sure, I could have claimed, "It's not my fault. That happened on Wally's watch. I had nothing to do with it." That response, however, would not get anyone a bonus. Instead I pulled out my "I'm guilty" defense, and it worked like a charm. As soon as the Accounting Director stopped erupting like Mount St Helens, we could get down to work. We settled in, rolled up our sleeves, and went to work on the problem (not the argument). In a day and a half, the $2 million mistake was now a $200,000 mistake, Accounting was back on Plan, and everyone got their bonuses. As you might imagine, thereafter, I had a lot of good friends in Accounting.

One last word about personal development. As you do your job, do it well, to the best of your ability. Those who strive to do an excellent job are the ones who get a chance to work on a higher level. Keep your eyes open and analyze your work periodically to identify what things energize you and what things drain you of energy. When you look around for opportunities to grow, you want to add more of the energizing stuff and less of the rest. Don't be afraid to ask for what you want. Your superiors are probably not mind readers. It's ok to tell them what future advancement you are considering and ask them to keep you in mind.

Ethics

Our personal ethics matter in the marketplace. Management consultant Peter Drucker once made the observation that there's no such thing as business ethics—just ethics. Academics often argue about ethical breakdowns in the marketplace. The core debate is, "Is it just a few bad apples or does something in this barrel turn good apples bad?" I think it's both. People develop a personal sense of ethics which dictates where they draw lines and set boundaries in their behavior. I also think organizational culture can undermine personal ethics and cause us to do things we would not have done on our own.

Ethics is often a hot topic in business circles. It's a hot topic because we seem to have such a shortage of good ethics in American institutions. According to Daniel Yankelovich, our confidence in the ethics of business leaders has been declining for decades. Polls indicate that 87 percent of the public think there has been a decline of social morality; 90 percent see a threat to the family and a decline in family values.[128]

If you live on Main Street, we rant about the risky behavior of Wall Street which almost put our economy into another Great Depression and the outrageous bonuses awarded to the culprits. Government bailouts for irresponsible business leaders drive taxpayers crazy. Corporate life is ripe with examples of organizations who tossed out all moral values in the pursuit of profits—Enron, World Com, Tyco, Global Crossing, Bernie Madoff, and others. But the blame doesn't stop here.

Our political leaders are often caught with fewer moral scruples than a used car salesman. Trust in government leaders, of all stripes, is at an all-time low, and with good reason. Immorality, abuse, lies, and cover-ups have even spread through the Catholic Church to the point they have tainted the top officials. In fact it's hard to find any institution or arena of American life which has earned our trust because of high moral standards and demonstrated ethical behavior.

My advice is you should strive to behave with the highest standards of ethics in your work and personal life regardless of what others around you do. People say Warren Buffet practices "old fashioned values" in his business dealings. I would say he demonstrates the point that in the long run, good ethics are rewarded and bad ethics are exposed and punished.

Holding to your personal ethics can pay off even when it goes against the grain of your industry or standard industry practices. S. Truett Cathy began Chick-Fil-A as a single fast food stand serving chicken sandwiches in South Georgia. In spite of the fact that he insisted on holding to his Christian values (all Chick-Fil- A restaurants are closed on Sunday so employees can attend church and be with family), his chain prospered. Today it is the largest privately held restaurant chain in America and the basis of Cathy's estimated $4 billion net worth.

Personal Ethics

Ethics is a lot simpler than we often make it to be. When you hear this topic taught in business school or in other public forums, it seems so vague, so ill-defined, and so relativistic—like trying to nail Jell-O to the wall.

Yet the truth is, we all have a clearly defined sense of right and wrong. As Tim Keller says, "We all have a pervasive, powerful, and unavoidable belief not only in moral values but also in moral obligation…. All human beings have moral feelings. We call it a conscience. When considering doing something we feel would be wrong, we tend to refrain."[129]

We not only have an inner conviction about right and wrong for ourselves, we have a strong belief that there are external standards which make certain behaviors wrong and immoral for anyone. All human beings have this notion that there are certain ways we should or should not behave, even if we don't always live out those convictions.

We all have ethical standards, even if it's as simple as "Do unto others as you would have them do unto you." This Golden Rule, originally shared by Jesus in the New Testament, is still widely accepted and disseminated in American culture.

Toe the line! Protect yourself and your career. Don't do that which you feel is unethical. Guard your reputation. It's easy to lose, and a good reputation is the best asset you can have to build a strong career. There is one other asset that will prove invaluable to your long-term career success.

No matter what line of work you eventually enter into, there is one skill that will make or break your progress or success in that field. It does not matter if you are an astronaut, a food service worker, a nurse, or a carpenter – if you want to grow to achieve your potential in any field, you must learn to build relational capital. Having found a good job in a compatible corporate culture for you, read on to learn how you can develop the single most important ability in maximizing your new position.

Chapter 20

Strong Careers are Built on Relational Capital

Born in the Bronx, Lloyd Blankfein was raised in the New York City public housing project known as Linden Houses. He was raised by his father, a postal clerk, and his mother, a receptionist. As a boy he worked as a concession vendor at Yankee Stadium in the summer while attending public schools for his elementary and secondary education. Valedictorian of his class at Thomas Jefferson High School, Blankfein was the first in his family to attend college, going Harvard on a merit scholarship.

Today, Blankfein is the CEO and Chairman of Goldman Sachs, the one of the strongest US investment banks, and one of the highest paid executives on Wall Street. Over the past three years, Blankfein earned in excess of $100 million. Today Blankfein's 30th floor office on the tip of Manhattan Island allows him to look across the city into the rough neighborhood containing the Linden housing projects where he began his rise to his current position of power and influence.[130]

To what should we ascribe his success? It certainly was not that he came from one of the families of wealth and influence that sit atop New York society. It was not the quality of his education, although being able to turn an ordinary urban public school experience into a full scholarship to Harvard is noteworthy. Nor is it his connections in investment banking. When Blankfein first applied to work at Goldman in the 1980's, he was rejected. Eventually, he snuck in through the back door. Goldman acquired J. Aron & Co, a precious metals trading firm, where Blankfein worked as a gold coin and bar salesman. He worked his way up to the top through the trading floor, a rare accomplishment in the investment banking business.

Those who know his story contend Blankfein's success is due to the quality of his relationships in the business. Here is a guy who worked hard and learned fast but who also made a lot of friends on his way up the corporate ladder. Even as CEO he still likes to get out and wander the trading floor talking to staff members. According to employees, Blankfein will often send messages or chat on his mobile in the middle of the night discussing conditions in the world markets and giving advice on future activities. His staff describes him as the antithesis of the typical Wall Street stuffed shirt, but instead sees him as an open, transparent kind of person.

Relationships and Success

Success in the real world is not primarily driven by your educational attainments or by your technical skills. I am aware that this is not what you've been told by other authority figures, but let's face it; they are in the business of selling education or technical training.

A research study among CEOs of large organizations found soft skills far more important to their long-term success than technical talent. Across all these CEO's, they claim that only 15% of their success in the workplace is due to their technical skills. The largest part of their career success was ascribed to their relational skills – their ability to work well with other people. Like Lloyd Blankfein at Goldman Sachs, these CEOs found it was not family background, connections with good society or even a good education which allowed them to progress rapidly in their careers. Instead, they credit most of their success to having learned to build relational capital in the workplace, a skill almost anyone can learn.

In *Seven Habits of Highly Successful People*, the late Stephen Covey suggests you should begin with the end in mind. Think about where you want to go in your career. Ideally, you want a career which will grow to develop and utilize all of your unique abilities and interests. We are not talking about unbridled ambition – those who strive to get ahead simply to get ahead or to gain power over people. That kind of ambition is a recipe for disaster for the long-term health of your career. Instead, we are talking about the process of discovering who you are, what you can do, and what you can contribute to others. You do not want to spend your whole career in first gear if you have a fifth speed overdrive in your transmission.

Learning to manage the people element of your career, what we call building relational capital, offers these advantages for your vocation. First, it will give you much better information sources than simply waiting for the official memo to come out. Building positive relationships can result in help and support when you need it. When you run into an obstacle, it's great to have people who can lend you a hand. Focusing on relationships can actually produce friends, both workplace friends and even friends you socialize with outside work hours.

Another benefit of building relational capital is to develop allies at work. When you want to advocate a position with management, it helps to have others who will reinforce your view. You will want to seek out mentors. These are more experienced people who can help you grow your capacity and exposure at work. You will also want to mentor others yourself. **Having supporters in the organization - below you, with peers, and above you – is essential if you hope to get promoted and if you want to succeed in your job tasks at work.** Do not step on people on the way up the corporate ladder – it will come back to haunt you. Instead, make friends.

Finally, your relationships at work offer the potential to turn into genuine community and to let you give back to others. We give back not because it will help us win our next promotion. We give back because it helps us relate to the human experience. This makes us better able to lead and manage other people in organizational life, people who are also immersed in the human experience, as we are.

Friends Help Your Performance

Learning to make friends at work is critical to your effectiveness on a day-to-day basis and to your long-term success. Friends allow you to tap into unofficial information channels. Every workplace has some kind of office politics going on. They don't all look like a canned TV program (think *The Office*) or like the Macavellian politics of a government agency. The "grapevine" in any organization is a means of transmitting information, testing out ideas, and gathering worker feedback in an informal way before management commits to any course of action.

In short, you want friends who will tell you what's coming in over the grapevine. How to do that? Ask questions, listen to people, and never reveal your sources. If you betray a trust and attach a name to a tidbit – "Jackie told me…" you will be shut out of the info flow. Just say, "I hear some people are concerned about…" Never use the grapevine to back bite or start rumors about others. This will also shut out sources. If you help others, be positive in your informal communications, and support others with information – people will do the same for you. I've often found out about relevant developments, which would eventually impact my area, in a casual conversation in the hallway, by the water cooler, or in the lunchroom. Advanced "unofficial" warnings can make all the difference in how you handle upcoming change.

If you make friends at work, you will also find you can get help when you need it. It may be as simple as getting a younger colleague to explain how to run some high tech software program, which my wife does quite often in her school environment. In turn, when younger teachers need help selecting leveled reading books for their grade, they know to approach Martie for help. The normal shipping process may take three days and a wad of paperwork, but if you have friends, you can often walk your project down to the Shipping Room and get it out this afternoon. When your annual budget is due, your back is against the wall, and you can't figure out a solution – it sure is nice to know someone in Accounting who you can ask to help rescue your budget.

Building friends at work also has this benefit – you will have friends! Who can't use a few friends? Coming to work and laboring alongside folks you like and who like you can turn a dull and difficult assignment into something more meaningful and enjoyable.

Often times working with people who have become your friends is pleasure enough. But sometimes, these people will become friends outside of the office and may have more influence in your life than you could ever imagine.

One of my early management jobs was for a corporation in Chicago. I got to know the top secretary in the advertising department both from work contacts and from the fact she attended my church. One day Lois asked me to do her a favor. Her boss had been promoted, and the new advertising manager was coming to work the next Monday. She asked if I would take this fellow to lunch on his first day. "He's new here, he doesn't know anybody. Please, it would be a real favor to me." Reluctantly, and after much arm-twisting, I agreed to handle this task. Karl, her new boss, turned out to be a pretty interesting guy. Eventually we became friends. We did things together with our families. Karl became a mentor in my role as a parent, as his kids were about ten years ahead of mine. We became fast friends, even though we only worked together for about four years, and to this day, 30 years later, Karl is still one of my best friends in the world. It turns out I wasn't doing Lois or Karl a favor, I was doing me a favor.

Being a Friend

The easiest way to understand how to build relational capital at work is to simply think about personal friendships. When you think about the kind of person you would like to have as a friend, what characteristics come to mind?

Honesty pops into my mind. If someone isn't straightforward, and I sense he's twisting or distorting the truth when he speaks, I don't feel he'd make a good friend.

I also look for people who are kind. I watch them interact with children, pets, and especially those who are their social inferiors. All these interactions give us an accurate insight about whether this is a kind person.

For me, another key question is to ask how well this person communicates? When I speak to him, do I sense he's open and teachable? Does he look for new information from the opinions and views of others, or is he just locked into his own preconceived notions? Some people I've met can be incredibly stubborn, bullheaded, dogmatic – stuck on one point of view…their own! Can this person carry on a dialogue or a discussion? Or is it all "tell" and little "ask?" Is he interested in what I have to say? Is he a good listener? This is absolutely required to establish the kind of communication between two people which can eventually lead to friendship.

There are other aspects that improve people's friendship potential. Are they encouraging and positive? It's not much fun to be with critical folks who run everything down. A person who has a constantly dark and stormy outlook on life is not good company. Instead, look for someone who is positive about life. This beats hanging out with whiners and complainers. Are they willing to take time for you? Are they available when you want to hang out?

Attributes like these—honesty, kindness, teachability, listening, encouraging, being positive, and available—are what we look for in a person we want to be friends with. If you determine to be this kind of a friend to people you encounter in your workplace, you will find you are making friends and growing your relational capital.

Competence and Compassion

Earlier, in Chapter Seven, we talked about the importance of competence and compassion in the workplace. It may be terribly obvious, but it bears repeating -- these two attributes will make a major contribution to your ability to make friends in the marketplace.

Bain and Company, the well-known Boston-based management consulting firm, once hired a communications professor from Harvard Business School to help them figure out why some of the partners were having trouble convincing audiences to follow Bain's management advice. The professor from the B-School came in and listened to the partners present and then reported back to management. Following is a summary of his findings.

"When an audience listens to a speaker give a presentation, there are three questions they ask themselves. First, does the speaker know what he is talking about? Is he competent to address this subject? Second, is he being honest? Third, does he care about me? Only if an audience reacts in the affirmative to all three questions, will they grant high credibility to the speaker and be willing to follow his advice."[131] In this case, the Bain partners kept coming up short on compassion and failed to convince the audience.

Why does compassion matter? Building friendships at work is not just trying to score points and work your way up the corporate ladder. Often we find individuals at work who focus solely on impressing superiors. How we treat our peers in the organization may be more indicative of what our character is really like. And in most cases, our peers will have a much more accurate sense than our supervisors do of what our real person is like. Smart leaders are aware of this tendency and take it into account when it's time to promote someone.

The real litmus test for compassion is how we treat those who are lower than we are in the organization. These may be people who report to us, secretarial staff, maintenance workers, or the receptionist at the front desk. **How we treat our inferiors will give the most accurate picture of what our heart is like.**

People want to help and to help along the careers of those they sense are genuine human beings who care about them as people. Yes, you should always be at work building your network of friends both inside and outside the marketplace. As you do this, try to focus on these folks, not just as contacts you might later want to use, but as real human beings you have the privilege of getting to know. Show a genuine interest in them, their concerns, their careers, and even their life outside of work.

Somewhere down the road in your career, your investment in friends will pay off in a promotion. Or not, depending on your willingness to develop the habit of making friends. In the first market research group I managed, I had an analyst who was very bright and capable, performing at a high level. When a new position opened in the marketing department, everyone assumed my analyst, Elaine, had a lock on the position. She had outstanding qualifications and the management team who had worked with her gave her high marks. Yet, she did not get the job.

I nosed around afterwards trying to figure out what went wrong. Apparently the secretary to the Executive Vice President pulled the rug on her nomination. The secretary told her boss that an informal poll of many of the secretaries revealed a common perception that Elaine was snooty, looked down on them, and generally treated them with disrespect. No promotion. Apparently Elaine worked at impressing her bosses, but overlooked making friends with the "little people."

Listening and Learning

Work on your active listening skills. This is a powerful way to make friends. When you ask people how they are doing, stop, give them direct eye contact, and be prepared to listen. People want to be heard, need to be heard, and are often not heard in the workplace. Learn to ask questions. When you ask a coworker how they are, take the time to actually listen. When they respond, practice your active listening skills, and ask a follow-up question. This shows that you're paying attention, and you really care about what they have to say.

When I was promoted to Group Brand Manager at the tender age of 28, I had three sales forces reporting to me. One group, the Telemarketing Sales Group, was composed of about 15 people who were so wildly unhappy, their supervisor was afraid they would set the building on fire. As I walked the halls of the corporation, I would regularly be accosted by disgruntled staff from this department.

My strategy to diffuse the situation was simple. I'd stop, let them talk and listen. On occasion, I'd nod encouragingly and say, "I see what you mean." After they blurted out their pent up concerns for 15 minutes, I'd say something like this, "Thanks, Terry. I really appreciate your sharing your insights with me. I don't know what I can do about it, but I will research the situation and get back to you." Sometimes they had a good idea or two. Often I'd be thinking, "That is totally wacky!" but I'd still be smiling and appreciative.

The amazing thing was that as soon as most of the unhappy staff felt they had been heard, they were no longer up in arms. I was not able to do much to change things, but because they felt respected and cared for, I soon became a hero in that department. Surprisingly enough, when their attitudes changed, their sales went up and their commission checks grew fat and healthy. A win-win for all – just from active listening.

Networking

From the information we shared in the section on career transitions, you should be aware of the importance of building your network of friends and contacts. This team of relationships, both inside your firm, industry, and community, are vitally important. These folks will help you carry out your daily tasks. They will help you when you are angling for that promotion. And they will help you when you are seeking a new job.

Rob Cross and Robert Thomas recently profiled a highly successful technology executive in charge of a global business unit of about 7,000 employees. In the authors' analysis they determined this woman's outstanding success can be traced back to her social network (the real world kind, not the virtual kind) built up over 20 years in business. It's not a large network, but it both supports and challenges her. The executive claims her motto is simple: "Make friends so that you have friends when you need friends." She also says, "Luck happens through networks where people give first and are authentic in all they do." The authors conclude that network size usually doesn't matter. Top executives have diverse but select friends from a variety of places, rather than sheer numbers. This business leader's network includes people from her own firm, peers both inside and outside her firm, colleagues from professional associations, a few close friends who can be really honest, and some very different people who challenge and stretch her creativity and personal growth.[132]

How do you build a network? One relationship at a time. Get involved. Volunteer to join cross functional teams in the office. These may seem like thankless assignments, but they often give you a chance to meet and rub elbows with some interesting people. Be sure to attend office parties, client events and other social gatherings. Attend industry gatherings and community business events. Volunteer to serve in some of these groups.

Business meetings, mixers, conferences and other functions provide opportunities to build relationships. While many of us shudder at the thought of having to go to another uncomfortable business mixer, you might want to rethink that. Everyone else at the function probably feels just like you do. Look at this as an opportunity to build friendships and amass relational capital. Think of this as an opportunity where you can provide some ease to others who are feeling painfully awkward and out of place. Simply look for someone who seems more uncomfortable than you to approach.

Many of us reply to this notion by saying, "Well, I'm never sure what to say. I'm not very good at small talk." Well, work on it! Small talk is just another way to help other people feel comfortable and get to the point where they can relax and have a normal conversation. Build up your reservoir of small talk. I like to throw out nuggets about my childhood and my hometown, like the time my fifth-grade buddies and I went camping in the snow in February. This gives your listener a springboard to share interesting aspects of their own childhood and hometown.

When appropriate, ask meaningful questions about things that are important to them. Simply put, everyone's favorite topic is themselves. Ask questions that get them to talk about themselves. They will take it from there. Ask about their spouse, their children, and other relationships they've mentioned to you previously.

Honestly, this is not that hard. All you have to do is walk up, stick out your hand and say, "Hi. I'm Bruce Dreisbach.... So, how are you connected to this (group / host)? Tell me about your business? What kinds of things does your job involve? Do you have a family? Did you grow up around here? What do you like to do for fun?" If you want to learn more about how to make yourself and others feel more comfortable in awkward business or social settings you might read *How To Work A Room* by Susan RoAne.

Three Kinds of Friendships

We were made for community. Seeing as you spend the vast majority of your adult life at work, it is really reasonable to seek to build some community there. Our American culture is so fiercely skewed in the direction of the individual that we're often deceived into believing a person should aspire to strong, rugged independence. As demonstrated by the Marlboro Man or characters played by John Wayne, or Matt Damon in the Bourne movies, our culture reveres this image of the isolated individual. But it's just the opposite of how humans have been designed to flourish.

Why settle for loneliness and isolation if you don't have to? Let me suggest three principle friendships you ought to seek out in the marketplace.

First, we can build up one another in peer-to-peer relationships. Look for a group of colleagues you can encourage. Breaking bread together is a great way to build relationships. If you bring your lunch in a brown paper bag, go outside with your coworkers in nice weather and eat it around a table with other people. If you have a break room, take your lunch and a friendly attitude to share with others. One of my friends makes delicious dried apple slices which he frequently brings in and shares with co-workers at lunch. They beg for the recipe, but he never gives away the secret—it provides a unique way to connect to others. If you're running out for a cheese steak, offer to pick up a sandwich for a colleague. If you dash out for lunch at McDonalds, invite a co-worker to go along. If he too busy for lunch, volunteer to pick up lunch and bring it back for him.

You don't need an agenda to build friendships with peers. Just an open attitude, a willingness to ask questions, and active listening skills. At M&M/Mars a number of the brand managers I worked with would periodically go out after work and hoist a few brews at a local pub. The sessions were great opportunities to get to know colleagues in a more personal way. We shared a lot about our families, our kids, our recreational interests, and our life concerns.

A second kind of relationship you ought to seek out is to find a mentor. This is a more experienced person in your firm who you, and others, respect and admire. Seek them out and ask if they would occasionally give you some time where you can ask questions, solicit their advice and benefit from their wisdom. Most experienced workers will grant this request because they have probably benefitted from a mentor sometime during their career.

My first professional job in market research was working for a mid-sized research supplier in Princeton, New Jersey. The president of the firm was a very effective executive and took a personal interest in me. This was perhaps my first mentoring relationship in the marketplace, and it had a profound impact on my life which I can still see today. The process wasn't formal; my boss simply invited me out to lunch every few weeks. There was never any agenda, but he did ask probing questions. He let me talk, and he shared from his own wealth of professional experience.

I was a naive 25-year-old with little social capital and no exposure to the business world. The boss shared from his own mistakes at my age and taught me the importance of integrity in the business world. He coached the development of my professional skills, taught me strong work ethics, and even took me on sales calls to important clients in Manhattan. He took risks with me, sending my wife and I on our first business trip—an overnight road trip to Pepperidge Farm in Connecticut. We were amazed he would risk both the firm's money and a key client relationship to someone as 'green' as I was. This mentoring relationship fueled both my growth as a person in the marketplace and my role as a professional in the field of market research.

The third kind of relationship you should have is to be a mentor to younger staff. You need to give back and help others climb the organizational ladder. Investing in protégés will not only enhance your reputation, it will give you a built-in fan club you can draw on in later years.

When I worked in Manhattan, one of my mentoring relationships was with Jose Ramirez. Jose was a real New Yorker, raised in an immigrant Puerto Rican family in the projects of the Bronx. I, on the other hand, was a white hick from New Hampshire. Much of a mentoring relationship involves discussions about work-related issues. Yet, a great deal of good also comes from building a sense of friendship and community.

Jose and I were like aliens from opposing planets trying to learn to speak each other's language. We had long rambling conversations where I explained to Jose how to fish for trout, trap coyotes, build tree stands, and hunt whitetail deer with a bow and arrow. Jose was fascinated, even going so far as to set up an urban archery range in his backyard—although he had to open the back door and shoot through his one-car garage to get enough distance to the target!

For his part Jose taught me how to walk and talk like I was actually from New York. He knew the stance, the swagger, the walk of every urban tribe from the Bowery to Harlem, and into the Bronx, Queens, and

Brooklyn. By the time Jose was done with me, the panhandlers on Broadway never bothered me—they thought I was a local!

We did other things during our weekly lunch meetings - actually talking about business, Jose's ideas to grow his job, and better ways to interact with other areas. While I had 150 people who reported to me, Jose offered a great read on middle management in my organization. Through his eyes I got the perspective of many people I never had a chance to talk with. But our building community was foundational. Jose and I demonstrated that two very different kinds of people can find common ground and communicate through friendship. At the same time, we improved our ability to communicate with others at work and to accomplish our jobs.

Experience Community and Give Back to Others

The famous author and thinker, Henry James, one of the key thinkers and writers of the early 19th century, once made a comment which gets right to the heart of our rationale for building relational capital. James was saying goodbye to his nephew Billy, his brother William's son, as the boy was preparing to return to school. Of all the elaborate, subtle, impenetrable things James could have chosen to say to his nephew, here is what he said. "There are three things that are important in human life. The first is to be kind. The second is to be kind. The third is to be kind."[133]

We live in a world of need. The individuals who populate our workplace are often experiencing significant need in their lives. When we are willing to see co-workers as fellow human beings sharing the human experience and are willing to meet them at any point of need, we begin the process of building community.

As you get to know co-workers, ask questions, and begin to listen; you'll find ways to get involved in the lives of your colleagues. Being sensitive to the needs around you and reacting in practical ways can really help build bridges of friendship. Cut some fresh flowers from your garden and bring them to a coworker in the office. If your vegetable garden is booming with zucchini squash and tomatoes, bring in the overflow to hand out at work. If a colleague has a baby or loses a loved one, offer to bring over a meal. Send your secretary a nice card and a note of appreciation on her work anniversary.

As we mentioned before, giving back to others and building community are not things we do to score a promotion. We do it because it helps us relate to the human condition – in ourselves and in others. By connecting to the humanness in others, we become better workers and better leaders.

When you consider the needs of those in the marketplace, don't just stop with the people who are present in your workplace. There may be many others you're connected to who aren't at work each day. Think about folks who may have been laid off by your firm or by other firms in your industry. Think about people who have retired. Think about those who are family members or neighbors to those who are in your workplace. Consider the needs of others who are simply in your community where your workplace is located.

Your community probably has a number of organized efforts aimed at helping those who are less fortunate. You might be able to volunteer at a soup kitchen, a homeless shelter, or a food pantry. My local rescue mission runs a youth outreach program for inner-city children, and they always need volunteers for it. Habitat for Humanity helps build low cost houses for needy people.

ABC News once did a story on a school bus driver named Jorge Munoz from Queens, New York. During his evening commute, he would pass a group of homeless people who were obviously hungry. He got together with his family and started cooking meals for them. Every night for the past four years, Munoz, his family, and a few friends return home from work, and makes up 120 to 140 home-cooked meals which they then take out and distribute to the hungry.[134]

Wherever you are in your career, we want to underscore the importance of building relational capital at every stage. Make a new commitment to become more proactive about building relational capital. You need a network to succeed. You need friends at work so it actually becomes a place you enjoy spending the bulk of your life. And you need something more than your job or career to enjoy life.

Chapter 21

Building Balance into Your Life

Joe Gibbs built an outstanding career in American sports, first as an NFL coach, then as an NHRA Pro Stock team owner and finally as the owner of NASCAR Championship team Joe Gibbs Racing. Gibbs, who has always been recognized for working long hours and having a fierce work ethic, built a dynasty with the Washington Redskins who he coached twice for a total of 16 years. In his first stint as head coach, Gibbs led his team to eight playoff appearances, four NFC Championship titles, and three Super Bowl titles. Gibbs' NASCAR career has similar highlights with his team winning three different championships under his ownership.

In hindsight Gibbs now has significant regrets about how he lived his life. At age 68 Coach reflects on his career and says "it is more important to be remembered for words and wisdom than for wins." Gibbs also regrets "squandering too much personal time in favor of professional success, particularly as a workaholic NFL coach and laments the missing years with his sons. Gibbs even went so far as to take his sons out to lunch and give them this advice. "Don't do what I did, with your kids. What we are going to leave on this earth won't be races won or the Super Bowls. It's influence over others."[135]

A Life with Regrets

A successful career is only one component of a fulfilling life. Those who give themselves completely to work most often find themselves filled with regrets at the end of their work life. I can't tell you how many colleagues I know who thought they were pursuing success in the marketplace, but woke up one day and discovered they had squandered their lives on nothing but work and at the end of their career had little or nothing to show for it.

Early in my professional life, I worked closely with a man in his mid 40s who had four children. Les was a hard working guy, always the first in the office and always the last to leave at night. One day we were eating lunch together and he said, "I had a terrible thought last night when I realized my oldest daughter is graduating from high school this month. She is 18 years old, and I don't know her. I've always been too busy with work, and now I realize I've missed my chance. I'm never really going to get to know her. I don't have any kind of relationship with my other three kids, either. They are like strangers who live in my house." At the time I was young, married, and with no children in sight, but I never forgot that lesson. There is no way I wanted to live the sort of life where I ended up not really knowing my kids.

Recently I had breakfast with a friend who told me about one of his neighbors. This couple had both grown up poor. When they married and went to work, they aspired to have all of the fun things money could buy. Their attraction to material things started long before they moved next door to Joel and his family. The husband worked as a salesman and made good money, but the job required a lot of out-of-town travel. Yet, he could not say no to his wife and her endless desire for new acquisitions. They built an in-ground swimming pool, an addition to the house, and installed new landscaping. Her car constantly needed upgrading, and her vacations had to be extravagant. This constant demand for material things sucked at their income until the husband worked longer and longer hours. After a while, he was only home for less than a day on the weekend. Work, work, work was his life.

Eventually, the wife became lonely, and all her new toys were not addressing that issue. She started sleeping with various men on her street and in the neighborhood. Pretty soon, this got back to her workaholic husband and the whole situation blew up. That put an end to the marriage, all the material possessions, and the over commitment to work--all at a very painful cost to those involved.

Work is only part of what makes your life rewarding. Work needs to be integrated into the context of a holistic life. A life skewed toward work can ruin everything else you hold dear. Here is how you can cultivate that critical balance in your life.

Building Margins into your Life

What does it mean to live a life with margins? Quite simply, having margins is having the capacity to absorb the unexpected in life. It's having the capacity to embrace new opportunities that come along without having all your circuit breakers blow. It means having the capacity to cope with change when change can give you room to grow and prosper in new ways.

So many people who think they are pursuing the American Dream are actually living on overload. They remind me of the pet hamster I had as a kid. He loved to get in his wheel and run constantly, for hours without end. I don't know if he was under the impression he was going anywhere, but what was clear from my vantage point – he was running flat out, but never made progress. So many people live lifestyles where we are absolutely flat out. We are running as hard as we can and don't even have the time or energy to ask if we are getting anywhere.

How can you tell if your life is on overload? Overload is when you are *always* in a hurry. Overload is when fatigue is a constant part of your life. Overload is when you are anxious about many things. Overload is when your budget is in the red. Overload is when you are too distracted to listen or think. Overload is when your relationships suffer because of a lack of focused attention. Overload is when you never have time to reflect and think about the bigger picture and what priorities are important in your life. The sure sign you have a problem? Overload is when you are too busy to to finish the book you've been reading on finding margins in your life.

What does it look and feel like to have margin in your life? A person who has margin has time to finish the book on finding margins - then read it a second time! A person living with margin has energy. This person has enthusiasm for surprise and the adventure in each day. The person with margin has finances in the black. This person is secure, confident and calm.

Margin is the space that once existed between ourselves and our limits. It is the reserve held against contingencies and unanticipated situations. Margin is the reservoir of emotional energy, physical energy, time and finances that lead to a life of balance and health. Those who discover how to live with margins learn to enjoy a life with contentment, simplicity, balance and rest.[136]

How are your reserves and margins? Here is a startling statistic which should put the fear of God in most American workers. Research shows that most American wage earners are only two paychecks from becoming homeless! Put another way, most middle class Americans live with so little margin that if they had an economic disaster of some kind, one that cost them the equivalent of two paychecks, they could easily tumble down the path which leads to bankruptcy and homelessness. Most often this happens when the major bread winner loses her job or when someone in the family suffers from a catastrophic illness or accident. This sudden drop off in income eats up meager savings, credit card debt explodes, the mortgage or rent can't be made and suddenly the family faces eviction.

Building in Margin

Building margin back into your life is done by increasing your reserves. Putting boundaries on your work life and seeking to balance work with other activities and relationships will help you build reserves and restore margins.

My first business mentor used to tell associates this story about a young lumberjack in the Big North Woods of northern Minnesota. Larry the Lumberjack was a tall strapping fellow who walked into camp early one Monday morning. The crew chief hired him on the spot and put him to work felling logs like the other young men. Boy, could Larry swing that axe! At the end of the first day he cut 50% more logs than any other lumberjack in camp. On Tuesday he just held his own and by Wednesday his production was way off. Thursday morning the crew chief approached Larry and said, "I'm sorry, son, but I'm going to have to let you go. You are just not cutting enough logs." Young Larry said, "I don't understand. I'm working twice as hard as the other guys." The crew chief looked at him for a moment and asked, "Do you ever stop to sharpen your axe?"

According to my mentor, the moral of the story is that you need to take time to sharpen your axe. People who stop working, who take some time off, and do something else to refresh their creativity and energy out produce those who simply work long hours. In that firm work hours were from 8:30 AM until 4:30 PM. If the boss caught you working late, he would haul you into his office to find out why. In his view if you could not get your work done between 8:30 and 4:30, you were doing something wrong in how you managed your time. Or you needed some help to get a life outside of work.

I (Katybeth) have found my out-of-work activities serve to calm me down and energize me, both of which greatly benefit my work. In college I took a ceramics class just because I thought it sounded fun. Ten years later, I am still playing with clay and look forward to my Tuesday evening classes at the local cultural arts center as a much needed dose of creative therapy. I'm also passionate about food—I like to eat it, cook it, shop for it, and talk about it. Four years ago, my husband and I joined a Community Supported Agriculture (CSA) group with a local farm. As members, we are invited to volunteer at the farmer's market, stocking and selling the veggies. My husband says, "I'm a Veggie Pusher!" Even though five hours in the sun can get warm in the summer, I have such a great time talking about food and meet all sorts of interesting people. I also take a yoga class at lunch, and many of the women in the class have become good friends. In fact we have "Yoga Sister Happy Hours" after work! Though I wouldn't want to do any of these things full time, my hobbies are extremely energizing and give me interesting things to explore outside of my day job.

In my case (Bruce) I have a wide interest in outdoor activities, including all types of fishing, hunting, trapping, hiking, camping, canoeing, sailing, golfing, growing flowers, and vegetable gardening. I do like a few indoor activities including reading, painting, writing, conversation, and sitting in front of a wood fire. My father-in-law was a lawyer who worked until he was 91. He once confided to me, the reason he kept working long after his peers had retired was that he had never bothered to develop any hobbies as an adult. So other than his legal work, there was little in life that held any interest for him. As a result of that conversation, I began to develop a large palate of outside interests early in my career. These activities have not only enriched my life, they have made me a better worker.

There are no limits to the number of meaningful activities which are worthy of your time and attention outside of work. A friend who is a physician, belongs to the Brotherhood of the Jungle Cock, an organization of adults who are dedicated to teaching youngsters to fly fish. Other friends serve as adult leaders for Girl Scouts or Boy Scouts. I have mentored a local 9-year-old lad in fishing while his dad teaches other neighborhood boys football and baseball. Some of my buddies from church take regular camping trips designed to introduce boys without dads and parents who have never camped to one of our favorite recreational activities.

Defining Success

We need to think very carefully about how we define success. How do you define success? When you get 10 or 20 years down the road in your career, or when you approach the end of your career, what will make you think or feel you have had some success? What do you really want to do with your life? What will make you proud?

Author Peter Buffett offers some keen insights on this issue. Buffett says, "Here's a hint: It's about who you are rather than what you do." According to Buffett, many graduates and young adults are recalibrating their definition of success. Not just in response to the altered economic landscape produced by the Great Recession, but in recognition that our self-esteem and peace of mind are inevitably connected to our view of success. Buffett says many recent grads have seen the danger of a worldview which defines success only in terms of money and career advancement. In an economy where so many things can be taken away by circumstances beyond your control, it is a gamble to base both your self-esteem and peace of mind on such temporary factors.

The result is an increasing movement by people who have determined to use their talents to help the human race rather than simply joining the rat race. This change in focus, from worrying about how the world will reward our work, to concentrating on what we can accomplish in the world through the use of our time and talents, is a major shift in mindset. It offers a win – win for both the individual looking to make an impact in the world and for those who benefit from these efforts.[137]

Life Outside of Work

Is there life outside work? You might be surprised to discover that there is a great deal of life outside of the office. If you begin to explore, what for many is a neglected arena, you may be surprised at what you find. For lots of people, the things they get involved with outside of work light up their lives and re-energize their experience at work. For others the sense of self-worth and accomplishment from outside activities far surpass anything that goes on in the marketplace.

This spring, as we have been writing this book, a series of record-breaking floods and tornados have ripped through the heartland of our nation bringing death and destruction to large swaths of the Mid-west and the South. Many people have responded to these natural disasters by pitching in to help. "Mark Carr woke up Wednesday morning in Rocky Ford, Colorado, determined to help tornado survivors. He loaded a couple of chainsaws and his three children into his truck and set off to drive 600 miles to Joplin, Missouri, where help is needed." Mark and his family plan to spend a week in Joplin doing whatever needs to be done.

He is not alone in his desire to help. In Tuscaloosa, Alabama, more than 14,000 people have registered as volunteers after last month's deadly tornado. I saw a news story about a team of firemen from the Mid-Atlantic states who have been responding to the need for search and rescue workers in natural disaster areas. They invest their vacation time to go and help others in need. Their first trip was to Haiti in December 2010. This spring they responded after the tornados in Tuscaloosa, the flooding on the Mississippi, and were in Joplin, Missouri, helping find survivors. Another group of firemen from New Jersey organize and go into disaster areas specifically to help local firemen, who as first responders are often too busy to help with their own family's needs.[138]

A good college friend of mine, worked for many years as a high school English teacher and school guidance counselor. In the summer he enjoyed doing construction and roofing houses. One summer he took a church mission trip overseas where he and a team built some much needed facilities in an impoverished Third World country. Chuck found this experience profoundly moving and rewarding. In his early fifties, he quit his job as a teacher and went to work running his own roofing company. This line of work pays well and gives him the flexibility to go on frequent overseas missions adventures. Now he can take four-month-long mission trips each year and his United States-based roofing work pays for his mission trips as well as his own living.

Sometimes you need a pedestrian job to free you up to do something really worthwhile. This is strategic career planning at its finest. When I was first married, my wife and I spent two summers at a small church outside Schenectady, New York. We were recruited to help lead the summer youth program for kids in the church and the surrounding community. As we began to know the people in this small hamlet, I discovered that the most influential man in town was a fellow who worked as the custodian in the local elementary school. This gentleman was a powerful influence for good and had a profound impact on kids and adults in town. He could easily have gone to seminary and been a pastor but instead choose to "work down" in a job that gave him maximum contact with citizens in town, the chance to serve others, and the time to build a multitude of caring relationships. In all my years in the marketplace, I've never met another person with as high a level of personal impact as this humble janitor.

Giving Back

Life is not just about striving and achieving and getting your share of the pie. Life, in its richest sense, is also about giving to others. An old proverb I have often followed goes like this, "Give and it will be given to you. A good measure, pressed down, shaken together and running over, will be poured into your lap. For with the measure you use, it will be measured to you."

There are no limits to the number of ways you can give back to meet genuine human needs in your community. When I worked in the concrete jungle of Manhattan, I used to love to travel uptown into Harlem to see some of the community gardens people had cultivated on vacant lots. Harlem, above 125th Street, is a pretty tough neighborhood, but to see and smell and touch an oasis of beautiful growing plants amidst the grime of the city always put fresh life into my soul. All over America, city dwellers are planting fruit trees on public land and offering free blackberries, plums and loquats to the public- free for the picking. These experiments in green living mobilize community residents and teach about sustainable, healthy living.[139]

In the last big recession, a couple of guys in a church on Boston's South Shore got concerned about how many people they knew who had been laid off and were having trouble finding work. They decided to start a "Career Transition Support Group," through their church. The program was simple. It offered people a place to come talk about their struggles, offered constructive advice and encouragement to each other, and provided a network to use to help find a new job. At first they simply advertised through members of their congregation and their friends. That was successful so they started advertising locally and then regionally. These groups multiplied and grew in size and effectiveness. Eventually the participants convinced the two founders to go into business full time offering career transition services. Within a year of hanging out their shingle, they were drawing paying clients from all over the Boston metro area and were booked to capacity.

A friend in Richmond, Virginia, was struck by the high number of hungry kids in school. He learned that 14 million kids nationally go to bed hungry in the United States. Almost 37 million people, one out of eight Americans, had need of emergency food help last year. Keith decided to get some friends at church to help him solicit donations and hand out food. Each week sees dozens of needy families, adults and kids, show up to take advantage of Keith's local food bank.

At the opposite end of home-grown efforts to give back and meet needs is DC Central Kitchens which has distributed over 17 million meals and helped over 620 men and women gain full-time employment over the past 18 years. DC Central Kitchens was the brainchild of Robert Egger, who started out to run a nightclub. That's right – a nightclub. At the age of 12, Eggers saw the Bogart film Casablanca and, much to his father's dismay, fell in love with the idea of opening the greatest nightclub in the world. Eggers eventually did get into the nightclub business and worked his way into several management positions. One evening he went with some friends who were helping at a church which was handing out meals to homeless people. Eggers realized that while these people were buying food to give to hungry people, his friends in the restaurant and catering business were throwing tons of food away every night. Eggers put the two needs together and the outcome was DC Central Kitchens, which collects close to two tons of food every day, converts it into 4,500 meals, and delivers them through partner agencies to serve seniors, kids, folks in shelters and recovery programs.

Homelessness is a facet of American life which exists in every corner of our nation. It's much easier to see in urban settings, but it is also widespread in rural areas. My wife, who teaches special needs kids, sees a constant revolving door of students who drift through her programs, never staying long enough to learn, mostly because of unstable living situations. It does not take much. An eviction here, a domestic dispute, a lost job, and a child is evicted with the family and moves out of district. After three of four such forced relocations in the first several grades, you have a student who has fallen behind in reading and other basic skills. Those who hit fourth grade with a serious learning deficit are most likely to end up dropping out of high school. One third of our kids in America fail to graduate from high school, often because of a poor home situation, rather than any lack of interest in learning. Think about their career prospects!

A friend and I sometimes volunteer at the cold weather shelter in our town. The biggest eye opener for me was who is actually living in homeless shelters. Until I volunteered, I always had the impression, perhaps formed by pictures of denizens of Skid Row in the Bowery in New York City, that homeless people were individuals who had once had good jobs and families, but who were now degraded by alcohol and drug addictions to the point of living on park benches or in cardboard boxes.

Was I wrong! At least a third of the occupants of our shelter were intact families with children, with both parents, and parents who have jobs. When you watch two small children, and a Mom and Dad struggle to bed down for the night in a room with 22 other homeless people, it changes your view on what's important. Later I learned that nationally, the average age of a homeless person in the US is nine. These folks have had some tough breaks, lost a job, had a health crisis without insurance and ended up living in a car. They simply do not have enough in savings to pay for first and last month's rent plus the security deposit, nor is there much affordable housing available. These folks are just like the two-thirds of working Americans who are two paychecks from being homeless.

Generally, about a third of those in homeless shelters are people with mental health issues, addiction problems, and those who have made bad choices in life. But many can be helped, and most people in there just need a hand up, not a hand out. With appropriate assistance, the majority of these folks can get a second chance at life. The question is what to do to help.

Thirteen year old Zach Bonner has been helping the hurt and homeless in Tampa for half his life. He started by handing out drinks of water from his little red wagon to survivors of Hurricane Charley in 2004. He expanded his outreach, and with the help of his mother, started a foundation to help the needy. "It was just something I felt I could do," he says. "When you are in preschool or kindergarten, they are teaching you to share and give to others. And I had a really good time doing it, so I wanted to continue." [140]

We always think social problems like homelessness are so big there is nothing we can do to help. Not true. With a little imagination, you can find a constructive way to help someone in need. Ultimately, none of these problems are solved in their macro version, on a national basis of millions of needy people. The way we make an impact is on the individual level – we can help create change – one person at a time.

A friend's daughter away at college organized a group of girlfriends who meet one evening a week for two hours. The agenda is simple: They drink tea, chat about their lives, and knit hats, mittens, and scarves for homeless people. Periodically, these items are taken to a homeless shelter for distribution. I'm told they call themselves the "Bitch & Stitch Club," but whatever their nickname, they have found a great way to build community and give back to others.

The problem of homelessness may look too big to tackle if you simply look at raw numbers across all 50 states. But if you look at the problem through the eyes of people and organizations who could help – the enormous becomes quite manageable. When the late Senator Mark Hatfield from Oregon was in the US Senate, his committee studied the problem of homelessness from a national perspective. Hatfield suggested if every church in America adopted one homeless person, couple, or family, the problem of homelessness would cease to exist in the USA.

In Cambridge, Massachusetts, the local housing authority runs a unique program designed to help students caught in homelessness get extra help with their school work so they can graduate and go onto college. The founders of this program recognized that there are generational patterns of poverty and dependence on public housing. Without the intervention of this academic tutorial program, many kids will be in the line for public assistance in the next generation. "The Cambridge Workforce program was originally set up to teach "life skill" lessons, such as how to balance a checkbook. As the program succeeded in keeping more of these children in school, it gradually expanded to include college preparatory work." Volunteers and interns help students prepare for state and national tests; they assist them with selecting colleges and completing all the required paperwork. They even take students on college tours both in and out of state. Today this program serves 140 lower income students and has been so successful the Governor is working to replicate it across the state. [141]

Perhaps my favorite charitable giving program is that of the "Secret Santas." "The tradition dates back to 1971, when the owner of a Mississippi diner gave Larry Stewart, a homeless man, a free breakfast. When Stewart later became a successful businessman in Kansas City, Missouri, he handed out money to people at dollar stores, Laundromats and bus stations." Stewart died in 2007, but the tradition has expanded to a number of cities and many individuals. This past Christmas several dozen Secret Santas worked the streets of Phoenix handing out $100 bills to people in need. Among the recipients surprised by Secret Santas: a blind man waiting for a bus, a veteran just back from Iraq, and a waitress with three kids and a cancer stricken husband.[142]

Sacred Idleness

The final topic we want to touch on is so remote, so irrelevant, and so unheard of in today's over-wired and overly busy world. It may come as a shock to you. Try not to laugh. **If you want balance in your life, you need to build in time to do nothing.** Too muchness is not a new problem. Over 100 years ago the Scottish poet, author and preacher George MacDonald said, "Work is not always required of a man. There is such a thing as sacred idleness, the cultivation of which is now fearfully neglected."

Recent research indicates that the average American does not use all of his or her vacation time in any given year. That is amazing! Americans don't actually get much vacation time. When I worked for Mars, Inc., the large multinational, I learned that my counterparts in England or France started with five weeks of vacation per year. In Spain they were given six weeks of vacation plus two hours off for a nap every workday. In America we started with a paltry two weeks annual vacation!

Why is it we can't take time to stop and smell the flowers? Somehow we have swallowed the American cultural myth which says a busy person is a successful person. That the busier you are the more valuable must be your life. Many of us are so entrapped by our electronic technology that we are missing life itself. Our relationships suffer, our sense of balance and perspective is undermined, we are distracted, anxious, and frankly, not much fun to be with.

Digital technology reporter Daniel Sieberg found he was living under the tyranny of his own electronics, and it was sucking the joy out of his life. He says, "Say you spend a total of two hours each day posting on Facebook or Twitter, mindlessly surfing the Web, sculpting your online image, or all of the above. It does not seem like much, but over the course of a year it adds up to roughly 30 days – an entire month vanished in the ether. What do you have to show for it? What else could you have accomplished in that time?"[143]

Perhaps you need to go on a digital diet? One of my daughters did that recently taking a month off Facebook to "cleanse her system and get her perspective back." She reports the experiment paid many dividends. Perhaps you just need to find an hour a day to take a walk in the outdoors, listen to the birds, and gently restore your sanity. One friend goes off once a week for two hours to play with his young children in a park with a playground. He tells me his objective is to "achieve pleasurable boredom." Another man I know, who is now in his early 70s, takes off every summer for a day-long hike in the White Mountains of New Hampshire. His goal is to climb a suitable peak, sit comfortably taking in the view, and to re-evaluate his life. Where he has come from in the past year. Where he is today. And where he wants to go in the future. He calls it his "Vision Quest."

Poet William Wadsworth talks about the payback from solitude, reflection, and contemplation. The closing stanza of his poem *Daffodils*, reads,

> *"For oft, when on my couch I lie*
> *In vacant or in pensive mood,*
> *They flash upon that inward eye*
> *Which is the bliss of solitude;*
> *And then my heart with pleasure fills,*
> *And dances with the daffodils."*

Here is the hard truth: if you never learn to slow down and smell the flowers, you will have nothing in your reservoir of internal resources to fuel you through difficult times. If you never take time to develop some hobbies, find some creative outlets outside of work, or find ways to give back; you will miss much of what truly makes life sweet. If you never take time to turn off the world, go for a walk in nature, and just see clouds drift by; you will never get the big perspective on what makes your life special, worth living, and where you want to go with your end game. It really is true, what Socrates said about his own life, "The unexamined life is not worth living."

Conclusion

As we bring this volume to a close, I hope a few of the key points that we have made resonated with your own feelings and thoughts as you seek to find your way in the world of career and vocation. Remember, work is meant to be a blessing in our lives. Work is about more than earning a living -- it's a journey of discovery! Work is a unique opportunity that we are given to discover our own unique self and to make a special contributions to the world in which we live. Work is the place that allows us to grow to maturity and become the total person we were meant to be.

The pursuit of appropriate work, the search for our own sweet spot, puts us on the path to discovering how we are made and what makes us special. You are unique! There is no one else in the world quite like you. This is a good thing. As you open the process of self-discovery, you will gain clear guidance for career choices which bring you to your competence and leave you feeling fulfilled.

Practical advice can help you land the job you want and then grow that job into a career. Take the time to sort through the tools we've given you: finding a square hole for your square peg, building relational capital which helps you reach your potential, understanding both the world of work and the world outside of work. Together these guiding forces will allow you to take charge of your work life and grow a career that fits your interests, makes use of your strengths, and provides economic rewards for your efforts.

APPENDIX

Job Fit Factors for
Bruce Dreisbach

- Mandate to Develop/Create/Rebuild (I am an Architect of Change.)

- Marketing-based: Linking consumer need to products/services of company

- Role as Consumer Advocate within organization

- Room for cross functional work

- A supportive team to help with execution

- Organization with strong leader who provides authority and direction

- Area of responsibility where I can create/develop/strategize

- Freedom to manage for results

- Results-driven evaluation and accountability

- Allows for the use of management leverage to contribute through and with others

Reader Check List

Here's a handy check list to make sure you squeeze every bit of help from this volume as you seek your sweet spot.

Section One: Search for Daily Meaning / Daily Bread
- What's your motivation? Honestly? (Chapter (C- 5)
- Is your focus on the money? The prestige? (C-5)
- Do you feel you are being pressured? Externally? Internally? (C-5)
- Have you invested in home work for yourself? (C-5)
- Is fear of failure holding you back? (C-5)
- Describe your passions & major strengths. (C-7)
- Are you planning for job transitions now? (C-8)

Section Two: Finding the Unique You
- Discover your inner road map. (C-10).
- Ask for help. (C-10)
- Solitude is required to find the unique you. (C-10)
- What's your heart tell you? (C-11)
  - Motivated Abilities Pattern
  - Strong Interest Inventory
  - StrengthsFinder 2.0
  - Temperament Tests
- What's your history & experience tell you? (C-13)
- Do you need more experience to learn about yourself? (C-13)
- Try Analytical Hindsight. (C-13)
- Put it all together: Your Hedgehog Principle (C-14)

Section Three: Finding a Job You Love
- Invest enough time to clarify your dreams, passions.(C-15)
- Define your best strengths. (C-15)
- Research your economic opportunities. (C- 15)
- Target prospect industries & companies. (C15)
- Research Corporate Culture: which best fits your needs? (C-15, C-18)

- Develop your Cover Letter & Resume. (C-15)
- Network to meet the right people. (C-15)
- Set up Informational Interviews. (C-16)
- Follow up appropriately. (C-16)
- Invest at least 40 hours a week to work on landing a job. (C-16)
- Interview Dos and Don'ts. (C-16)
- Be willing to be humble. (C-16)
- Is your training relevant? (C-16)
- Do you need a college degree? (C-16)
- Check your hobbies for a potential business concept. (C-16)
- Should you start your own business? (C-9, C-16)
- Managing your boss. (C-19)
- Managing relationships at work. (C-19, C-20)
- Build balance into your life. (C-21)

ENDNOTES

[1] Joel, Billy, Lyrics of *Allentown*, 1981

[2] Saslow, Eli, "In Recession, One Road Led Back Home," *The Washington Post*, 11/22/09, p.A1

[3] Ashburn, L., "Seeking Purpose, Passion," *USA Today*, 03/25/2010, p.11-B

[4] Murry, L.., *Atlanta Constitution Journal,* 3/10/2002, E-3

[5] Bakke, D.W., *Joy at Work* (New York: PVG, 2005, pp.46-47)

[6] Buechner, F., *Listening To Your Life* (New York: Harper, 1993, p.58)

[7] Terkel, S., *Working* (New York: NY Press, 1993)

[8] CareerBuilder.com

[9] Ibid

[10] Yankalovich, D., *Putting Work Ethic to Work*, 1983. Public Agenda Foundation

[11] Greenburg, H.M., Report for The MRSC, 1976 (Princeton, NJ)

[12] Sampson, R., *Managing the Managers*, (New York: McGraw Hill, p.158)

[13] Miller, A.F., *Why You Can't be Anything You Want to Be*, (Grand Rapids, MI: Zondervan, 1999, p.93)

[14] Rath, T., *Strengths Finder 2.0* (New York: Gallup Press, 2007, pp.ii-21)

[15] Mattson, M.T. & Ivancevich, J.M., *Controlling Work Stress* (San Francisco,CA: Joseey-Bass, 1987)

[16] www.cowboylyrics.com/lyrics/paycheck-johnny/take-this-job-and-shove-it-19045.html

[17] Fox, J.M. & Levin, J., *USA Today*, 11/11/2009, p5-D

[18] Hunter, D. & Hall, K. *The Washington Post*, 2/14/2010, p.A-7

[19] *USA Today*, 8/27/12, p. 8A

[20] "Time or Money," *Parade Magazine*, 09/02/2012, p.4

[21] Oberg, J. NBC News special to MSNBC, 01/27/2006

[22] Klinck, B., "Researchers Get Down & Dirty," *USA Today,* 3/22/2010, p.5-D

[23] Buechner & Frederick, *Listening To Your Life* (New York: Harper One, 1993, pp.185-186)

[24] Drucker, P.F. *The Effective Executive* (New York: Harper & Row, 2007 p.72)

[25] Miller Jr., A., *Why You Can't Be Anything You Want To Be* (Grand Rapids, MI: Zondervan, 1999, pp.95-96)

[26] McBride, M., "That Special Feeling," *Guideposts* (November 2006), p.69

[27] Pipher, M., *Writing To Change The World* (New York: Riverhead Books, 2006, pp.44-45)

[28] Guinness, O., *The Call* (Nashville, TN: Thomas Nelson, 2003, p.28)

[29] Yahoo Finance / Parade survey of 26,612 Parade.com visitors

[30] Keller,T., *Counterfeit Gods*, (New York: Dutton Publishing, 2009, pp. ix-x)

[31] Marklein, M.S., "Freshman Have Making Money on Their Minds," *USA Today* (January 21, 2010), p. D-7

[32] As quoted by Mary Piper, *Writing To Change the World*, Riverhead Books, NY, NY 2006, p.12

[33] Robbins & Wilner, 2001, p.61-62

[34] Robbins & Wilmer, 2001, p.26

[35] Robbins & Wilmer, pp.31-32

[36] Levitt, S.D. & Dubner, S.J., *Freakonomics* (New York: Harper, 2009)

[37] http://www.netmba.com/mgmt/ob/motivation/mcclelland/

[38] Studs Terkel, *Working*, 1997. NY, NY, New Press, p7

[39] Mattson & Miller, *Finding a Job You Can Love*, (Nashville, TN: Thomas Nelson, 1982, pp.25-32)

[40] Gladwell, M., *Outliers* (New York: Little & Brown, 2008, p.149)

[41] Pink, D., *Drive* (New York: Riverhead, 2009)

[42] Sheinin, D., "The Postgame Show", *The Washington Post*, 7/26/2009, p.D-1

[43] Dilanian, K. & Watson, T., "Shriver Gave Heart and Soul," *USA Today*, 08/12/2009, p.5-A

[44] Brown, S. & Dungy, T., "Overcoming Adversity On and Off the Field," The 700 Club, http://www.cbn.com/entertainment/sports/700club_tonydungy100906.aspx

[45] Ibid

[46] Peel, W.C. & Larrimore, W., *Going Public with Your Faith* (Grand Rapids, MI: Zondervan, 2003, pp.64-65)

[47] Thompson, M., "The Sea Witch," *Time Magazine,* 03/03/2009, p.11-B

[48] (http://abcnews.go.com/print?id=4003180

[49] Swindoll, C.R, *Quest For Character* (Portland, OR: Multnomah, 1987, pp.177-181)

[50] Ibid

[51] Elmer, V., "To Get To the Top, Don't Look Down on the Bottom Rung," *The Washington Post*, 06/13/2010, p.H1

[52] Wilson, P. & Olsen, P.R., "Career Switch Can Work," *Atlanta Constitution Journal*, 03/28/2010, p.1-G

[53] Davidson, P., "Being jobless for 6 months or more 'grinds on you,'" *USA Today*, 10/08/2009, p.B-1

[54] USA Today Snapshots, *USA Today*, September 27, 2010, pA-1

[55] Ashburn, L., "Seeking Purpose, Passion," *USA Today*, 03/25/2010, p.11-B

[56] Wolf, R., "When Retiring Means Giving Back," *USA Today*, 1/28/2011, p. A-1

[57] Ashburn, L.., 2010

[58] de Bonvoisin, A., "The Change Guarantee," *Guideposts*, May 2009, p.63

[59] Cain, S., *Quiet* (New York: Crown Publishers, 2012, pp.218-219)

[60] Hicks, D.A., *Money Enough* (San Francisco, Jossey-Bass, 2010, pp.89-90

[61] Davidson, P., "Second Careers," *USA Today*, 07/31/2009, p.A-1

[62] Carey, C., "Trade Schools Serve New Purpose," *USA Today*, 07/20/2009, p.5D

[63] Morrison, J., "Desperately Seeking Workers," *USA Today*, 01/22/2008, p.8B

[64] della Cava, M., "Jobless? Join the Club," *USA Today*, 12/17/2008, p.D1

[65] Reiner, A., "Brand Me," *AARP Magazine*, January, 2011, pp.58-63

[66] Reiner, A., "Brand Me," *AARP Magazine*, January, 2011, p.61

[67] Chisholm, V.,"On My Own, With God's Help," Higher Than The Top, 1993, (Nashville, TN: Dimensions for Living, p.23

[68] Shell, A.,"Financial Plans Evolve with Life," *USA Today*, 01/31/2011, p.B1

[69] Welch, J. & Welch, S., *Winning* (New York: Harper Business, 2005, pp.265-266)

[70] Lucado, M., *A Hat for Ivan* (Wheaton, IL: Crossway, 2004)

[71] Carvel, T.,*The Beginning of Something Very Good" Higher Than the Top* (Nashville,TN: Dimensions for Living, 1993, pp.21-22)

[72] Buechner, F., *Listening To Your Life*, (New York: Harper One, 1992, p.290

[73] Fong-Torres, B., "Go After What You Love," *Parade Magazine*, 4/25/2010, p.4

[74] Batterson, M., *Wild Goose Chase* (Colorado Springs: Multnomah, 2008, p.17)

[75] Jobs, S., "Stay Hungry, Stay Foolish," *Fortune*, 09/05/2005, pp.31-32

[76] Miller, A.F., *Why You Can't Be Anything You Want To Be* (Grand Rapids, MI: Zondervan, 1999, p.93)

[77] Isbister, Dr. N. & Robinson, M., *Who do You Think You Are?* (London: Harper Collins, 1999)

[78] Grutter, J. & Hammer, A.L., *Strong Interest Inventory User's Guide* (CPP, Inc., 2005)

[79] Rath, T., *StrengthsFinder 2.0* (New York: Gallup Press, 2007)

[80] Rath, 2007, p ii-iii

[81] Bolton, R. & Grover Bolton, D., *Social Style/Management Style*, (New York: Amacon, 1984)

[82] Kiersey, D. & Bates, M., *Please Understand Me* (Del Mar, CA: Prometheus Nemesis, 1984)

[83] Trent, J., *The Treasure Tree* (Nashville, TN: Thomas Nelson, 1998)

[84] Gladwell, M., *Outliers: The Story of Success* (New York: Little-Brown, 2008, pp. 50-55)

[85] Child, L., "My Good Life After Being Fired," *Parade Magazine*, 6/26/2009, p14

[86] Fuller, B., "Beads and Baskets," *Guideposts*, May 2009, p. 59

[87] Redenbacher, O., "Funny Looking Farmer with the Funny Sounding Name," in *Higher Than the Top*, (Nashville: Dimensions for Living, 1993)

[88] Collins, J., *Good to Great* (New York, Harper, 2001, pp.95-96)

[89] Collins, p.96

[90] Collins, p.109

[91] Collins, p.114

[92] Midgette, A., "The Upbeat," *The Washington Post Magazine*, 9/10/2010, pp.9-14

[93] Swindoll, pp.169-171

[94] Dewey, C., "Kiplinger's Personal Finance," *The Washington Post*, 09/26/2010, p.G3

[95] Draper, D., Hull, J. and Hurteau, D., "I'd Rather Be...," *Field & Stream*, July 2010, pp.65-61

[96] Krantz, M., "Why Aren't Thriving US Companies Hiring More," *USA Today*, 4/6/2011, p.B2

[97] Dugas, C., "Doing Post-Grad Study in Job Hunting," *USA Today*, 11/26/2010, p.4B

[98] Petrecca, L., "More Grads Use Social Media to Job Hunt," *USA Today*, 04/05/2011, p.1B

[99] Elmer, V., "Author Urges Job Seekers to Go Beyond Web," *The Washington Post*, 08/09/2009, p.H1

[100] Archer, M., Cracking the Hidden Job Market, *USA Today*, 1/18/2011, p.5B

[101] Elmer, 8/9/09

[102] Archer, M., 1/18/11

[103] Welch, 2005, p.259

[104] Welch, 2005, p.271

[105] Singletary, M., "They Were Noticed but not Hired," *The Washington Post*, 01/23/2011, p.G1

[106] Dugas, C., 11/26/10

[107] Perez, A.J., "Football Assistant Paying his Dues," *USA Today*, 11/12/2009, p.C1

[108] Canavan, K., "Ready to change careers?" *USA Today*, 6/14/2010, p.5B

[109] Shatzman, C., "Good Works," *Family Circle*, 4/1/2010, p.52

[110] Vanderkam, L., "Handmade Is the New Black," *USA Today*, 1/26/10, p.9A

[111] Zac, D., "Reinvent Your Life," *The Washington Post*, 8/5/2007, p.M4

[112] Zac, D., 2007, p.M1

[113] Zac, D., 2007, p.M4

[114] Robbins & Wilner, 2001, p.125

[115] Robbins & Wilner, 2001, p.93

[116] Robbins & Wilner, 2001, pp.107-108

[117] Robbins & Wilner, 2001, pp.110-111

[118] Marklein, M.B., "Do Too Many People Go to College," *USA Today*, 08/21/2008, p.15B

[119] Lowrey, A., "How law school went from being a sure thing to being a bum deal," *The Washington Post*, 10/31,2010, p.G4

[120] Marklein, MB, 8/21/2008, p.15B

[121] Vanderkam, L., "Many Grads Gamble on Education," *USA Today*, 9/22/10, p.11A

[122] Singletary, M., "Avoid the College Bubble," *The Washington Post*, 10/31/2010, p. B1

[123] McFarland, K., "Why Zappos Offers New Hires $ to Quit," *Bloomberg Business*, 09/19/2008

[124] Johnson, S., *Who Moved My Cheese?*, (New York: Putnam, 2002)

[125] Maese, R., "Called Down Another Aisle," *The Washington Post*, 04/10/2011, p.1D

[126] Fisher, A., "Help! My Boss is Driving me Nuts!", CNNMoney.com, 08/28/2009

[127] Kaufman, S, Convergence Recruiting Solutions, notes from e-mail, 12/19/2009

[128] Nash, L. & McLennan, S., *Church on Sunday, Work on Monday* (San Francisco: Jossey-Bass, pp.31-33)

[129] Keller, T., *The Reason for God* (New York: Riverhead, 2008, pp.151-152)

[130] Gogoi, P., "Goldman's big rebound raises some eyebrows," *USA Today On line*, 9/17/2009

[131] Byker, Dr. Don, Harvard Business School, in a personal conversation

[132] Cross, R., & Thomas, R., "Research Report for the Network Roundtable," University of Virginia, 2006

[133] Buechner, F., *Listening to Your Life* (New York: Harper One, 1992, p.293)

[134] http://www.democraticunderground.com/discuss/duboard.php

[135] Ryan, N., "Gibbs Shares Life Playbook," *USA Today*, 6/30/2009, p.7C

[136] Swenson, R.A., *Margins: Restoring Emotional, Physical, Financial and Time Reserves to Overloaded Lives*, NavPress, 2004

[137] Buffett, P., "How should college grads define success," *USA Today*, 5/26/11, p.11A

[138] Keen, J.,"Volunteers fan out to MO, AL after tornados," *USA Today*, 5/27/11, p.8A

[139] Jones, B., "More urbanites have their pick of fresh fruit," *USA Today*, 3/9/10, p.3A

[140] Grossman, C.L., "Beliefnet's Most Inspiring." *USA Today,* 12/16/09, p.7D

[141] Vaznis, J., "A place for dreams and a better future," *Boston Globe*, 11/29/09, p.B1

[142] Eversley, M, "Anonymous Santas strike in Arizona," *USA Today*, 12/23/09, p.A3

[143] Sieberg, D., "Overrun by Technology," *The Washington Post*, 5/29/11, p.B1

Bibliography

Adams, Scott, *The Dilbert Principle,* 1999

Bakke, Dennis W., *Joy At Work*, 2005

Barker, Joel Arthur, *Paradigms*, 1992

Batterson, Mark, *Wild Goose Chase*, 2008

Bolles, Richard Nelson, *How to Find Your Mission in Life*, 2005

Bolton, R. & Bolton, D., *Social Style / Management Style,* 1994

Buechner, Frederick; *Listening to Your Life*, 1993

Collins, Jim; *Good to Great*; 2001

Collins, Jim & Porras, Jerry, *Built To Last*, 1994

Deal, Terrance & Kennedy, Alan, Corporate Cultures, 1982

DePree, Max; *Leadership Is An Art*, 1989

Dimensions For Living, *Higher Than the Top*, 1993

Drucker, Peter F., *The Effective Executive*, 1966

Ehrereich, Barbara, *Nickel & Dimed*, 2001

Fisher, Roger & Ury, William, *Getting To Yes*, 1981

Frankel, Alex, *Punching In*, 2007

Gelbert, Doug, *Who The Heck was Oscar Mayer?;* 1996

Gladwell, Malcolm, *Outlier*, 2008

Hunter, James C, *The Servant*, 1998

Isbister, Nick & Robinson, Martin, *Who Do You Think You Are?;* 1999

Johnson, Dr. Spencer, *Who Moved My Cheese?*, 2002

Keller, Timothy, *Counterfeit Gods*, 2009

Mattson, Ralph & Miller, Arthur, *Finding A Job You Can Love;* 1982

Maxwell, John C., *Leadership 101;* 1994

McCorrmack, M., *What They Don't Teach You at Harvard Business School*; 1894

McGinnis, Alan Loy, *Bring Out the Best in People*, 1985

Miller, Jr., Arthur F., *Why You Can't be Anything You Want to Be*, 1999

Peter, Lawrence J & Hull, Raymond, *The Peter Principle*, 1969

Peters, Thomas J & Waterman, Robert H Jr., *In Search of Excellence*; 1982

Pierce, Jon L. & Newstrom, John W., *Leaders*, 2006

Pitcher, Patricia, *Artists, Craftsmen & Technocrats*, 1995

Rath, Tom, *StrengthsFinder 2.0*, 2007

RoAne, Susan, *How to Work a Room*, 1988

Robbins, Alexandra, & Wilner, Abby, *Quarterlife Crisis*, 2001

Schein, Edgar H, *Organizational Culture & Leadership*, 2004

Stevens, R. Paul, *The Other Six Days*, 1999

Trevino, Linda K.,& Nelson, Katherine A; *Managing Business Ethics*, 2007

Trompenaars, F. & Hampton-Turner, C., *Riding the Waves of Culture*, 1998

White, Jerry, *Honesty, Morality & Conscience*, 1996

www.ingramcontent.com/pod-product-compliance
Lightning Source LLC
Chambersburg PA
CBHW071711170526
45165CB00005B/1972

* 9 7 8 1 5 0 0 9 9 9 9 5 7 *